THE
DEAD SEA SCROLLS
DECEPTION

THE
DEAD SEA
SCROLLS
DECEPTION

Michael Baigent
and
Richard Leigh

JONATHAN CAPE
LONDON

First published 1991
© Michael Baigent and Richard Leigh 1991
Jonathan Cape, 20 Vauxhall Bridge Road, London SW1V 2SA

Michael Baigent and Richard Leigh have asserted their right
under the Copyright, Designs and Patents Act, 1988
to be identified as the authors of this work

A CIP catalogue record for this book
is available from the British Library

ISBN 0–224–02761–1

Phototypeset by Falcon Graphic Art Ltd
Wallington, Surrey
Printed in Great Britain by
Mackays of Chatham PLC, Chatham, Kent

Dedication

L'abbaye de la fontaine vive,
Avec sa chapelle lucide
Ou Nostres Dames nous genent
D'y habiter dans la cave
Voutée.

Les rouleaux de foins
Sous un linceul de sel,
Et la cloche au ficelle
Ou se trouve un seul moin
Maussade.

Mais autour du chastel
L'héraut proclame
La sorcellerie
De la druidesse-dame
Et sa chat séduit le soleil.

Jehan l'Ascuiz

The authors and publishers would like to thank the following for permission to reproduce photographs:

The executors of the estate of John Allegro (3, 8–10, 14–15, 17, 19–27; Michael Baigent (28–38, 40); Cambridge University Library (1); Israel Antiquities Authority (6–7, 11–13, 18); Israeli Government Press Office (39); William Reed (2); John L. Trever (5); Sabine Weiss/RAPHO (16) and Yigael Yadin (4).

Contents

Acknowledgments

We should like to thank Robert Eisenman for the generosity with which he made available to us his time, his energy and his insights. We are particularly grateful for the light he has cast on the relationship between the Dead Sea Scrolls and the New Testament, and on the social, political and religious forces at work in the historical backdrop. Our debt to him will become more than apparent in the course of the following pages. We should also like to thank Heather Eisenman.

We should like to thank Mrs Joan Allegro for the access she provided to her husband's material and for her sympathy and support in our undertaking.

We should like to thank the staff of Jonathan Cape, specifically Tom Maschler, Tony Colwell, Jenny Cottom, Lynn Boulton and Helen Donlon; and Alison Mansbridge our editor for her suggestions and the patience she displayed in the most arduous circumstances.

We should like to thank Rod Collins for fostering fiscal well-being and peace of mind.

We should like to thank our agent Barbara Levy for presiding over the project, as well as Ann Evans, who co-instigated it and has now found a new vocation as medium for the wandering and restless shade of Jehan l'Ascuiz.

Finally, we should like to thank the staffs of the British Library Reading Room, and of the London Library.

And, it goes without saying, we should like to thank our ladies.

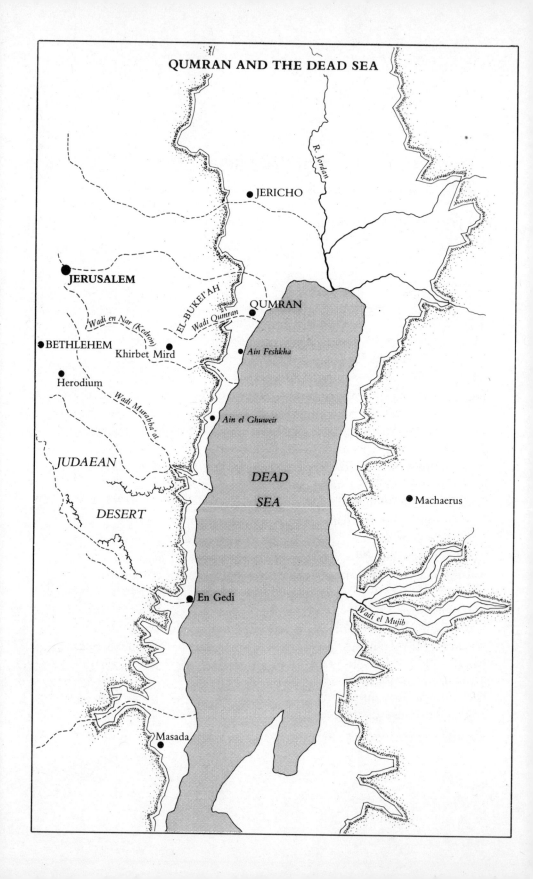

QUMRAN AND THE DEAD SEA

JERICHO

R. Jordan

JERUSALEM

QUMRAN

Wadi en Nar (Kedron)   EL-BUKEI'AH   *Wadi Qumran*

BETHLEHEM

Khirbet Mird

Ain Feshkha

Herodium

Wadi Murabba'at

Ain el Ghuweir

JUDAEAN

DEAD

SEA

Machaerus

DESERT

En Gedi

Wadi el Mujib

Masada

Preface

THE FOUR DEAD SEA SCROLLS

Biblical manuscripts dating back to at least
200 BC are for sale. This would be an ideal
gift to an educational or religious institution
by an individual or group. Box F 206.

S uch was the advertisement that appeared in the *Wall Street
Journal* on 1 June 1954. Were an advertisement of this sort
to appear today, it would no doubt be thought some species of
practical joke, not entirely in the best of taste. Alternatively, it
might be regarded as a coded message – to mask an arms deal,
for example, or something involving espionage.

Today, of course, the Dead Sea Scrolls are well enough known,
if only by name. Most people, while having an extremely nebulous idea of what they are, will at least have heard of them. If
nothing else, there exists an awareness that the scrolls are in some
way genuinely precious items, archaeological evidence of immense
importance. One doesn't expect to find a specimen of them while
digging in one's back garden. One doesn't regard them even as one
might the rusted weapons, the domestic utensils and appliances, the
remnants of equipment or apparel that might be found at, say, the
site of some Roman excavation in Britain.

The discovery of the Dead Sea Scrolls in 1947 generated a flurry
of excitement both in scholarly circles and among the general public.

But by 1954 that excitement had been skilfully defused. The scrolls, it was assumed, had revealed everything they were going to reveal, and this was made to seem less dramatic than had been expected. In consequence, the advertisement for their sale elicited no particular public interest when it appeared on page 14 of the *Wall Street Journal*. Immediately below it was an advertisement for industrial steel tanks, electric welders and other equipment. In the adjacent column were lists of premises for rent and situations vacant. It was the equivalent of offering items of Tutankhamun's treasure amidst lots of surplus plumbing or computer supplies. This book will show how such an anomaly could have occurred.

In tracing the progress of the Dead Sea Scrolls from their discovery in the Judaean desert to the various institutions that hold them today, we found ourselves confronting a contradiction we had faced before – the contradiction between the Jesus of history and the Christ of faith. Our investigation began in Israel. It was to extend to the corridors of the Vatican, and, even more ominously, into the offices of the Inquisition. We also encountered a rigidly maintained 'consensus' of interpretation towards the content and dating of the scrolls, and came to understand how explosive a non-partisan examination of them might be for the whole of Christian theological tradition. And we discovered how fiercely the world of orthodox biblical scholarship was prepared to fight to retain its monopoly of available information.

For Christians today, it is perfectly possible to acknowledge the Buddha, for example, or Muhammad, as historical individuals, just as one might Caesar or Alexander, and to differentiate them from the legends, the traditions, the theologies that have become associated with them. So far as Jesus is concerned, however, such differentiation is altogether more difficult. At the very heart of Christian belief, history and theology are inextricably entangled. Each suffuses the other. Yet each, if looked at separately, is a potential threat to the other. It is therefore easier, and safer, to blur the demarcation lines between them. Thus, for the faithful, two quite distinct figures are fused into one. On the one hand, there is the historical individual, the man who, according to most scholars, actually existed and walked the sands of Palestine two thousand years ago. On the other hand, there is the man–god of Christian doctrine, the divine personage deified, extolled and promulgated by St Paul. To examine this personage as an historical individual – to regard him, that is, as one might regard Muhammad or the Buddha, Caesar or Alexander – is still, for many Christians, tantamount to blasphemy.

During the mid-1980s, we were engaged in precisely such blasphemy. In researching the project we'd undertaken at the time, we were trying to separate history from theology, to distinguish the historical Jesus from the Christ of faith. In the process, we blundered head-on into the muddle of contradictions that confronts all researchers into biblical material; and like all researchers before us, we found ourselves bewildered by that muddle.

In the kind of research we'd embarked on, scriptural accounts, needless to say, could provide only the most meagre aid. As historical documents and testimony, the Gospels, as every scholar knows, are notoriously unreliable. They are essentially accounts of stark mythic simplicity, seemingly occurring in an historical limbo. Jesus and his disciples appear centre stage of an extensively stylised tableau, from which most of the context has been stripped away. Romans and Jews mill confusingly in the background, like extras on a film set. No sense is conveyed of the social, cultural, religious and political circumstances in which Jesus' drama is embedded. One is, in effect, confronted with an historical vacuum.

The Acts of the Apostles fleshes out the picture only slightly. From the Acts, one derives at least a tenuous sense of a milieu – of internecine strife and doctrinal squabbles amongst Jesus' immediate followers, of a coalescing movement which will gradually take the form of 'Christianity', of a world that extends beyond the circumscribed confines of Galilee and Judaea, of the geographical relation of Palestine to the rest of the Mediterranean. But there is still no accurate rendering of the broader social, cultural, religious and political forces at work. Everything is focused on, and restricted to, St Paul. If the Gospels are stylised, the Acts are no less so, albeit in a different way. If the Gospels are reduced to the stark oversimplification of myth, the Acts comprise a kind of picaresque novel – a picaresque novel, moreover, intended for specifically propagandist purposes and with

Paul as protagonist. There may be some insight into Paul's mentality, attitudes and adventures, but there is no reliable perspective on the world in which he moved. From the standpoint of any historian, any responsible chronicler, no account of the epoch would have been complete without some reference to Nero, say, and the burning of Rome. Even within Palestine, there were developments of momentous importance to those living at the time. In AD 39, for example, Herod Antipas, Tetrarch of Galilee, was exiled to the Pyrenees. By AD 41, both Galilee and Judaea – administered by Roman procurators since AD 6 – had been conferred on King Agrippa, and Palestine was united under a single non-Roman monarch (puppet though he might be) for the first time since the days of Herod the Great nearly half a century before. None of these developments is so much as mentioned in the Acts of the Apostles. The effect is akin to reading a biography of, say, Billy Graham which makes no mention of his friendships with presidents and other prominent individuals, no mention of Kennedy's assassination, no mention of the civil rights movement, the war in Vietnam, the transformation of values during the 1960s, Watergate and its aftermath.

Contrary to Christian tradition, Palestine two thousand years ago was as real as any other historical setting – that of Cleopatra's Egypt, for example, or of Imperial Rome, both of which impinged upon it. Its reality cannot be reduced to a bald mythic simplicity. Whoever Jesus or Paul were, and whatever they did, must be placed against the backdrop of broader events – against the swirl of personalities, groups, institutions and movements that operated in 1st-century Palestine and composed the fabric of what is called history.

To obtain any real sense of this period, we, like every other researcher, had to turn to other sources – Roman accounts, historical chronicles compiled by other writers of other orientations, allusions in later documents, apocryphal texts, the teachings and testimony of rival sects and creeds. Jesus himself was, needless to say, seldom mentioned in these sources, but they furnish a comprehensive and detailed picture of the world in which he moved. In fact, Jesus' world is better documented and chronicled than, for example, that of King Arthur, or of Robin Hood. And if Jesus himself remains elusive, he is no more so than they.

It was therefore with surprise and zest that we plunged into the background of the 'historical Jesus'. But no sooner had we done so than we found ourselves confronted by a problem that besets all researchers into biblical history. We found ourselves confronted by an apparently bewildering spectrum of Judaic cults, sects and sub-sects, of political and religious organisations and institutions, which seemed sometimes to be militantly at odds with one another, sometimes to overlap.

It quickly became apparent to us that the labels used to differentiate between these various groups – Pharisees, Sadducees, Essenes, Zealots, Nazorenes – were neither accurate nor useful. The muddle remained, and Jesus seemed to have connections of one kind or another with virtually all its components. Thus, for example, insofar as anything could be established about him at all, he appeared to have come from a Pharisee family and background, and to be steeped in Pharisaic thought. Several modern commentators have stressed the striking parallels between Jesus' teachings, especially the Sermon on the Mount, and those of Pharisee exponents such as the great Hillel. According to at least one commentator, Jesus 'was himself a Pharisee'.

But if Jesus' words were often interchangeable with those of official Pharisee doctrine at the time, they also appear to draw heavily on mystical or 'Essene' thought. John the Baptist is generally recognised as having been an Essene of some sort, and his influence on Jesus introduces an obvious Essene element into the latter's career. According to scriptural accounts, however, John's mother – Jesus' maternal aunt, Elizabeth – was married to a priest of the Temple, thereby giving both men Sadducee connections. And – most sensitive of all for later Christian tradition – Jesus clearly seems to have included Zealots among his followers: Simon Zealotes, for example, or Simon the Zealot, and possibly even Judas Iscariot, whose name, as it comes down to us, may derive from the fierce Sicarii.

In itself, of course, the mere suggestion of association with the Zealots was highly provocative. Was Jesus indeed the meek lamblike saviour of subsequent Christian tradition? Was he indeed wholly non-violent? Why, then, did he embark on violent actions, such as overturning the tables of the money-changers in the Temple? Why is he portrayed as being executed by the Romans in a fashion reserved exclusively for revolutionary activity? Why, before his vigil in Gethsemane, did he instruct his followers to equip themselves with swords? Why, shortly thereafter, did Peter actually draw a sword and lop off the ear of a minion in the High Priest's entourage? And if Jesus was in fact more militant than generally depicted, was he not also, of necessity, more politically committed? How, then, could one explain his preparedness to 'give unto Caesar' what was Caesar's – assuming that to be an accurate transcription and translation of his words?

If such contradictions surrounded Jesus during his lifetime, they also appeared to have survived him, continuing for at least another forty-odd years after his reported death. In AD 73, the fortress of Masada, having withstood a sustained Roman siege, was at last overrun, but only when its defending garrison committed mass suicide. The defenders of Masada are generally acknowledged to have been Zealots – not a religious sect, according to conventional interpretations, but adherents of a political and military movement. As it has been preserved for posterity, however, the doctrine of the garrison's defenders would appear to have been that of the Essenes – the allegedly non-violent, mystically oriented sect who were believed to have disowned all forms of political, not to say military, activity.

Such were the contradictions and prevailing confusion we found. But if we were flummoxed by it all, so, too, were professional scholars, 'experts' far more deeply versed in the material than ourselves. After threading a path through the maze, virtually every reliable commentator ended up at odds with his colleagues. According to some, Christianity arose as a quietist, mystery-school form of Judaism, which couldn't therefore have any connection with militant revolutionary nationalists such as the Zealots. According to others, Christianity was itself, at first, a form of revolutionary Judaic nationalism, and couldn't possibly have anything to do with pacifist mystics like the Essenes. According to some, Christianity emerged from one of the mainstreams of Judaic thought at the time. According to others, Christianity had begun to deviate from Judaism even before Paul appeared on the scene and made the rupture official.

The more we consulted the 'experts', the more apparent it

became that they *knew*, effectively, little more than anyone else. Most disturbing of all, we encountered no one theory or interpretation that satisfactorily accommodated all the evidence, all the anomalies, inconsistencies and contradictions.

It was at this point that we came upon the work of Robert Eisenman, Chairman of the Department of Religious Studies and Professor of Middle East Religions at California State University in Long Beach. Eisenman had been an undergraduate at Cornell at the same time as Thomas Pynchon. He studied Comparative Literature there under Vladimir Nabokov, receiving his BA in Physics and Philosophy in 1958, and his MA in Hebrew and Near Eastern Studies from New York University in 1966. In 1971 he was awarded a PhD in Middle East Languages and Cultures by Columbia University, having concentrated specifically on Palestinian history and Islamic law. He has also been an External Fellow of the University of Calabria in Italy and a lecturer in Islamic law, Islamic religion and culture, the Dead Sea Scrolls and Christian origins at the Hebrew University in Jerusalem. In 1985–6, he was Research Fellow in Residence at the William F. Albright Institute of Archaeological Research in Jerusalem, and in 1986–7 Visiting Senior Member of Linacre College, Oxford, and Visiting Scholar at the Oxford Centre for Postgraduate Hebrew Studies.

We came upon Eisenman's work initially in the form of a slender text cumbersomely entitled *Maccabees, Zadokites, Christians and Qumran*, which was published in 1983 by E.J. Brill of Leiden, Holland. The book was precisely the sort of thing one might expect from such an author writing for an academic publisher. There were more footnotes than there was text. There was a presupposition of enormous background knowledge and a forbidding welter of sources and references. But there was also a central thesis of exhilarating commonsense and lucidity. As we hacked our way through the density of the text, the questions that had perplexed us began to resolve themselves, clearly and organically, without ingeniously contrived theories, and without crucial fragments being ignored.

We drew extensively on Eisenman's work in the first section of *The Messianic Legacy* (London, 1986). Our conclusions owed much to the perspective he had opened for us on biblical scholarship and the historical background to the New Testament. However, certain questions remained unanswered. We could not have known it at the time, but we had overlooked a crucial link – a link that has, over the last five years, become a focus for controversy, a topic for front-page articles in national newspapers. That link proved to be the information provided by the Dead Sea Scrolls.

At the centre of the puzzle, we were to discover, was a hitherto unknown connection between the Dead Sea Scrolls and the elusive figure of St James, Jesus' brother, whose dispute with Paul precipitated the formulation of the new religion subsequently known as Christianity. It was this link that had been painstakingly concealed by a small enclave of biblical scholars, whose conveniently orthodox interpretation of the scrolls Eisenman came to call the 'consensus'.

According to Robert Eisenman:

> A small group of specialists, largely working together, developed a consensus . . . In lieu of clear historical insight . . . preconceptions and reconstructions, such as they were, were stated as facts, and these results, which were used to corroborate each other, in turn became *new* assumptions, that were used to draw away a whole generation of students unwilling (or simply unable) to question the work of their mentors.[1]

The result has been the upholding of an official orthodoxy of interpretation – a framework of assumptions and conclusions which, to outsiders, appears to have the solidity of established and undisputed fact. In this fashion, many of the so-called *données*, the 'givens' of history, were produced. Those responsible for developing the consensus view of Christianity have been able to exercise a monopoly over certain crucial sources, regulating the flow of information in a manner that enables its release to serve one's own purpose. This is the phenomenon explored by Umberto Eco in *The Name of the Rose*, where the monastery, and the library within it, reflect the medieval Church's monopoly of learning, constituting a kind of 'closed shop', an exclusive 'country club' of knowledge from which all but a select few are banned – a select few prepared to toe the 'party line'.

Those purveying the 'party line' can bolster the authority they arrogate to themselves by claiming that they alone have seen the relevant sources, access to which is closed to all outsiders. For outsiders, assembling the disparate available fragments into a coherent order amounts to an exercise in semiotics – and in the realm of semiotic exercises it becomes perfectly possible to hold the Knights Templar responsible for everything, and Umberto Eco himself responsible for the collapse of the Banco Ambrosiano. Thus, most outsiders, in the absence of any access to the relevant sources, have no choice but to accept the interpretations of the 'party line'. To challenge those interpretations is to find oneself labelled at best a crank, at worst, a renegade, apostate or heretic. Few scholars have the combination of courage, standing and expertise to issue such a challenge and hold on to their reputations. Robert Eisenman, whose currency and credibility have placed him among the most prominent and influential figures in his field, has done so. His story provided the impetus for this book.

I
THE DECEPTION

1

The Discovery of the Scrolls

E ast of Jerusalem, a long road slopes gradually down between barren hills sprinkled with occasional Bedouin camps. It sinks 3800 feet, to a depth of 1300 feet below sea-level, and then emerges to give a panoramic vista of the Jordan Valley. Away to the left, one can discern Jericho. In the haze ahead lie Jordan itself and, as though seen in a mirage, the mountains of Moab. To the right lies the northern shore of the Dead Sea. The skin of water, and the yellow cliffs rising 1200 feet or more which line this (the Israeli) side of it, conduce to awe – and to acute discomfort. The air here, so far below sea-level, is not just hot, but palpably so, with a thickness to it, a pressure, almost a weight.

The beauty, the majesty and the silence of the place are spell-binding. So, too, is the sense of antiquity the landscape conveys – the sense of a world older than most Western visitors are likely to have experienced. It is therefore all the more shocking when the 20th century intrudes with a roar that seems to rupture the sky – a tight formation of Israeli F-16s or Mirages swooping low over the water, the pilots clearly discernible in their cockpits. Afterburners blasting, the jets surge almost vertically upwards into invisibility. One waits, numbed. Seconds later, the entire structure of cliffs judders to the receding sonic booms. Only then does one remember that this place exists, technically, in a state of permanent war – that this side of the Dead Sea has never, during the last forty-odd years,

3

made peace with the other. But then again, the soil here has witnessed incessant conflict since the very beginning of recorded history. Too many gods, it seems, have clashed here, demanding blood sacrifice from their adherents.

The ruins of Qumran (or, to be more accurate, Khirbet Qumran) appear to the right, just as the road reaches the cliffs overlooking the Dead Sea. Thereafter, the road bends to follow the cliffs southwards, along the shore of the water, towards the site of the fortress of Masada, thirty-three miles away. Qumran stands on a white terrace of marl, a hundred feet or so above the road, slightly more than a mile and a quarter from the Dead Sea. The ruins themselves are not very prepossessing. One is first struck by a tower, two floors of which remain intact, with walls three feet thick – obviously built initially with defence in mind. Adjacent to the tower are a number of cisterns, large and small, connected by a complicated network of water channels. Some may have been used for ritual bathing. Most, however, if not all, would have been used to store the water the Qumran community needed to survive here in the desert. Between the ruins and the Dead Sea, on the lower levels of the marl terrace, lies an immense cemetery of some 1200 graves. Each is marked by a long mound of stones aligned – contrary to both Judaic and Muslim practice – north–south.

Even today, Qumran feels remote, though several hundred people live in a nearby kibbutz and the place can be reached quickly and easily by a modern road running to Jerusalem – a drive of some twenty miles and forty minutes. Day and night, huge articulated lorries thunder along the road, which links Eilat in the extreme south of Israel with Tiberius in the north. Tourist buses stop regularly, disgorging sweating Western Europeans and Americans, who are guided briefly around the ruins, then to an air-conditioned bookshop and restaurant for coffee and cakes. There are, of course, numerous military vehicles. But one also sees private cars, both Israeli and Arab, with their different coloured number-plates. One even sees the occasional 'boy racer' in a loud, badly built Detroit monster, whose speed appears limited only by the width of the road.

The Israeli Army is, needless to say, constantly in sight. This, after all, is the West Bank, and the Jordanians are only a few miles away, across the Dead Sea. Patrols run day and night, cruising at five miles per hour, scrutinising everything – small lorries, usually, with three heavy machine-guns on the back, soldiers upright behind them. These patrols will stop to check the cars and ascertain the precise whereabouts of anyone exploring the area, or excavating on the cliffs or in the caves. The visitor quickly learns to wave, to make sure the troops see him and acknowledge his presence. It is dangerous to come upon them too suddenly, or to act in any fashion that might strike them as furtive or suspicious.

The kibbutz – Kibbutz Kalia – is a ten-minute walk from Qumran, up a short road from the ruins. There are two small schools for the local children, a large communal refectory and housing units resembling motels for overnight tourists. But this is still a military zone. The kibbutz is surrounded by barbed wire and locked at night. An armed patrol is always on duty, and there are numerous air-raid shelters deep underground. These double for other purposes as well. One, for example, is used as a lecture hall, another as a bar, a third as a discothèque. But the wastes beyond the perimeter remain untouched by any such modernity. Here the Bedouin still shepherd their camels and their goats, seemingly timeless figures linking the present with the past.

In 1947, when the Dead Sea Scrolls were discovered, Qumran was very different. At that time the area was part of the British mandate of Palestine. To the east lay what was then the kingdom of Transjordan. The road that runs south along the shore of the Dead Sea did not exist, extending only to the Dead Sea's north-western quarter, a few miles from Jericho. Around and beyond it there were only rough tracks, one of which followed the course of an ancient Roman road. This route had long been in total disrepair. Qumran was thus rather more difficult to reach than it is today. The sole human presence in the vicinity would have been the Bedouin, herding their camels and goats during the winter and spring, when the desert, perhaps surprisingly, yielded both water and grass. In the winter, or possibly the early spring, of 1947, it was to yield something more – one of the two or three greatest archaeological discoveries of modern times.

5

The precise circumstances attending the discovery of the Dead Sea Scrolls have already passed into legend. In a number of particulars, this legend is probably not entirely accurate, and scholars were bickering over certain points well into the 1960s. It remains, however, the only account we have. The original discovery is ascribed to a shepherd boy, Muhammad adh-Dhib, or Muhammad the Wolf, a member of the Ta'amireh tribe of Bedouin. He himself later claimed he was searching for a lost goat. Whatever he was doing, his itinerary brought him clambering among the cliffs at Qumran, where he discovered an opening in the cliff-face. He tried to peer inside but, from where he stood, could see nothing. He then tossed a stone into the blackness, which elicited a sound of breaking pottery. This, needless to say, impelled him to further exploration.

Hoisting himself upwards, he crawled through the aperture, then dropped down to find himself in a small cave, high-ceilinged and narrow, no more than six feet wide and perhaps twenty-four long. It contained a number of large earthenware jars, about two feet tall and ten inches wide, many of them broken. Eight are generally believed to have been intact, though the quantity has never been definitively established.

According to his own account, Muhammad became frightened, hauled himself back out of the cave and fled. The next day, he returned with at least one friend and proceeded to explore the cave and its contents more closely. Some of the earthenware jars were sealed by large 'bowl-like' lids. Inside one of them, there were three leather rolls wrapped in decaying linen – the first of the Dead Sea Scrolls to see the light in nearly two thousand years.[1]

During the days that followed, the Bedouin returned to the site and at least four more leather rolls were found. At least two jars were removed and used for carrying water. When proper archaeological excavation began, it revealed a substantial number of sherds and fragments – enough, according to reliable estimates, to have constituted no fewer than forty jars. There is no way of knowing how many of these jars, when first discovered, were empty and how many actually contained scrolls. Neither is there any way of knowing how many scrolls were taken from the cave and, before

6

their significance became apparent, secreted away, destroyed or used for other purposes. Some, it has been suggested, were burned for fuel. In any case, we were told that more scrolls were taken from the cave than have previously been recorded, or than have subsequently come to light. Altogether, a total of seven complete scrolls were to find their way into the public domain, along with fragments of some twenty-one others.

At this point, accounts begin to grow increasingly contradictory. Apparently, however, thinking the scrolls might be of some value, three Bedouin took all they had found – three complete parchments according to some sources, seven or eight according to others – to a local sheik. He passed the Bedouin on to a Christian shopkeeper and dealer in curios and antiques, one Khalil Iskander Shahin, known as 'Kando'. Kando, a member of the Syrian Jacobite Church, contacted another Church member residing in Jerusalem, George Isaiah. According to reliable scholars, Kando and Isaiah promptly ventured out to Qumran themselves and removed a number of additional scrolls and/or fragments.[2]

Such activities were, of course, illegal. By the law of the British mandate – a law subsequently retained by both Jordanian and Israeli governments – all archaeological discoveries belonged officially to the state. They were supposed to be turned over to the Department of Antiquities, then housed in the Palestine Archaeological Museum, known as the Rockefeller, in Arab East Jerusalem. But Palestine was in turmoil at the time, and Jerusalem a city divided into Jewish, Arab and British sectors. In these circumstances, the authorities had more pressing matters to deal with than a black market in archaeological relics. In consequence, Kando and George Isaiah were free to pursue their clandestine transactions with impunity.

George Isaiah reported the discovery to his ecclesiastical leader, the Syrian Metropolitan (i.e. Archbishop) Athanasius Yeshua Samuel, head of the Syrian Jacobite Church in Jerusalem. Academically, Athanasius Yeshua Samuel was a naïve man, untutored in the sophisticated scholarship needed to identify, much less translate, the text before him. The late Edmund Wilson, one of the earliest and most reliable commentators on the Qumran discovery, wrote of Samuel that he 'was not a Hebrew scholar and could not make out what the manuscript was'.[3] He even burned a small piece of it and smelled it, to verify that the substance was indeed leather, or parchment. But whatever his academic shortcomings, Samuel was also shrewd, and his monastery, St Mark's, contained a famous collection of ancient documents. He thus had some idea of the importance of what had passed into his hands.

Samuel later said he first learned of the Dead Sea Scrolls in April 1947. If chronology has hitherto been vague and contradictory, however, it now becomes even more so, varying from commentator to commentator. But some time between early June and early July Samuel requested Kando and George Isaiah to arrange a meeting with the three Bedouin who'd made the original discovery, to examine what they'd found.

When the Bedouin arrived in Jerusalem, they were carrying at least four scrolls and possibly as many as eight – the three they'd originally found themselves, plus one or more from whatever they or Kando and George Isaiah had subsequently plundered. Unfortunately, the Metropolitan had neglected to mention the Bedouin's impending visit to the monks at the monastery of St Mark. When the Bedouin appeared with their dirty, crumbling and ragged parchments, themselves unshaven and insalubrious-looking, the monk at the gate turned them away. By the time Samuel learned of this, it was too late. The Bedouin, understandably resentful, wanted nothing further to do with Metropolitan Samuel. One of them even refused to have any further dealings with Kando, and sold his portion of the scrolls – a 'third' share which amounted to three scrolls – to the Muslim sheik of Bethlehem. Kando managed to purchase the shares of the remaining scrolls, and sold them in turn to the Metropolitan for a reported £24. This cache was believed at first to consist of five scrolls, but proved eventually to contain only four, one of them having broken in two. Of the four texts, one was a well-preserved copy of the book of Isaiah from the Old Testament, the parchment of which unrolled to a length of twenty-four feet. The other three, according to the nomenclature later adopted by scholars, included the 'Genesis Apocryphon', a commentary on the 'Book of Habakkuk' and the so-called 'Community Rule'.

Shortly after the Bedouin's abortive visit to Jerusalem – in late

July according to some reports, in August according to others – Metropolitan Samuel sent a priest to return with George Isaiah to the cave at Qumran. Being engaged in illicit activities, the pair worked by night. They examined the site at length and found at least one additional jar and some fragments; they also conducted, apparently, some fairly extensive excavations. When the first official research party reached the location a year later, they discovered an entire section of the cliff-face had been removed, making a large entrance into the cave below the smaller hole originally explored by the Bedouin. What this enterprise may have yielded remains unknown. In researching this book, we interviewed certain people who insisted that George Isaiah, during the course of his nocturnal explorations, found a number of other scrolls, some of which have never been seen by scholars.

Having obtained at least some of the scrolls, Metropolitan Samuel undertook to establish their age. He first consulted a Syrian expert working at the Department of Antiquities. In this man's opinion, the scrolls were of fairly recent date. The Metropolitan then consulted a Dutch scholar working with the Ecole Biblique et Archéologique Française de Jérusalem, an institution run by Dominican monks and financed, in part, by the French government. He was intrigued, but remained sceptical about the scrolls' antiquity, describing subsequently how he returned to the Ecole Biblique and consulted 'a prominent scholar' there, who lectured him about the prevalent forgeries floating around amongst dodgy antique dealers.[4] As a result, he abandoned his research on the matter, and the Ecole Biblique lost its opportunity to get involved at the beginning. Only the relatively untutored Metropolitan, at this point, seems to have had any inkling of the scrolls' age, value and significance.

In September 1947, the Metropolitan took the scrolls in his possession to his superior, the Patriarch of the Syrian Jacobite Church in Homs, north of Damascus. What passed between them is not known, but on his return the Metropolitan again dispatched a party of men to excavate the cave at Qumran. Presumably he was acting on the Patriarch's instructions. In any case, he obviously believed there was more to be discovered.

Metropolitan Samuel's visit to Syria in September had coincided with the arrival there of Miles Copeland, who had joined the OSS during the Second World War, had remained with that organisation when it became the CIA and went on to become a long-serving operative and station chief. In a personal interview, Copeland told how, in the autumn of 1947, he had just been posted to Damascus as the CIA's representative there. In the circumstances then prevailing, there was no need to operate under particularly deep cover, and his identity seems to have been pretty much an open secret. According to Copeland, a 'sly Egyptian merchant' came to see him one day and claimed to possess a great treasure. Reaching into a dirty sack, the man then pulled out a scroll, the edges of which were already disintegrating – fragments were flaking off into the street. When asked what it was, Copeland, of course, couldn't say. If the merchant left it with him, however, he promised he would photograph it and get someone to study it.

In order to photograph it, Copeland and his colleagues took the scroll up on to the roof of the American Legation in Damascus and stretched it out. A strong wind was gusting at the time, Copeland remembered, and pieces of the scroll peeled away, wafted over the roof and into the streets of the city, to be lost for ever. According to Copeland, a substantial portion of the parchment vanished in this manner. Copeland's wife, an archaeologist herself, said she could not help wincing every time she heard the story.

Using photographic equipment supplied by the American government, Copeland and his colleagues took, he reported, some thirty frames. This, he said, was not sufficient to cover the entire length of the scroll, which must, therefore, have been considerable. Subsequently, the photographs were taken to the American embassy in Beirut and shown to a prominent official there, a man versed in ancient languages. The official declared the text to be part of the Old Testament book of Daniel. Some of the writing was in Aramaic, he said, some in Hebrew. Unfortunately, however, there was no follow-up. Copeland returned to Damascus, but the 'sly Egyptian merchant' was never seen again and the photographs were left in a drawer.[5] No one, to this day, knows what became of them, or of the scroll itself, although fragments of a Daniel scroll were subsequently found at Qumran, five years after the incident Copeland described.

If the scroll Copeland saw and photographed was indeed a text of Daniel, it has never become public.

Although it was precisely at this time that Metropolitan Samuel was in Syria with the scrolls he had purchased, it is unlikely that the scroll Copeland saw was one of these, since only three of the scrolls in his possession could be unrolled at all, and only one – the twenty-four-foot-long Hebrew text of Isaiah – would have taken more than thirty frames of film to photograph. If this is what Copeland saw, why should it have been identified as Daniel, not Isaiah, and why should the writing have been identified as both Hebrew and Aramaic? It is possible, of course, that the CIA official was mistaken. But when we repeated Copeland's story to a prominent Israeli researcher, he was intrigued. 'It might be very interesting,' he said, in confidence. 'It might be a scroll that hasn't been seen yet.' If we could obtain any further information, he said, 'I'll exchange with you . . . additional data concerning missing scrolls.'[6] Which implies, needless to say, that such data exist and have never been made public.

While Copeland's photographs were being examined in Beirut, Metropolitan Samuel was persisting in his efforts to confirm the age of the scrolls in his possession. A Jewish doctor who visited his monastery put him in touch with scholars from Hebrew University. They in turn put him in touch with the head of Hebrew University's Department of Archaeology, Professor Eleazar Sukenik. On 24 November, before Sukenik came to view the scrolls held by the Metropolitan, a secret meeting occurred between him and a figure subsequently identified only as an Armenian antique dealer. Neither had had time to obtain the requisite military passes. They were therefore obliged to meet at a checkpoint between the Jewish and the Arab zones of Jerusalem, and to talk across a barrier of barbed wire. Across this barrier, the Armenian showed Sukenik a fragment of a scroll on which Hebrew writing could be discerned. The Armenian then explained that an Arab antique dealer from Bethlehem had come to him the day before, bringing this and other fragments alleged to have been found by Bedouin. Sukenik was asked if they were genuine and if Hebrew University were prepared to purchase them. Sukenik requested a second meeting, which occurred three days later. This time he had a pass, and was able to look closely at a number of fragments. Convinced they were important, he resolved to go to Bethlehem to see more, dangerous though such an undertaking was at the time.

On 29 November 1947, Sukenik slipped furtively out of Jerusalem and made the clandestine trip to Bethlehem. Here he was told in detail how the scrolls had been discovered and was shown three scrolls which were for sale – those which the Metropolitan had missed – and two of the jars that contained them. He was allowed to take the scrolls home, and was studying them when, at midnight, dramatic news came over the radio: a majority of the United Nations had voted for the creation of the state of Israel. At that moment, Sukenik resolved to purchase the scrolls. They seemed to him a kind of talismanic portent, a symbolic validation of the momentous historical events that had just been set in motion.[7]

This conviction was shared by his son, Yigael Yadin, then chief of operations for the Haganah – the semi-clandestine militia which during the struggle for independence in 1948 was to evolve into the Israeli Defence Forces. For Yadin also the discovery of the scrolls was to assume an almost mystical significance:

> I cannot avoid the feeling that there is something symbolic in the discovery of the scrolls and their acquisition at the moment of the creation of the State of Israel. It is as if these manuscripts had been waiting in caves for two thousand years, ever since the destruction of Israel's independence, until the people of Israel had returned to their home and regained their freedom.[8]

Towards the end of January 1948, Sukenik arranged to view the scrolls held by Metropolitan Samuel. The meeting, again, was to be clandestine. It was to occur in the British sector of Jerusalem, at the YMCA, where the librarian was a member of the Metropolitan's congregation. Security was particularly tight here, the YMCA being situated directly across the road from the King David Hotel, which had been bombed, with great loss of life, in 1946. To enter the zone, Sukenik had to obtain a pass from the British District Officer, Professor Biran.

Endeavouring to pass himself off as just another scholar, Sukenik carried a handful of library books with him and made his way to the YMCA. Here, in a private room, he was shown the Metropolitan's scrolls and allowed to borrow them for inspection. He returned them to the Metropolitan on 6 February, unable to raise sufficient funds to purchase them. By that time, the political and economic situation was too tense for any bank to authorise the requisite loan. The local Jewish authorities, faced with the prospect of impending war, could not spare anything. No one else was interested.

Sukenik tried to bring down the price, and the Syrian agent representing the Metropolitan arranged to meet him a week later. By that time, Sukenik had contrived to raise the money required. He heard nothing, however, from the Metropolitan or the agent, until some weeks later a letter arrived from the Syrian declaring that the Metropolitan had decided, after all, not to sell. Unknown to Sukenik, negotiations were already in train by then with American scholars who had photographed the scrolls and insisted a much better price could be elicited for them in the United States. Sukenik, needless to say, was mortified by the lost opportunity.

Metropolitan Samuel had contacted the Jerusalem-based Albright Institute (the American School of Oriental Research) in February, and a complete set of prints had been sent by the Institute to the acknowledged expert in the field, Professor William F. Albright, at Johns Hopkins University. On 15 March, Professor Albright replied confirming Sukenik's conviction of the importance of the discovery, and setting the seal of approval on the Qumran texts. He also, unwittingly, provided support for those intent on attributing to the scrolls the earliest date possible:

> My heartiest congratulations on the greatest manuscript discovery of modern times! There is no doubt whatever in my mind that the script is more archaic than that of the Nash Papyrus . . . I should prefer a date around 100 BC . . . What an absolutely incredible find! And there can happily not be the slightest doubt in the world about the genuineness of the MS.[9]

On 18 March, a suggested press release was drawn up. In the meantime, the scrolls had been taken to Beirut and placed in a bank there for safekeeping. Later in the year, Metropolitan Samuel was to pick them up, and in January 1949 he took them to the United States, where they were to spend the next few years in a New York bank vault.

On 11 April, the first press release appeared, issued by Yale University, where Professor Millar Burrows – director of the Albright Institute – was head of the Department of Near Eastern Languages. The press release was not entirely truthful. No one wanted swarms of amateurs (or rivals) to descend on Qumran, and so the discovery was alleged to have been made in the library of Metropolitan Samuel's monastery. But for the first time, fully a year after they'd initially surfaced, the existence of the Dead Sea Scrolls became known to the general public. On page 4 of its edition for Monday, 12 April 1948, *The Times* ran the following article under the headline 'ANCIENT MSS. FOUND IN PALESTINE':

> New York, April 11
> Yale University announced yesterday the discovery in Palestine of the earliest known manuscript of the Book of Isaiah. It was found in the Syrian monastery of St Mark in Jerusalem, where it had been preserved in a scroll of parchment dating to about the first century BC. Recently it was identified by scholars of the American School of Oriental Research [the Albright Institute] at Jerusalem.
>
> There were also examined at the school three other ancient Hebrew scrolls. One was part of a commentary on the Book of Habakkuk; another seemed to be a manual of discipline of some comparatively little-known sect or monastic order, possibly the Essenes. The third scroll has not been identified.

It was not an article calculated to set the world of scholarship aflame. So far as most readers of *The Times* were concerned, it would have meant little enough, and would anyway have been effectively up-staged by other news on the same page. Fourteen German SS officers who'd commanded extermination squads on the Eastern Front were sentenced to hang. According to the chief prosecutor, the judgment 'was a landmark in the campaign against racial intolerance and violence'. There were also reports of a massacre in the Holy Land the previous Friday. Two Jewish terrorist

14

organisations – the Irgun and the Stern Gang – had wiped out the Arab village of Deir Yasin, raping girls, exterminating men, women and children. The Jewish Agency itself expressed 'horror and disgust' at what had happened. In the meantime, according to other reports on the page, there was fighting in Jerusalem. Arab artillery had bombarded the western quarter of the city at dusk. Quantities of new field-guns had arrived from Syria and were aimed at Jewish sectors. The city's water supply had again been cut off. Rail supplies had been disrupted. Renewed fighting for the Tel Aviv–Jerusalem road was expected to be imminent. Elsewhere in the Holy Land, Arab terrorists had murdered two British soldiers, and Jewish terrorists one. (Forty-two years later, while this was being checked and copied from microfilm in a local library, there was a bomb alert and the premises had to be evacuated. *Plus ça change . . .*)

Hostilities in the Middle East were to continue for another year. On 14 May 1948 – the day before the British mandate was scheduled to expire – the Jewish People's Council met in the Tel Aviv Museum and declared their own independent state of Israel. The response from adjacent Arab countries was immediate. That very night, Egyptian aircraft bombed Tel Aviv. During the six and a half months of fighting that followed, Israel was to be invaded by troops from Egypt, Saudi Arabia, Transjordan, Syria, Iraq and Lebanon, while the King of Transjordan proclaimed himself monarch of all Palestine.

The final ceasefire took effect on 7 January 1949. According to its terms, the large central section of what had formerly been Palestine was to remain Arab. This territory was occupied and then annexed by Transjordan, which on 2 June 1949 began to call itself simply Jordan. Thus Qumran passed into Jordanian hands, along with the Arab east side of Jerusalem. The border between Israel and Jordan – the Nablus road – cut through the centre of the city.

Amidst these dramatic historical events, the scrolls attracted little public attention or interest. Behind the scenes, however, political, religious and academic forces were already beginning to mobilise. By January 1949, the Department of Antiquities for Transjordan and Arab Palestine had become involved, under the auspices of its director, Gerald Lankester Harding. So had Father

15

Roland de Vaux, director, since 1945, of another institution – the Dominican-sponsored Ecole Biblique, situated in the Jordanian-controlled eastern sector of Jerusalem, and for the last sixty years a centre of French–Catholic biblical scholarship in the city.

A year and a half had now elapsed since the scrolls were first found. To date, however, no trained archaeologist had visited the site of the discovery. The Albright Institute had tried, but the war, they decided, rendered any such endeavours too dangerous. It was at this point that a Belgian air-force officer, Captain Philippe Lippens, appeared on the scene. Lippens had arrived in Jerusalem as a member of the United Nations Truce Supervision Organisation. But he was also Jesuit-trained, and a graduate of the Oriental Institute at the University of Louvain. He had read of the scrolls, and now approached de Vaux, who until then appears to have been sceptical about their significance. If he managed to locate the cave of the original discovery, Lippens asked, would de Vaux confer legitimacy on the undertaking by acting as technical director for subsequent excavations? De Vaux assented.

On 24 January, Lippens established the support of a British officer commanding a brigade of the Jordanian Arab Legion, and, through this officer, the support of Lankester Harding in Amman. With Harding's blessing, the British Army's archaeological officer was despatched to Qumran, to search for the cave in which the original discovery had been made. He was accompanied by two Bedouin from the Arab Legion, who located the cave on 28 January. Inside, they found remains of the linen in which the scrolls had been wrapped and numerous pieces of pottery. A fortnight or so later, early in February, Harding and de Vaux visited the cave together. They found enough shards for more than forty jars and the remains of thirty identifiable texts, as well as many more unidentifiable fragments. Within another fortnight, the first official archaeological expedition had been mounted.

In the years that followed, scrolls became big business indeed, and traffic in them came to constitute an extremely lucrative cottage industry. Fragments were being smuggled to and fro in dirty wallets, in cigarette boxes, in assorted other makeshift containers. Forgeries began to appear, and wily local merchants had no shortage of gullible purchasers. The popular press portrayed anything resembling ancient parchment as immensely valuable. In consequence, Arab dealers were loath to settle for anything less than hundreds of pounds, and on at least one occasion a thousand – and this, it must be remembered, was in the days when a house could be mortgaged for £1500.

When Metropolitan Samuel took his scrolls to the United States, Jordanian radio reports claimed he was asking a million dollars for them. Fears arose that scrolls would be bought not only for private collections and as souvenirs, but also as investments. At the same time, of course, the scrolls themselves were dangerously fragile, requiring special conditions of light and temperature to preserve them from further deterioration. In many of them, indeed, the process of deterioration was already irreversible. As the black market burgeoned, so did the prospect of ever more valuable material being lost irretrievably to scholarship.

Responsibility to do something about the matter devolved upon Gerald Lankester Harding of the Department of Antiquities. Harding concluded it was less important to insist on the letter of the law than to rescue as many scrolls and fragments as he could. In consequence, he adopted a policy of purchasing scroll material from whomever happened to have it. This affected the legal status of such material by tacitly acknowledging that anyone who possessed it had a legitimate claim to it. In their negotiations and transactions, Harding's agents were authorised to ignore all questions of legality and (up to a point) price. He himself, being fluent in Arabic, befriended not just dealers, but the Bedouin as well, and let it be known he would pay handsomely for anything they might obtain. Nevertheless, Metropolitan Samuel was accused of having 'smuggled' his scrolls out of the country, and the Jordanian government demanded their return. By that time, of course, it was too late. Eventually, the Bedouin of the Ta 'amireh tribe were given what amounted to a 'cave-hunting monopoly'. The Qumran area became, in effect, a military zone, and the Ta 'amireh were charged with policing it, 'to keep other tribes from muscling in on the scroll rush'.[10] Whatever the Ta 'amireh found, they would take to Kando, who would remunerate them.

Kando would take the material to Harding and be remunerated in turn.

In October 1951, members of the Ta 'amireh tribe arrived in Jerusalem with scroll fragments from a new site. Both Father de Vaux of the Ecole Biblique and Harding were away, so the Bedouin approached Joseph Saad, director of the Rockefeller Museum. Saad demanded to be taken to the site in question. The Bedouin went off to consult, and failed to return.

Saad obtained a jeep, a letter of authority from the archaeological officer of the Arab Legion and some armed men and drove to the first Ta 'amireh camp he could find, outside Bethlehem. The next morning, as he was driving into Bethlehem, he saw one of the men who had approached him the day before. Dispensing with all niceties, Saad proceeded to kidnap the Bedouin:

> As the Jeep slewed to a stop, Saad called the man over and immediately demanded more information about the cave. Fear came into the Arab's eyes and he made as if to move on. The soldiers leapt down from the jeep and barred his way. Then, at a nod from Saad they lifted the man bodily and pushed him into the back of the truck. The driver let in the clutch and they roared off back the way they had come.[11]

Subjected to this sort of persuasion, the Bedouin agreed to co-operate. Saad obtained reinforcements from a nearby military post, and the contingent headed off down the Wadi Ta 'amireh towards the Dead Sea. When the terrain became impassable, they abandoned the jeep and began to walk. They walked for seven hours, until they came to a wadi with walls hundreds of feet high. Far up in the cliff-face, two large caves could be seen, with clouds of dust issuing from them – the Bedouin were already inside, collecting what they could. At Saad's arrival, a number of them emerged. The soldiers accompanying Saad fired into the air and the Bedouin dispersed. Of the two caves, one, when the soldiers reached it, proved to be huge – twenty feet wide, twelve to fifteen feet high and extending some 150 feet back into the cliff. It was the next morning before Saad got back to Jerusalem. Exhausted after his expedition (which had included fourteen hours of walking), he went to sleep. He woke later in the day to find Jerusalem in a state of upheaval. Friends of the Bedouin had spread the news of his 'kidnapping' and incarceration. One commentator observed afterwards that it was 'perhaps' a mistake to have used force: this served to drive documents underground and made the Bedouin more reluctant to relinquish what they found.[12]

Saad's expedition led to the discovery of four caves at Wadi Murabba'at, just over eleven miles south of Qumran and some two miles inland from the Dead Sea. The material found here was less difficult to date and identify than that from Qumran, but of nearly comparable import. It derived from the early 2nd century AD – more specifically, from the revolt in Judaea orchestrated by Simeon bar Kochba between AD 132 and 135. It included two letters signed by Simeon himself and furnished new data on the logistics, economics and civil administration of the rebellion, which had come within a hair's-breadth of success – Simeon actually captured Jerusalem from the Romans and held the city for some two years. According to Robert Eisenman, this insurrection was a direct continuation of events dating from the previous century – events which involved certain of the same families, many of the same underlying principles, and perhaps also Jesus himself.

Shortly after the discovery of the caves at Murabba'at, activity around Qumran began to gather momentum. Having returned from Europe, Father de Vaux began to excavate the site, together with Harding and fifteen workers. These excavations were to continue for the next five years, until 1956. Among other things, they exhumed a complex of buildings, which were identified as the 'Essene community' spoken of by Pliny.

Pliny himself perished in AD 79, in the eruption of Vesuvius which buried Pompeii and Herculaneum. Of his works, only the *Natural History* survives – which, however, deals with both the topography and certain events in Judaea. Pliny's sources are unknown, but his text refers to the sack of Jerusalem in AD 68, and must therefore have been composed some time after that. There was even for a time a legend, now discredited, that, like Josephus, he accompanied the Roman army on its invasion of Palestine. In any case, Pliny is one of the few ancient writers not just to mention the Essenes by

19

name, but to locate them geographically. He locates them, quite specifically, on the shores of the Dead Sea:

> On the west side of the Dead Sea, but out of range of the noxious exhalations of the coast, is the solitary tribe of the Essenes, which is remarkable beyond all the other tribes in the whole world, as it has no women and has renounced all sexual desire, has no money, and has only palm-trees for company. Day by day the throng of refugees is recruited to an equal number by numerous accessions of persons tired of life and driven thither by the waves of fortune to adopt their manners . . . Lying below the Essenes was formerly the town of Engedi . . . next comes Masada.[13]

De Vaux took this passage as referring to Qumran, assuming that 'below the Essenes' means 'down', or to the south. The Jordan, he argued, flows 'down', or south, to the Dead Sea; and if one continues further south, one does indeed come to the site of Engedi.[14] Other scholars dispute de Vaux's contention, maintaining that 'lying below' is to be understood literally – that the Essene community was situated in the hills *above* Engedi.

Whether Qumran was indeed Pliny's community or not, de Vaux was spurred on to further efforts. In the spring of 1952, he endeavoured to wrest the initiative from the Bedouin and make a systematic survey of all caves in the vicinity. The survey was conducted between 10 and 22 March 1952 by de Vaux, three other members of the Ecole Biblique and William Reed, the new director of the Albright Institute. They were accompanied by a team of twenty-four Bedouin under the authority of three Jordanian and Palestinian archaeologists.[15] Not surprisingly, perhaps, it was the Bedouin who did all the work, clambering up the steep, often precipitous cliff-faces and exploring caves. The archaeologists preferred to remain below, compiling inventories, drawing up maps and charts. As a result, the survey was not very comprehensive. The Bedouin, for example, chose not to divulge the existence of certain caves they had found. Several scrolls did not come to light until much later. And one is known never to have been recovered from the Bedouin.

Altogether, the survey encompassed some five miles of cliff-face.

It examined 267 sites according to de Vaux, 273 sites according to William Reed. According to de Vaux, it yielded thirty-seven caves containing pottery. According to Reed, it yielded thirty-nine. The official map produced at the conclusion of the expedition shows forty.[16] Shards were found for more than a hundred jars, a highly speculative figure. Such imprecision is typical of Qumran research.

But if the 1952 survey was amateurish, it also produced one genuinely important discovery. On 20 March, two days before the end of the survey, in the site designated Cave 3, a research team found two scrolls – or, rather, two fragments of the same scroll – of rolled copper. The writing on it had been punched into the metal. Oxidisation had rendered the metal too brittle to be unrolled. Before it could be read, the scroll would have to be sliced open in a laboratory. Three and a half years were to pass before the Jordanian authorities allowed this to be done. When they at last consented, the cutting was performed in Manchester under the auspices of John Allegro, a member of de Vaux's team. The first segment of the scroll was finished in summer 1955, the second in January 1956.

The scroll proved to be an inventory of treasure – a compilation or listing of gold, silver, ritual vessels and other scrolls. Apparently, at the commencement of the Roman invasion, this treasure had been divided into a number of secret caches; and the 'Copper Scroll', as it came to be known, detailed the contents and whereabouts of each such cache. Thus, for example:

ITEM 7. In the cavity of the Old House of Tribute, in the Platform of the Chain: sixty-five bars of gold.[17]

According to researchers, the total hoard would have amounted to some sixty-five tons of silver and perhaps twenty-six of gold. To this day, there is some argument as to whether the treasure ever in fact existed. Most scholars, however, are prepared to accept that it did and that the scroll comprises an accurate inventory of the Temple of Jerusalem. Unfortunately, the locations indicated by the scroll have been rendered meaningless by time, change and the course of two millennia, and nothing of the treasure has ever been found. A number of people, certainly, have searched for it.

★

21

In September 1952, six months after the official survey, there surfaced a new source of scrolls. It proved to be a cave within some fifty feet of the actual ruins of Qumran, which de Vaux and Harding had excavated in 1951. Here, at the site demarcated Cave 4, the largest discovery of all was made – again, predictably, by the Bedouin. Some years would be required to piece this material together. By 1959, however, most of the fragments had been organised. The work was conducted in a large room, which came to be known as the 'Scrollery', in the Rockefeller Museum.

The Rockefeller Museum – or, to give it its official name, the Palestine Archaeological Museum – had first opened in 1938, during the British mandate, and was built from funds donated by John D. Rockefeller. It contained not only exhibition space, but also laboratories, photographic dark-rooms and the offices of the Department of Antiquities. Shortly before the mandate ended in 1948, the museum had been turned over to an international board of trustees. This board was made up of representatives of the various foreign archaeological schools in Jerusalem – the French Ecole Biblique, for example, the American Albright Institute, the British Palestine Exploration Society. For eighteen years, the Rockefeller was to exist as an independently endowed institution. It managed to retain this status even through the Suez Crisis of 1956, when many of its staff were recalled to their home countries. The only casualties of the crisis were Gerald Lankester Harding, dismissed from his post as director of the Department of Antiquities, and the scrolls themselves. During hostilities, they were removed from the museum, placed into thirty-six cases and locked up in a bank in Amman. They were not returned to Jerusalem until March 1957, 'some of them slightly moldy [sic] and spotted from the damp vault'.[18]

In 1966, however, the Rockefeller, with the scrolls it contained, was officially nationalised by the Jordanian government. This move was to have important repercussions. It was also of questionable legality. The museum's board of trustees did not object, however. On the contrary, the president of the board transferred the museum's endowment fund from London, where it had been invested, to Amman. Thus the scrolls and the museum housing them became, in effect, Jordanian property.

A year later, the Middle East erupted in the Six Day War, and Jordanian East Jerusalem fell to Israeli troops. At five o'clock on the morning of 6 June 1967, Yigael Yadin was informed that the museum had been occupied by an Israeli paratroop unit.

After becoming, in 1949, chief of staff of the Israeli Defence Forces, Yadin had resigned in 1952 and studied archaeology at Hebrew University, earning his PhD in 1955 with a thesis on one of the Dead Sea Scrolls. That year he began teaching at Hebrew University. In 1954 he had travelled to the USA on a lecture tour. There, after speaking at Johns Hopkins University, he met Professor William F. Albright and asked why the American had published only three of Metropolitan Samuel's four scrolls. Albright replied that Samuel was anxious to sell the scrolls and would not allow the fourth to be published until a purchaser had been found for all of them. Could a purchaser not be found in the States, Yadin asked: 'Surely a few million dollars for such a purpose is not too difficult to raise.' Albright's reply was astonishing. The scrolls, he said, would probably sell for as little as half a million. Even so, however, no American institution or individual appeared to be interested.[19]

There were, in fact, two reasons for this apparent apathy. In the first place, facsimile editions of the first three scrolls had already been produced; and this, for most American researchers, obviated the need for the originals. More significant, however, was the legal status of the scrolls' ownership. The Jordanian government had branded Metropolitan Samuel 'a smuggler and a traitor', claiming he had had no right to take the scrolls out of Jordan; and the Americans, by virtue of publishing the contraband texts, were accused of collusion in the 'crime'. This, needless to say, deterred prospective purchasers, who had no desire to lay out a substantial sum of money, only to find themselves embroiled in complex international litigation and, quite possibly, end up with nothing. Yadin, on the other hand, had no need to fear the Jordanians. Relations between his country and theirs couldn't possibly sink any lower.

On 1 June, Yadin was telephoned by an Israeli journalist stationed in the States, who called the advertisement in the *Wall Street Journal* to his attention. Yadin resolved immediately to obtain the scrolls, but recognised that a direct approach might jeopardise everything.

In consequence, he worked almost entirely through intermediaries, and it was a New York banker who replied to the advertisement. A meeting was arranged for 11 June 1954, a price of $250,000 for the four scrolls was agreed on and a wealthy benefactor found to provide the requisite money. After a number of frustrating delays, the transaction was completed at the Waldorf Astoria on 1 July. Among those present was a distinguished scholar, Professor Harry Orlinsky, whose role was to ensure the scrolls were indeed genuine. In order to conceal any Israeli or Jewish interest in the deal, Orlinsky introduced himself as 'Mr Green'.

The next day, 2 July, the scrolls were removed from the vault of the Waldorf Astoria and taken to the Israeli Consulate in New York. Each scroll was then sent back to Israel separately. Yadin returned home by ship, and a code was arranged to keep him informed of each scroll's safe arrival. Details of the transaction were kept secret for another seven months. Not until 13 February 1955 did a press release reveal that Israel had acquired the four scrolls of Metropolitan Samuel.[20] Along with the three scrolls previously purchased by Sukenik, they are now in the Shrine of the Book, which was established specifically to house them.

By the end of 1954, then, there were two entirely separate bodies of scroll material and two entirely separate cadres of experts working with them. In West Jerusalem, there were the Israelis, addressing themselves to the scrolls acquired by Sukenik and Yadin. In East Jerusalem, at the Rockefeller, there was a team of international scholars operating under the direction of de Vaux. Neither group communicated with the other. Neither had any contact with the other. Neither knew what the other possessed or what the other was doing, except for what leaked out in scholarly journals. In several instances, specific texts were fragmented, some pieces being in Israeli hands, some at the Rockefeller – which made it, of course, that much more difficult to obtain any sense of the whole. So ridiculous was the situation that certain individuals were tempted to do something about it. Former Major-General Ariel Sharon reported that, in the late 1950s, he and Moshe Dayan devised a plan for an underground raid on the Rockefeller, to be conducted through Jerusalem's sewer system.[21] The plan, needless to say, was never implemented.

Now, however, in 1967, hearing of the capture of the Rockefeller, Yadin immediately dispatched three colleagues from Hebrew University to ensure that the scrolls were safe. He recognised the implications of what had happened. Because the Rockefeller Museum was no longer an international institution, but a Jordanian one, it would pass into Israeli hands as a spoil of war.

2
The International Team

Yigael Yadin recounted the events of 1967 to David Pryce-Jones in an interview conducted early in 1968. He was aware, he said, that other scrolls were around, and that Kando, the dealer involved in the original discovery, knew where they were. He therefore sent other staff members from Hebrew University, accompanied by three officers, to Kando's house in Bethlehem. Kando was taken under escort to Tel Aviv. When he emerged after five days of interrogation, he took the officers back to his home and produced a scroll which had been hidden there for six years. This proved to be an extremely important discovery – the 'Temple Scroll', first published in 1977.[1]

Pryce-Jones also interviewed Father de Vaux, who was highly indignant at what had occurred. According to Pryce-Jones, de Vaux called the Israelis 'Nazis': 'His face flushed as he claimed the Israelis would use the conquest of Jerusalem as a pretext to move all the Dead Sea Scrolls from the Rockefeller and house them in their Shrine of the Book.'[2] He also feared for both his own position and his access to the Qumran texts, because, as Pryce-Jones discovered, 'Father de Vaux had refused to allow any Jews to work on the scrolls in the Rockefeller'.[3]

De Vaux's fears, in fact, proved groundless. In the political and military aftermath of the Six Day War, the Israelis had other matters on their plate. Yadin and Professor Biran, who from 1961 to 1974 was director of the Israeli Department of Antiquities, were therefore prepared to maintain the status quo, and de Vaux was left in charge of the scrolls, with the stipulation that their publication be speeded up.

A cache of some eight hundred scrolls had been discovered in Cave 4 in 1952. To deal with the sheer quantity of this material, an international committee of scholars had been formed, each member of which was assigned certain specific texts for study, interpretation, translation and eventual publication. Owing nominal allegiance to the Jordanian Department of Antiquities, the committee in reality functioned under the virtually supreme authority of Father de Vaux. He subsequently became editor-in-chief of the definitive series on the Dead Sea Scrolls, the multi-volume *Discoveries in the Judaean Desert*, published by Oxford University Press. He was to retain his prominence in the field until his death in 1977.

Roland de Vaux was born in Paris in 1903 and studied for the priesthood between 1925 and 1928 at the seminary of Saint Sulpice, learning Arabic and Aramaic in the process. In 1929, he joined the Dominican Order, under whose auspices he was sent to the Ecole Biblique in Jerusalem. He began teaching regularly at the Ecole in 1934 and served as its director from 1945 until 1965. Between 1938 and 1953, he edited the Ecole's magazine, *Revue biblique*.

To those who met or knew him, de Vaux was a striking and memorable personality, something of a 'character'. A heavy smoker, he wore a bushy beard, glasses and a dark beret. He also, invariably, wore his white monk's robes, even on excavations. A charismatic man, known for his vigour and enthusiasm, he was an eloquent lecturer and an engaging raconteur, with a flair for public relations. This made him an ideal spokesman for the enterprise on which he was engaged. One of his former colleagues described him to us as a good scholar, if not a particularly good archaeologist.

But behind his personable façade, de Vaux was ruthless, narrow-minded, bigoted and fiercely vindictive. Politically, he was decidedly right-wing. In his youth, he had been a member of Action Française, the militant Catholic and nationalist movement which burgeoned in France between the two world wars, which extolled the cult of 'blood and soil' and expressed more than a little sympathy for the dictatorships in Germany, Italy and, on Franco's triumph, Spain.

Certainly he was ill-suited to preside over research on the Dead
Sea Scrolls. In the first place, he was not just a practising Catholic, but also a monk, and this could hardly conduce to balance or
impartiality in his handling of extremely sensitive, even explosive,
religious material. Moreover, he was hostile to Israel as a political
entity, always referring to the country as 'Palestine'. On a more
personal level, he was also anti-Semitic. One of his former colleagues
testifies to his resentment at Israelis attending his lectures. After
interviewing de Vaux, David Pryce-Jones stated that 'I found him
an irascible brute, slightly potty too.'⁴ According to Magen Broshi,
currently director of the Israeli Shrine of the Book, 'de Vaux was a
rabid anti-Semite and a rabid anti-Israeli – but was the best partner
one could ask for'.⁵

This was the man, then, to whom responsibility for the Dead
Sea Scrolls was entrusted. In 1953, the board of trustees of the
Rockefeller Museum, whose president at the time was de Vaux himself, had requested nominations from the various foreign archaeological schools – British, French, German and American – then active
in Jerusalem. No Israelis were invited, despite the proximity of the
well-trained staff of Hebrew University. Each school was asked for
funds to help sustain the cost of the work.

The first scholar to be appointed under de Vaux's authority was
Professor Frank Cross, then associated with McCormick Theological
Seminary in Chicago and with the Albright Institute in Jerusalem.
Cross was the Albright's nominee, and began to work in Jerusalem
in the summer of 1953. The material assigned to him consisted of
specifically biblical texts – scroll commentaries, that is, found in
Cave 4 at Qumran, on the various books of the Old Testament.

Material of a similar nature was assigned to Monsignor Patrick
Skehan, also from the United States. At the time of his appointment,
he was director of the Albright Institute.

Father Jean Starcky, from France, was nominated by the Ecole
Biblique. At the time, he was attached to the Centre Nationale de la
Recherche Scientifique. Starcky, an expert in Aramaic, was assigned
the corpus of material in that language.

Dr Claus-Hunno Hunzinger was nominated by the Germans.
He was assigned one particular text, known as the 'War Scroll',

as well as a body of material transcribed on papyrus rather than on parchment. He subsequently left the team and was eventually replaced by another French priest, Father Maurice Baillet.

Father Josef Milik, a Polish priest resettled in France, was another nominee of the Ecole Biblique, with which he was also affiliated. A disciple and close confidant of de Vaux, Milik received an especially important corpus of material. It included a quantity of Old Testament apocrypha. It also included 'pseudepigraphical' writings – texts in which a later commentator would try to impart authority to his words by ascribing them to earlier prophets and patriarchs. Most important of all, it included what was called 'sectarian material' – material pertaining specifically to the community at Qumran, their teachings, rituals and disciplines.

The British nominee to the team was John M. Allegro, then working for his doctorate at Oxford under Professor Godfrey R. Driver. Allegro went to Jerusalem as an agnostic. He was the only member of the team not to have specific religious affiliations. He was also the only philologist in the group and already had five publications to his credit in academic journals. He was thus the only one to have established a reputation for himself *before* working on the scrolls. All the others were unknown at the time, and made their names only through their work with the texts assigned them.

Allegro was assigned biblical commentaries (which proved in fact to be 'sectarian material' of the kind assigned to Milik) and a body of so-called 'wisdom literature' – hymns, psalms, sermons and exhortations of a moral and poetic character. Allegro's material seems to have been rather more explosive than anyone at the time had anticipated, and he himself was something of a maverick. He had, certainly, no compunction about breaking the 'consensus' de Vaux was trying to establish and, as we shall see, was soon to be ousted from the team and replaced by John Strugnell, also enrolled in a doctoral programme at Oxford. Strugnell became a disciple of Frank Cross.

According to what principles was the material divided, distributed and assigned? How was it determined who would deal with what? Professor Cross, when asked this question on the telephone, replied that the matter was resolved with 'discussion and easy consensus and with the blessing of de Vaux':

> Certain things were obvious; those of us who had full-time professorships could not take unknown and more complex problems. So we took biblical, the simplest material from the point of view of identification of material and putting stuff into columns and what-not. The people who were specialists in Aramaic, particularly Starcky – obviously the Aramaic stuff went to him. The interests of the several scholars, the opportunities for research, pretty much laid out what each of us would do. This was quickly agreed to and de Vaux gave his blessing. We didn't sit down and vote and there was no conflict in this. Basically the team worked by consensus.[6]

Professor Cross makes it clear that each member of the team knew what all the others were doing. All the material had been laid out and arranged in a single room, the 'Scrollery', and anyone was free to wander about and see how his colleagues were progressing.* They would also, of course, help one another on problems requiring one or another individual's special expertise. But this also meant that if any one of the team were dealing with controversial or explosive material, all the others would know. On this basis, Allegro, to the end of his life, was to insist that important and controversial material was being withheld, or at least delayed in its release, by his colleagues. Another independent-minded scholar who later became involved reports that he was in the 1960s instructed 'to go slow', to proceed in a deliberately desultory fashion 'so that the crazies

---

* 'Scrollery' was a large room containing some twenty trestle tables where scroll fragments were pressed under sheets of glass. Photographs dating from the 1950s show a complete and appalling lack of any environmental control for the material, much of which was already deteriorating. Windows are open, for example, curtains blowing in the breeze. No attempt has been made to exclude heat, humidity, wind, dust or direct sunlight. It is all a far cry from the conditions in which the scrolls are housed today. They are now in a basement room, under a special amber light. Temperature and humidity are rigorously controlled. Each fragment is held between sheets of thin silk stretched in perspex frames.

will get tired and go away'.[7] De Vaux wanted, so far as it was possible, to avoid embarrassing the Christian establishment. Some of the Qumran material was clearly deemed capable of doing precisely that.

It was certainly convenient for de Vaux that until 1967 the Rockefeller Museum lay in the Jordanian territory of East Jerusalem. Israelis were forbidden to cross into the sector, and this provided the anti-Semitic de Vaux with a handy pretext to exclude Israeli experts, even though his team of international scholars was supposed, at least theoretically, to reflect the widest diversity of interests and approaches. If politics kept the Israelis out of East Jerusalem, they could easily have been provided with photographs, or with some other access to the material. No such access was granted.

We raised the issue with Professor Biran, governor of the Israeli sector of Jerusalem at the time and subsequently director of the Israeli Department of Antiquities. He stated that the Jordanian authorities had been adamant in refusing to let Sukenik, or any other Israeli scholar, enter their sector of Jerusalem. In his capacity of governor, Biran had replied by authorising de Vaux's committee to meet in the Israeli sector and offering them safe conducts. The offer was refused. Biran then suggested that individual scrolls or fragments be brought over, to be examined by Israeli experts. This suggestion was similarly rejected. 'Of course they could have come,' Professor Biran concluded, 'but they felt that they had possession [of the scrolls] and would not let anyone else take them.'[8] In the existing political climate, the scrolls were a fairly low priority, and no official pressure was brought to bear on this academic intransigence.

The situation was rendered even more absurd by the fact that the Israelis, first at Hebrew University and then at the specially created Shrine of the Book, had seven important scrolls of their own – the three originally purchased by Sukenik, and the four Yigael Yadin managed to purchase in New York. The Israelis seem to have pursued and published their research more or less responsibly – they were, after all, accountable to Yadin and Biran, to the government, to public opinion and the academic world in general. But the team at the Rockefeller emerge in a rather less favourable light. Funded by substantial donations, enjoying time, leisure and freedom, they

31

convey the impression of an exclusive club, a self-proclaimed élite, almost medieval in their attitude to, and their monopolisation of, the material. The 'Scrollery' in which they conducted their research has a quasi-monastic atmosphere about it. One is reminded again of the sequestration of learning in *The Name of the Rose*. And the 'experts' granted access to the 'Scrollery' arrogated such power and prestige to themselves that outsiders were easily convinced of the justness of their attitude. As Professor James B. Robinson (director of another, more responsible, team which translated the texts found in the Egyptian desert at Nag Hammadi) said to us: 'Manuscript discoveries bring out the worst instincts in otherwise normal scholars.'[9]

If the international team were high-handed in monopolising their material, they were no less so in interpreting it. In 1954, just when the team were beginning their work, the dangers had already been anticipated, by a Jesuit scholar, Robert North:

> Regarding the date of the scrolls, or rather the triple date of their composition, transcription, and storage, there has recently attained a relative consensus which is both reassuring and disquieting. It is reassuring insofar as it proceeds from such a variety of converging lines of evidence, and provides a 'working hypothesis' as basis of discussion. But there is danger of a false security. It is important to emphasize the frailty of the evidences themselves . . .[10]

North's warnings were to be ignored. During the course of the subsequent decade, a 'consensus' view – to use his term and Robert Eisenman's – was indeed to emerge, or be imposed, by the international team working under de Vaux at the Rockefeller. A rigid orthodoxy of interpretation evolved, from which any deviation was tantamount to heresy.

This orthodoxy of interpretation, which grew progressively more dogmatic over the years, was enunciated in its entirety by Father Milik and published in France in 1957 under the title *Dix ans de découvertes dans le désert de Juda*. Two years later, Milik's work was to be translated into English by another member of de Vaux's international team, John Strugnell. By that time, the first English formulation of the consensus view had already appeared – *The*

Ancient Library of Qumran, by Professor Frank Cross, Strugnell's mentor, in 1958. The consensus view was summarised and given its final polishing touches by Father De Vaux himself in a series of lectures given to the British Academy in 1959 and published in 1961 as *L'archéologie et les manuscrits de la Mer Morte.* By then, its tenets were soundly entrenched. Anyone who presumed to challenge them did so at severe risk to his credibility.

In 1971, on Father De Vaux's death, an extraordinary situation developed. Although he did not in any legal sense own the scrolls, he nevertheless bequeathed his rights to them to one of his colleagues, Father Pierre Benoit, another Dominican and subsequently de Vaux's successor as head of the international team and of the Ecole Biblique. For Father Benoit actually to inherit de Vaux's rights, privileges and prerogatives of access and control was, as a scholastic procedure, unprecedented. From a legal point of view, it was, to say the least, extremely irregular. More extraordinary still, however, the scholarly world did not contest this 'transaction'. When we asked Professor Norman Golb of the University of Chicago why so dubious a procedure was allowed to occur, he replied that opposing it would have been 'a lost cause'.[11]

With de Vaux's behaviour as a precedent, other members of his team followed suit. Thus, for example, when Father Patrick Skehan died in 1980, he bequeathed rights to the scrolls in his custody to Professor Eugene Ulrich of Notre Dame University, Indiana. The scrolls that had been the preserve of Father Jean Starcky were similarly bequeathed – or, more euphemistically, 'reassigned' – to Father Emile Puech of the Ecole Biblique. Thus the Catholic scholars at the core of the international team maintained their monopoly and control, and the consensus remained unchallenged. Not until 1987, on the death of Father Benoit, were their methods to be contested.

When Father Benoit died, Professor John Strugnell was designated his successor as head of the international team. Born in Barnet, north London, in 1930, Strugnell received his BA in 1952 and his MA in 1955, both from Jesus College, Oxford. Although admitted to the PhD programme at Oxford's Faculty of Oriental Studies, he never completed his doctorate, and his candidature lapsed in 1958. In 1954, he had been admitted to de Vaux's team, had gone to Jerusalem and remained there for two years. In 1957, after a brief stint at the Oriental Institute of the University of Chicago, he returned to Jerusalem, becoming affiliated with the Rockefeller Museum where he worked as epigraphist until 1960. In that year, he was appointed Assistant Professor of Old Testament Studies at Duke University's Divinity School. In 1968, he moved to Harvard Divinity School as Professor of Christian Origins.

Strugnell's appointment as head of the international team was not entirely unimpeded. Since 1967, the Israeli government had been legally authorised to ratify all such appointments. In Father Benoit's case, the Israelis hadn't bothered to exercise their authority. In Strugnell's, for the first time, they asserted their own rights over the material. According to Professor Shemaryahu Talmon, a member of the committee that vetted Strugnell, his appointment was not ratified until certain conditions were met.[12] Among other things, the Israelis were troubled by the way in which certain members of the international team tended to play the role of 'absentee landlord'. Since the 1967 war, for example, Father Starcky had refused to set foot in Israel. Father Milik, de Vaux's closest confidant and protégé, had for many years lived in Paris, with photographs of some of the most vital scroll material, to which he alone has access. No one else is allowed to make photographs. Without Milik's consent, no one, not even on the international team, is allowed to publish on the material of which he has custody. To our knowledge, he has never, since the 1967 war, returned to Jerusalem to work on this material. *Time Magazine* describes him as 'elusive'.[13] Another publication, *Biblical Archaeology Review* (*BAR*), has twice reported that he refuses even to answer letters from the Israeli Department of Antiquities.[14] He has treated both other scholars and the general public with what can only be described as disdain.

Anxious to discourage such behaviour, the Israelis insisted that the new director of the scroll project spend at least some of his time in Jerusalem. Strugnell, who was reconsidering his position at Harvard in any case, complied by taking half-retirement from his post. He began to spend half of each year in Jerusalem, at the Ecole Biblique, where he had his own quarters. But there were other obligations which he failed to discharge. He did not publish the texts entrusted to him. His commentary on one of these texts – a fragment of 121 lines – has been expected for more than five years and has still not appeared. He wrote only one 27-page article on the material in his possession. Apart from this, he published an article on Samaritan inscriptions, a translation of Milik's study of Qumran and, as we shall see, a long and hostile critique of the one member of the international team to challenge the interpretation of the consensus. It is not a very impressive record for a man who spent a lifetime working in a field which depends on publication. On the other hand, he allowed selected graduate students to work on certain original texts for their doctoral degrees – thus earning prestige for them, for their mentor and for Harvard University.

In general, under Strugnell's auspices, the international team proceeded pretty much as they did before. It is interesting to compare their progress with that of scholars working on a different corpus of texts, the so-called 'Gnostic Gospels' discovered in Egypt, at Nag Hammadi.

The Nag Hammadi Scrolls were found two years before the Dead Sea Scrolls, in 1945. By 1948, they had all been purchased by the Cairo Coptic Museum. There was initially an attempt to establish a Qumran-style monopoly over the material, again by an enclave of French scholars, and as a result, work on them was retarded until 1956. No sooner did it finally get under way than it was interrupted by the Suez crisis. After this delay, however, the scrolls were in 1966 turned over to an international team of scholars for translation and publication. The head of this team was Professor James M. Robinson of the Institute for Antiquity and Christianity at Claremont Graduate School, California. When we spoke to Professor Robinson about the team in charge of the Qumran texts, he was scathing. The Qumran scholars, Professor Robinson said, 'no longer have to make reputations – all they can do is break them'.[15]

Professor Robinson and his team, in contrast, moved with impressive rapidity. Within three years, a number of draft transcriptions and translations were being made available to scholars. By 1973, the entire Nag Hammadi library was in draft English translation and was circulating freely amongst interested researchers. In 1977, the whole body of the Nag Hammadi codices was published, in facsimile and a popular edition – a total of forty-six books plus some unidentified fragments. It thus took Robinson and his team a mere eleven years to bring the Nag Hammadi Scrolls into print.[16]

Granted, the Qumran texts were more numerous and posed more complex problems than those from Nag Hammadi. But even allowing for this, the record of de Vaux's international team does not exactly inspire confidence. When they were formed in 1953, their declared objective and intention was to publish *all* the scrolls found at Qumran in definitive editions, forming a series to be issued by Oxford University Press as *Discoveries in the Judaean Desert of Jordan.*

The first volume appeared quickly enough, in 1955, and dealt with the fragments found in the original cave at Qumran, now officially designated Cave 1. Not until 1961, six years later, did the next volume appear; and this did not deal with Qumran texts at all, but with material found in the nearby caves of Murabba'at. In 1963, a third volume appeared, which dealt primarily with scroll fragments from Cave 2, Cave 3 and Caves 5–10. Of these fragments, the most complete and most important was the 'Copper Scroll', found in Cave 3. Apart from the 'Copper Scroll', the lengthiest text amounted to just over sixty lines, and most came to something between four and twelve lines. But the fragments also yielded two copies of a text known as 'The Book of Jubilees'. A copy of the same text would later be found at Masada, revealing that the defenders of the fortress used the same calendar as the Qumran community, and establishing closer connections between the two sites than de Vaux felt comfortable acknowledging.

The fourth volume of *Discoveries in the Judaean Desert* appeared in 1965, under the editorship of James A. Sanders. But Professor Sanders was not a member of de Vaux's team. The scroll he dealt with – a volume of psalms – had been found by the Bedouin in Cave 11 by 1956 and brought, along with a number of fragments, to the Rockefeller Museum. No purchaser being forthcoming, the material was locked in one of the museum's safes, to which no one was allowed access. Here it remained until 1961, when the Albright Institute was at last enabled to buy it, finance being provided by

Kenneth and Elizabeth Bechtel of the Bechtel Corporation, a giant American construction company with many interests in the Middle East (though none in Israel), many connections with the American government and at least some associations with the CIA. Professor Sanders's volume thus appeared independently of the framework and timetable established by de Vaux's international team.

In the meantime, however, the bulk of the most copious and most significant material – the material found in the veritable treasure trove of Cave 4 – continued to be withheld from both the public and the academic community. Now and again, small pieces and tantalising fragments would leak into scholarly journals. But not until 1968 did the first official publication of material from Cave 4, albeit a very small proportion, appear. It did so under the auspices of the one 'renegade' or 'heretic' on de Vaux's team, John Allegro.

As delays in releasing the Qumran material persisted, and the time between published volumes continued to lengthen, suspicions began to proliferate that something was seriously amiss. Critics voiced three suspicions in particular. It was suggested that de Vaux's team were finding their material too difficult, too complex. It was also suggested that they might deliberately be proceeding slowly, suppressing or at least retarding the release of certain material in order to buy time. And it was suggested that the team were simply lazy and idle, basking in comfortable sinecures which they would obviously be in no hurry to relinquish. It was further pointed out that no such delays had occurred with the pieces of Qumran material in American and Israeli hands. In contrast to de Vaux's team, American and Israeli scholars had wasted no time in bringing their material into print.

The sixth volume of *Discoveries in the Judaean Desert* did not appear until 1977, nine years after Allegro's work. A seventh volume was not issued until 1982, an eighth only in 1990 – and this latter did not deal with Qumran texts. As we have noted, draft translations of Nag Hammadi codices were in circulation within three years. In the case of the Qumran material, no such draft translations were ever made available by de Vaux's team, nor are they so today. The entire Nag Hammadi corpus was in print within eleven years. It is now approaching thirty-eight years since de Vaux's team began their work, and they have so far produced only eight volumes – less than twenty-five per cent of the material in their hands.[17] As we shall see, moreover, of the material which *has* appeared in print, very little of it is the material that really matters.

In an interview published in the *New York Times*, Robert Eisenman spoke of how 'a small circle of scholars has been able to dominate a field of research for several generations (even though some of these scholars have been defunct in this field for years) and to continue to do so through their control of graduate studies and placing their coterie of students and scholars in the most prestigious academic chairs'.[18] *Biblical Archaeological Review*, an influential journal published by the Washington lawyer Hershel Shanks, described de Vaux's international team as being 'governed, so far as can be ascertained, largely by convention, tradition, collegiality and inertia'.[19] According to *BAR*, the 'insiders' who hold the scrolls 'have the goodies – to drip out bit by bit. This gives them status, scholarly power and a wonderful ego trip. Why squander it?'[20] And at a conference on the scrolls at New York University in 1985, Professor Morton Smith, one of the most distinguished names in contemporary biblical studies, began by saying scathingly: 'I thought to speak on the scandals of the Dead Sea documents, but these proved too numerous, too familiar and too disgusting.'[21]

How have the members of the international team responded to such damning condemnation? Of the original international team assembled in 1953, only three at present remain alive. Joseph Milik, who has since left the priesthood, maintains, as we have seen, the life of an 'elusive' recluse in Paris. Professors John Strugnell and Frank Cross were at Harvard University Divinity School. Of these, Professor Cross proved the most accessible and allowed himself to be questioned about the delays in publication. In an interview with the *New York Times*, he admitted that progress had 'generally been slow' and offered two explanations. Most members of the team, he said, were engaged in full-time teaching and could get to Jerusalem to work on the material only during summer holidays. And the scrolls that have not yet been published, he added, are so fragmented that it is difficult to fit them together, much less translate them.[22] 'It's the world's most fantastic jig-saw puzzle,' he remarked on another occasion.[23]

It would, of course, be rash to underestimate the complexity of the work in which Cross and his colleagues were engaged. The myriad fragments of Qumran texts do indeed constitute a daunting jigsaw puzzle. Nevertheless, Cross's explanations are not altogether convincing. It is certainly true that members of the international team are active in teaching and have only limited time to spend in Jerusalem; but Cross did not mention that most of the work now being done on the scrolls is done with photographs, which do not require the researcher to travel anywhere. In fact, the state of photography at present often makes it easier, and more reliable, to deal with photographs than with original parchments. As for the complexity of the jigsaw, Cross himself contradicted his own argument. As early as 1958, he wrote that most of the scroll fragments then in the team's hands had already been identified – had been identified, in fact, by the summer of 1956.[24] According to John Allegro, writing in 1964, assembly and identification of all Cave 4 material – the most copious corpus – was 'nearly complete' by 1960/61.[25] Nor was the task of identifying material always as difficult as Cross might lead one to believe. In a letter to John Allegro, dated 13 December 1955, Strugnell wrote that £3000 worth of Cave 4 material had just been purchased (with Vatican funds) and identified *in one afternoon*.[26] Complete photographs of the material, he added, would require no more than a week.

Even before he breached the consensus of the international team, Allegro was anxious to speed things up and sceptical of the various reasons proffered for not doing so. But was it merely as a sop that de Vaux wrote to him on 22 March 1959 that all the Qumran texts would be published, and *Discoveries in the Judaean Desert* complete, by the middle of 1962, the date scheduled for Strugnell's concluding volume? In the same letter, de Vaux stated that work on the original texts would be finished by June 1960, after which they would be turned over to the various institutions that had paid for them. Today, more than thirty years after de Vaux's letter, survivors of his team and its new members still cling to the scrolls in their possession, insisting on the need for continued research. And, it is worth repeating, what has been voluntarily released is, for the most part, of least importance.

The Qumran texts are generally classified under two rubrics. On the one hand, there is a corpus of early copies of biblical texts, some with slightly variant readings. These are referred to as 'biblical material'. On the other, there is a corpus of non-biblical material consisting for the most part of documents never seen before, which can be labelled 'sectarian material'. Most outsiders, needless to say, instinctively assume the 'biblical material' to be of the greater interest and consequence – the simple word 'biblical' triggers associations in the mind which lead automatically to such a supposition. To our knowledge, Eisenman was the first to detect, and certainly the first to emphasise, the sophistry involved in this. For the 'biblical material' is perfectly innocuous and uncontroversial, containing no revelations of any kind. It consists of little more than copies of books from the Old Testament, more or less the same as those already in print or with only minor alterations. There is nothing radically new here. In reality, the most significant texts comprise not the 'biblical' but the 'sectarian' literature. It is these texts – rules, biblical commentaries, theological, astrological and messianic treatises – that pertain to the 'sect' alleged to have resided at Qumran and to their teachings. To label this material 'sectarian' is effectively and skilfully to defuse interest in it. Thus, it is portrayed as the idiosyncratic doctrine of a fringe and maverick 'cult', a small, highly unrepresentative congregation divorced from, and wholly peripheral to, the supposed mainstream of Judaism and early Christianity, the phenomena to which it is in fact most pertinent. Outsiders are thus manipulated into accepting the consensus – that the Qumran community were so-called Essenes and that the Essenes, while interesting as a marginal development, have no real bearing on broader issues. The reality, as we shall see, is very different, and the perfunctorily dismissed 'sectarian' texts will prove to contain material of an explosive nature indeed.

3
The Scandal of the Scrolls

I ronically enough, it was not a biblical scholar, not an expert in the field, but an outsider who first detected something suspect in the international team's position. The outsider was the distinguished American literary and cultural critic, Edmund Wilson, whom most university students in Britain and the States will have encountered through his work in fields far removed from Qumran and 1st-century Palestine. He is known for his own fiction – for *I Thought of Daisy* and, particularly, *Memoirs of Hecate County*. He is known as the author of *Axel's Castle*, an original and pioneering study of the influence of French symbolism on 20th-century literature. He is known for *To the Finland Station*, an account of Lenin's machinations and the Bolshevik hijacking of the Russian Revolution. And he is known for the grotesque, highly publicised literary feud he precipitated with his former friend, Vladimir Nabokov, by presuming to challenge Nabokov's translation of Pushkin's *Evgeny Onegin*.

As his controversy with Nabokov demonstrated, Wilson had no compunction about venturing into waters beyond his officially acknowledged expertise. But perhaps it was just such recklessness that Qumran research required – the perspective of an outsider, a

41

man capable of establishing some kind of overview. In any case, Wilson, in 1955, wrote a lengthy article for the *New Yorker* on the Dead Sea Scrolls – an article which, for the first time, made the scrolls a 'household phrase' and generated interest in them from the general public. In the same year, Wilson expanded his article and published it as a book, *The Scrolls from the Dead Sea*. Fourteen years later, in 1969, this text was expanded again, to encompass new material, and was reissued at virtually twice its former length. To this day, it remains one of the basic and most popular investigative works on the Qumran scrolls by an outsider. But even if Wilson was an outsider in the realm of biblical scholarship, he was certainly no mere amateur or dabbler; not even de Vaux's international team could impugn his integrity or 'high seriousness'. Wilson was thus able, on behalf of the literate public, to call them in some sense to account.

As early as 1955, Wilson detected a desire on the part of the 'experts' to distance the Qumran scrolls from both Judaism and Christianity. The 'experts', it seemed to him, were protesting rather too vehemently, and this aroused his suspicions:

> As soon as one sets out to study the controversies provoked by the Dead Sea Scrolls, one becomes aware of a certain 'tension' . . . But the tension does not all arise from the at first much disputed problems of dating, and the contention about the dating itself had, perhaps, behind it other anxieties than the purely scholarly ones.[1]

Wilson stressed how much the scrolls had in common with both rabbinical Judaism, as it was emerging during the 1st century AD, and with the earliest forms of Christianity; and he noted a marked 'inhibition', on the part of both Judaic and Christian-oriented scholars, to make the often obvious connections:

> One would like to see these problems discussed; and in the meantime, one cannot but ask oneself whether the scholars who have been working on the scrolls – so many of whom have taken Christian orders or have been trained in the rabbinical tradition – may not have been somewhat inhibited in dealing with such

questions as these by their various religious commitments . . . one feels a certain nervousness, a reluctance, to take hold of the subject and to place it in historical perspective.[2]

In accordance with scholarly decorum, Wilson is, of course, being tactful, couching a fairly serious charge in the most diplomatic of language. He himself had no compunction about taking hold of the subject and placing it in historical perspective:

If, in any case, we look now at Jesus in the perspective supplied by the scrolls, we can trace a new continuity and, at last, get some sense of the drama that culminated in Christianity . . . The monastery [of Qumran] . . . is perhaps, more than Bethlehem or Nazareth, the cradle of Christianity.[3]

It is, alas, characteristic and typical of biblical scholarship, and particularly of scholarship associated with the scrolls, that such a connection should be made not by the 'experts' in the field, but by an astute and informed observer. For it was Wilson who gave precise and succinct expression to the very issues the international team endeavoured so diligently to avoid.

These imputations about the bias of most biblical scholars were echoed to us personally by Philip Davies, Professor of Biblical Studies at the University of Sheffield and author of two books on the Qumran material. As Professor Davies pointed out, most scholars working with the scrolls were – and, for that matter, still are – Christian-oriented, with a background primarily in the New Testament. He knew a number, he said, whose research sometimes conflicted painfully with their most passionately held personal beliefs, and questioned whether objectivity, in such cases, was really possible. Professor Davies stressed the perennial confusion of theology with history. All too often, he said, the New Testament is taught not just as the former, but also as the latter – as a literal and accurate account of 1st-century events. And if one takes the New Testament – the Gospels and the Acts of the Apostles – as incontrovertible historical fact, it is impossible to do scholarly justice to the scrolls. Christian doctrine, in effect, 'dictates the agenda'.[4]

Because Edmund Wilson was an outsider, the international team could get away with adopting towards him an attitude of patronising condescension. He was too distinguished to be insulted or abused; but he could be ignored, or dismissed superciliously as an intelligent and well-intentioned amateur who simply did not understand the complexities and subtleties of the issues involved, and who, in his alleged naïveté, might make 'rash statements'.[5] It was thus that many scholars were intimidated against saying what they actually believed. Academic reputations are fragile things, and only the most audacious or secure individuals could afford to incur the risk involved – the risk of being discredited, of being isolated by a concerted critical barrage from adherents of the consensus. 'The scrolls are a fief', Shemaryahu Talmon, himself a prominent Israeli professor in the field, observed; and the scholars who monopolised them were, in effect, 'a cabal'.[6]

Not even such cabals, however, can be omnipotent in suppressing dissent. Edmund Wilson may have been an outsider, but deviation from the international team's consensus was beginning to surface within the cocooned sphere of biblical scholarship itself. As early as 1950, five years before Wilson's book, André Dupont-Sommer, Professor of Semitic Language and Civilisation at the Sorbonne, had presented a public paper which caused a sensation.[7] He addressed himself to one of the Qumran texts recently translated. It described, he explained to his audience, a self-styled 'Sect of the New Covenant', whose leader, known as the 'Teacher of Righteousness', was held to be a Messiah, was persecuted, tortured and martyred. The 'Teacher's' followers believed the end of the world to be imminent, and only those with faith in him would be saved. And albeit cautiously, Dupont-Sommer did not shrink from drawing the obvious conclusion – that the 'Teacher of Righteousness' was in many ways 'the exact prototype of Jesus'.[8]

These assertions provoked a squall of controversy and protest. Jesus' uniqueness and originality were held to be under attack, and the Catholic establishment, especially in France and the States, began to unleash its critical artillery. Dupont-Sommer himself was somewhat shaken by the reaction and, in subsequent statements, sought shelter behind more circumspect phraseology. Anyone who might have been inclined to support him was also, for a time, obliged to

1   Solomon Schecter surrounded by boxes of the manuscripts he obtained
from the Cairo *geniza* in 1896 and brought to Cambridge.

2 Muhammad adh–Dhib (right), who discovered the first cave of Dead Sea Scrolls.

3 Kando and George Isaiah, who first brought the scrolls to the attention of the Metropolitan of the Syrian Church.

4 Professor Eleazar Sukenik, who in 1947 was the first Israeli scholar to obtain and translate some of the Dead Sea Scrolls.

5 A portion of one of the scrolls, the 'Habakkuk Commentary', which tells of a battle between the leader of the Dead Sea community and two opponents, the 'Liar' and the 'Wicked Priest'.

יבוגרים יקץ איש
פורה עם ספוא
וֹחוֹשֶׁך אֹ
אֶת אֲ ...וֹאשֹר
עיוֹן לֹאֹחֹרֹיֹת אֹ
ֹדת אֲשֶׁר לֹמֹאֹנֹופֹא
הֹ דֹקֹר הֹאֹחֹרֹוֹן בֹפֹן
לֹפֹסֹוֹר בֹוֹל
רֹוֹם פֹטֹ אֹל אֹת
בֹא הֹנֹעֹר נֹקֹיֹם אֹת
די קֹלֹיֹם וֹגֹבֹרֹיֹם
בֹבֹבֹסֹלֹת
ולֹוֹא וֹצֹאֹעֹ

ובמי שור ולט לטות ולבוי את ערו והארץ
בא הוא אשר אמר לרשת משכנות לוא לו יאותן
וערא הוא ממנו מֹשֹפֹטי ושאתו ושא
פשרו על הכתואים אשר נחם...על כל
הגוֹאים
ובעצתו טל מחשבתם לקרוֹע ובכל ובריבם
ולבו עם טל העבים יקילו בעברים כוכי וחרו
לאכו ערב   נשר ופרשי טרשי מרוקֹ
ועובי בשר חֹ...ץ לאטול ביֹ...ל להבס רשֹא בנבֹת
נב דם קֹיֹיֹם   על הבתואון אשר
ורושו את הארץ בסוס   ובנבתמתם ומבריֹק
ובאו כאו חום חוֹן לאמֹ...   ...ל העבֹים עֹשֹר
ואֹן שבעה ובחֹמֹדֹן   ...רֹץ אֹף וֹעֹף X
אֹפֹנֹם ורֹבֹתֹו עֹקֹ...   הֹוֹא אֹשֹר
...דֹר אֹשֹרֹ X

6–7 Examples of scroll fragments purchased from the Bedouin after their identification and arrangement. Few of these thousands of fragments can be pieced together precisely.

8 *above* Father Josef Milik.

9 *right* Dr Frank Cross.

10 Excavations among the Qumran ruins: Father de Vaux and Father Milik with Gerald Lankester Harding of the Department of Antiquities.

11 One of the pots containing animal bones found during the excavations and never satisfactorily explained. They appear to be the remains of sacred meals.

12–13 The Qumran ruins during one of the excavations led by Father de Vaux and Gerald Lankester Harding.

14 Professor H. Wright Baker of Manchester University cutting the
'Copper Scroll' into segments in order for it to be translated. It proved to
contain a list of treasures from the Temple of Jerusalem.

15 The unopened 'Copper Scroll', found broken into two sections
in Cave 3 in 1952.

duck for cover. Yet the seed of doubt had been planted, and was eventually to bear fruit. From the standpoint of Christian theological tradition, that fruit was to be particularly poisonous when it burgeoned amidst the international team themselves, in the very precincts of the Rockefeller Museum's 'Scrollery'.

Among the scholars of Father de Vaux's original international team, perhaps the most dynamic, original and audacious was John Marco Allegro. Certainly he was the most spontaneous, the most independent-minded, the most resistant to suppression of material. Born in 1923, he saw service in the Royal Navy during the war and in 1947 – the year the first Dead Sea Scrolls were discovered – entered Manchester University as an undergraduate studying Logic, Greek and Hebrew. A year later, he transferred to the honours course in Semitic Studies. He also developed an interest in philology, the study of the origins of language, its underlying structure and development. Bringing his philological expertise to bear on biblical texts, he quickly became convinced that scripture could not be taken at face value and proclaimed himself an agnostic. In June 1951, he graduated with a BA, first-class honours, in Oriental Studies, and the following year received his MA for his thesis, 'A Linguistic Study of the Balaam Oracles in the Book of Numbers'. In October of that year, he enrolled in the doctoral programme at Oxford under the supervision of the distinguished Semitic scholar, Professor Godfrey R. Driver. A year later, Driver recommended him for the international team then being assembled by de Vaux, and Allegro was assigned the crucial material found in Cave 4 at Qumran. He departed for Jerusalem in September 1953. By that time, he had already published four acclaimed articles in academic journals – a track record more impressive than anyone else on the team could claim.

In 1956, Allegro published a popular book, *The Dead Sea Scrolls*, following this in 1968 with his own research on the texts and fragments from Cave 4 in the fifth volume of the definitive Oxford University Press series, *Discoveries in the Judaean Desert*. At this point, Allegro was one of the most esteemed and prestigious figures in the field of biblical scholarship. Yet within two years, he was to abandon his colleagues on the international team, turn his back upon the academic world and resign his university post at Manchester. He was also to be vilified and discredited. What had happened?

It quickly became clear, to the academic community in general as well as to the international team, that Allegro was the only one among them who was not only an agnostic, but also uninhibited about 'rocking the boat'. Unconstrained by any personal religious bias, he explained things, often impetuously, as he saw them; and he rapidly lost patience with his colleagues' refusal to countenance any theories, or even evidence, that might contradict the accepted 'party line' on Christian origins. In particular, he grew exasperated with the strained attempts to distance Christianity from the scrolls and the Qumran community. He insisted on the obvious connection between the two, and suggested that connection might be closer than anyone had hitherto believed – or, at any rate, dared to suppose.

The first major storm occurred in 1956, when Allegro agreed to give a series of three short talks on the Dead Sea Scrolls, to be transmitted on radio in the north of England on 16, 23 and 30 January. It was clear that he intended to accelerate the tempo of scroll research by injecting an element of excitement and con- troversy. 'I think we can look for fireworks', he wrote imprudently to John Strugnell, who was then in Jerusalem.[9] That statement, as Allegro failed to appreciate, was bound to set alarm bells ringing in the Catholic-dominated 'Scrollery'. Oblivious of this, he went on to say that 'recent study of my fragments has convinced me that Dupont-Sommer is more right than he knew'.[10] At the time, apparently, Strugnell was considering a career in the Church. Allegro quipped, 'I shouldn't worry about that theological job, if I were you: by the time I've finished there won't be any Church left for you to join.'[11]

Allegro's first and second broadcasts attracted little attention in Britain, but the second was written up by the *New York Times*, which misunderstood and misquoted him, yet generated a flurry of debate. The third talk, broadcast on 30 January, was followed on 5 February by an article in the *New York Times* which could not but cause a sensation. 'CHRISTIAN BASES SEEN IN SCROLLS', the headline proclaimed:

The origins of some Christian ritual and doctrines can be seen in the documents of an extremist Jewish sect that existed for more than 100 years before the birth of Jesus Christ. This is the interpretation placed on the 'fabulous' collection of Dead Sea Scrolls by one of an international team of seven scholars . . . John Allegro . . . said last night in a broadcast that the historical basis of the Lord's Supper and part at least of the Lord's prayer and the New Testament teaching of Jesus were attributable to the Qumranians.[12]

The same article hinted at trouble to come, quoting a Catholic scholar as saying that 'any stick now seems big enough to use against Christianity' provided it could be used 'to dislodge belief in the uniqueness of Jesus'.[13] Allegro, in fact, was beginning to trespass on very sensitive territory indeed. On 6 February, *Time Magazine* ran an article entitled 'Crucifixion Before Christ'. Two days later, *The Times* reported that three American religious leaders, one Jewish, one Catholic and one Protestant, had joined forces to refute Allegro and warn against any attempt to depict 'the Essenes' as precursors of Christianity.[14] All this controversy was, of course, finding its way back to de Vaux, together with requests that something be done. Allegro, however, appears to have been almost naively insouciant. On 9 February, he wrote to de Vaux claiming he was 'being accused of saying the most astonishing things, some of which are true, and are indeed astounding, others come from the bosoms of eager reporters'.[15]

It is clear in retrospect that Allegro never fully realised how sacrosanct the idea of Jesus' 'uniqueness' was, and that, as a result, he underestimated the lengths to which de Vaux and other members of the international team would go in order to distance themselves from his blunt approach. This was his only real mistake, so far – that of expecting his colleagues to accept his assertions without letting their own religious allegiances influence their judgment. In his own view, he was addressing his material as a disinterested scholar, and hoped they might eventually do likewise. His innocent gibe that, by the time he'd finished, there'd be no Church left for Strugnell to join, testifies to his conviction of how important and conclusive he felt his material to be – and to his excitement at the discovery.

On 11 February, de Vaux wrote back to Allegro, distinctly unamused. All the texts available to Allegro, de Vaux said, were also available to the other members of the team in Jerusalem. They had failed to find anything that supported Allegro's interpretation.

In his reply, on 20 February, Allegro attempted to stand his ground and at the same time repair the rift with his colleagues and defuse the public controversy: 'You will excuse me if I think that everyone in the world is going stark, raving mad. I am enclosing my broadcast talks, as you request, and if, after reading them, you are left wondering what all the fuss is about, you will be in precisely my position.'[16] Noting that Strugnell and Milik were alleged to be preparing rebuttals of his statements, he commented, 'I am not waging any war against the Church, and if I were, you may rest assured I would not let any loopholes in . . . I stand by everything I said in my three talks but I am quite prepared to believe that there may be other interpretations of my readings.'[17]

On 4 March, de Vaux replied, warning Allegro that a rebuttal was indeed being prepared. It would not be just from Strugnell and Milik, however. Neither would it be confined to a scholarly journal. On the contrary, it would take the form of a letter to *The Times* in London and would be signed by all the members of the international team.

Instead of being intimidated, Allegro was defiant. Not mincing words, he responded that a letter to *The Times* 'should be most interesting to the London public, who have never heard my broadcasts':

> I have already pointed out to you that these broadcasts were made on the local Northern station . . . You and your friends are now apparently going to draw the attention of the gutter press of this country to these passages, of which neither they nor the majority of their readers have heard, and start a witch hunt . . . I congratulate you. What will certainly happen is that the press, scenting trouble, will descend like hawks on me and want to know what it is all about . . . they will have added fuel in what appears on the face of it to be a controversy developing between the ecclesiastics of the Scroll team and the one unattached member.[18]

He went on to invoke Edmund Wilson, indicating just how worried de Vaux's team should be by the suspicions Wilson had voiced. In effect, he was attempting to use Wilson as a deterrent:

> Having regard to what Wilson has already said about the unwillingness of the Church to tackle these texts objectively, you can imagine what will be made out of this rumpus.
>
> With all respect I must point out to you that this nonsense of Wilson's has been taken seriously here. At every lecture on the Scrolls I give, the same old question pops up: is it true that the Church is scared . . . and can we be sure that *everything* will be published. That may sound silly to you and me, but it is a serious doubt in the minds of ordinary folk . . . I need hardly add what effect the signatures of three Roman priests on the bottom of this proposed letter will have.[19]

It seems clear that, by this time, Allegro was becoming nervous. On 6 March, he wrote to another member of the international team, Frank Cross, who had just been offered an appointment at Harvard University: 'I am awfully pleased about Harvard. Not only because this Christianity business is played out.'[20] But in the same letter, he admitted that the barrage of criticism was wearing him down and that he was feeling, both physically and mentally, 'at the end of my tether'. Certainly he had no desire to see the publication of a letter which alienated him publicly from the other members of the team and, by so doing, impugned his credibility.

By now, of course, it was too late. On 16 March 1956, the letter duly appeared in *The Times*, signed by Strugnell as well as by Fathers de Vaux, Milik, Skehan and Starcky, most of the team's 'big guns':

> There are no unpublished texts at the disposal of Mr Allegro other than those of which the originals are at present in the Palestine Archaeological Museum where we are working. Upon the appearance in the press of citations from Mr Allegro's broadcasts we are unable to see in the texts the 'findings' of Mr Allegro.
>
> We find no crucifixion of the 'teacher', no deposition from the cross, and no 'broken body of their Master' to be stood guard over

until Judgment Day. Therefore there is no 'well-defined Essenic pattern into which Jesus of Nazareth fits', as Mr Allegro is alleged in one report to have said. It is our conviction that either he has misread the texts or he has built up a chain of conjectures which the materials do not support.[21]

To publish this sort of accusation – especially in a letter to *The Times* – is remarkable behaviour. It patently reflects a conclave of academics 'ganging up' on one of their own members. Forced on to the defensive, Allegro replied with a letter to *The Times* of his own, which explained and justified his position:

> In the phraseology of the New Testament in this connection we find many points of resemblance to Qumran literature, since the sect also were looking for the coming of a Davidic Messiah who would arise with the priest in the last days. It is in this sense that Jesus 'fits into a well-defined messianic (not "Essenic" as I was wrongly quoted . . .) pattern'. There is nothing particularly new or striking in the idea.[22]

It is a reasonable enough statement, a legitimate correction of an important misquotation. It also indicates how eager Allegro's colleagues were to 'jump on him', to find an excuse for discrediting him. In any case, Allegro added, 'It is true that unpublished material in my care made me more willing to accept certain suggestions made previously by other scholars on what have appeared . . . to be insufficient grounds.'[23]

The bickering and ill-feeling continued until finally, on 8 March 1957, Allegro wrote angrily to Strugnell:

> You still do not seem to understand what you did in writing a letter to a newspaper in an attempt to smear the words of your own colleague. It was quite unheard of before, an unprecedented case of scholarly stabbing in the back. And, laddie, don't accuse me of over-dramatising the business. I was here in England . . . Reuters' man that morning on the 'phone to me was classic: 'But I thought you scholars stuck together! . . .' And when it was realised that in fact you were quoting things I never even said, the inference

was plain. This letter was not in the interests of scholarly science at all, but to calm the fears of the Roman Catholics of America . . . And what it all boiled down to was that you guys did not agree with the interpretation I put on certain texts – where I have quite as much chance of being right as you. Rather than argue it out in the journals and scholarly works, you thought it easier to influence public opinion by a scurrilous letter to a newspaper. And you have the neck to call it scholarship. Dear boy, you are very young yet, and have much to learn.[24]

As we have already noted, Allegro was the first of the international team to publish *all* the material entrusted to his charge. He remains the only one to have done so. John Strugnell, on the other hand, in accordance with the 'go-slow' policy of the team, has published virtually nothing of the substantial materials at his disposal. The only major work to which he did address himself, entitled 'Notes in the Margin', comprises 113 pages of criticism of Allegro, which Eisenman labels a 'hatchet-job'.

In the meantime, the damage had been done. The letter to *The Times* signed by de Vaux and three other ecclesiastics effectively gave free rein to the Catholic propaganda machine. Opprobrium and vilification intensified. In June 1956, for example, a Jesuit commentator published in the *Irish Digest* an article entitled 'The Truth about the Dead Sea Scrolls'. He attacked Wilson, Dupont-Sommer and, especially, Allegro. He then went on to make the extraordinary statement that the 'Scrolls add surprisingly little to our knowledge of the doctrines current among the Jews from, say, 200 BC to the Christian era'.[25] He concluded in positively inflammatory fashion: 'It was not from such a sect that "Jesus learned how to be Messiah" . . . Rather, it was from soil such as this that sprang the thorns which tried to choke the seed of the Gospel.'[26] Allegro was now being portrayed not merely as an erring scholar, but as a veritable Antichrist.

While this controversy was still raging around him, Allegro was already becoming involved in another. The new bone of contention was to be the so-called 'Copper Scroll', found in Cave 3 at

Qumran in 1952. As we have noted, the two fragments that made up the 'Copper Scroll' remained unopened for three and a half years. Speculation was rife about their contents. One researcher attempted to read the indentations showing through the copper and visible on the outside of the roll. It seemed to say, he suggested, something about treasure. This suggestion elicited a salvo of derision from the international team. It proved, however, to be quite correct.

In 1955, a year before his public dispute with his colleagues on the international team, Allegro had discussed the problem of the 'Copper Scroll' with Professor H. Wright-Baker of Manchester College of Technology. Wright-Baker devised a machine that could slice the thin copper into strips, thus rendering the text legible. The first of the two fragments was accordingly sent to Manchester, in Allegro's care, in the summer of 1955. Wright-Baker's machine performed its task, and Allegro quickly embarked on a translation of what had been revealed. The contents of the fragment proved so extraordinary that he kept them initially wholly to himself, not even divulging them to Cross or Strugnell, both of whom wrote to beg for details. His reticence cannot have improved his relations with them, but Allegro was in fact waiting for the second fragment of the scroll to arrive in Manchester. Any partial or premature disclosure, he felt, might jeopardise everything. For what the 'Copper Scroll' contained was a list of secret sites where the treasure of the Temple of Jerusalem was alleged to have been buried.

The second fragment was received in Manchester in January 1956. It was quickly sliced open and translated. Both fragments, along with accompanying translations, were then returned to Jerusalem. Only then did the real delays begin. De Vaux and the international team were worried about three things.

Their first concern was valid enough. If the contents of the scroll were made public and stories of buried treasure began to circulate, the Bedouin would be digging up the entire Judaean desert, and much of what they found might disappear for ever or elude scholarly hands and slip into the black market. Something of this sort was, in fact, already occurring. On discovering or learning of a potentially productive site, the Bedouin would set up a large black tent over it, loot it, pick it clean and sell their plunder privately to antique dealers.

De Vaux and the international team were also worried that the treasure inventoried in the 'Copper Scroll' might actually exist – might be a real treasure rather than an imaginary one. If it were indeed real, it would inevitably attract the attention of the Israeli government, who would almost certainly lay claim to it. Not only might this remove it from the authority of the international team. It might also trigger a major political crisis; for while Israel's claim might be legitimate enough, much of the treasure, and the scroll specifying its location, would have been found in Jordanian territory.

If the treasure were real, moreover, there were theological grounds for concern. De Vaux and the international team had been intent on depicting the Qumran community as an isolated enclave, having no connection with public events, political developments or the 'mainstream' of 1st-century history. If the 'Copper Scroll' did indeed indicate where the actual contents of the Temple lay hidden, Qumran could no longer be so depicted. On the contrary, connections would become apparent between Qumran and the Temple, the centre and focus of all Judaic affairs. Qumran would no longer be a self-contained and insulated phenomenon, but an adjunct of something much broader – something that might encroach dangerously on the origins of Christianity. More disturbing still, if the 'Copper Scroll' referred to a real treasure, it could only be a treasure removed from the Temple in the wake of the AD 66 revolt. This would upset the 'safe' dating and chronology which the international team had established for the entire corpus of scrolls.

The combination of these factors dictated a cover-up. Allegro at first colluded in it, assuming that delays in releasing information about the 'Copper Scroll' would only be temporary. In consequence, he agreed not to mention anything of the scroll in the book he was preparing – his general introduction to the Qumran material, scheduled to be published by Penguin Books later in 1956. In the meantime, it was arranged, Father Milik would prepare a definitive translation of the 'Copper Scroll', which Allegro would follow with another 'popular' book pitched to the general public.

Allegro had consented to a temporary delay in releasing information about the 'Copper Scroll'. He certainly didn't expect the delay to prolong itself indefinitely. Still less did he expect the international team to defuse the scroll's significance by dismissing the treasure it inventoried as purely fictitious. When Milik proceeded to do so, Allegro did not at first suspect any sort of conspiracy. In a letter to another of his colleagues, dated 23 April 1956, he gave vent to his impatience, but remained excited and optimistic, and referred to Milik with cavalier disdain:

> Heaven alone knows when, if ever, our friends in Jerusalem are going to release the news of the copper scroll. It's quite fabulous (Milik thinks literally so, but he's a clot). Just imagine the agony of having to let my [book] go to the press without being able to breathe a word of it.[27]

A month later, Allegro wrote to Gerald Lankester Harding, in charge of the Jordanian Department of Antiquities, and de Vaux's colleague. Perhaps he already sensed something was in the wind and was trying to circumvent de Vaux personally, to appeal to an alternative and non-Catholic authority. In any case, he pointed out that as soon as the press release pertaining to the 'Copper Scroll' was issued, reporters would descend *en masse*. To deal with this contingency, he suggested that Harding, the international team and everyone else involved close ranks and adopt a 'party line' towards the media. On 28 May, Harding, who had been warned and briefed by de Vaux, wrote back. The treasure listed in the 'Copper Scroll', he said, didn't appear to be connected with the Qumran community at all. Nor could it possibly be a real cache – the value of the items cited was too great. The 'Copper Scroll' was merely a collation of 'buried treasure' legends.[28] Four days later, on 1 June, the official press release pertaining to the 'Copper Scroll' was issued. It echoed Harding's assertions. The scroll was said to contain 'a collection of traditions about buried treasure'.[29]

Allegro appears to have been stunned by this duplicity. On 5 June, he wrote to Harding, 'I don't quite follow whether this incredible "traditions" gag you and your chums are putting out is for newspaper, government, Bedu or my consumption. Or you may even believe it, bless you.'[30] At the same time, however, he was still appealing to Harding as a possible ally against the phalanx of Catholic interests. Did not Harding think, he asked, that 'a bit more ready information on these scroll matters might not be a good idea? It's well known now that the copper scroll was completely open in January, and despite your attempts to squash it, it is also known that my translation went to you immediately . . . A little general information . . . saves a good deal of rumour-mongering, which has now taken on a somewhat sinister note.'[31] He adds that 'the feeling would get around that the Roman Catholic brethren of the team, by far in the majority, were trying to hide things'.[32] The same point is stressed in a letter to Frank Cross in August: 'In lay quarters it is firmly believed that the Roman Church in de Vaux and Co. are intent on suppressing this material.'[33] To de Vaux personally, he observed drily, 'I notice that you have been careful to keep it dark that the treasure is Temple possessions.'[34]

Allegro had originally believed a full translation of the text of the 'Copper Scroll' would be released fairly promptly. It must now have been clear to him that this wasn't going to occur. In fact, four years were to pass before a translation of the text appeared, and then it was published by Allegro himself, who by that time had lost all patience with the international team. He still would have preferred to publish his popular book after the 'official' translation, scheduled to be done by Father Milik, and was led to believe this would be possible. Milik's translation, however, was suddenly and unexpectedly subject to further delays, which may well have been deliberate. Allegro was asked to postpone his own publication accordingly. At one point, indeed, this request, transmitted through an intermediary, appears to have been attended by threats – from a member of the team whose name cannot be divulged for legal reasons. Allegro replied that, 'As conveyed to me, the request was accompanied by the expression of some rather strange sentiments originating, it was said, from yourself and those for whom you were acting. There appeared even to be some forecast of consequences were I not to accede to this request.'[35] The recipient of this letter wrote back sweetly that Allegro must not imagine himself the victim of persecution.[36] Thus, when Allegro went ahead with his own publication, he found himself in the embarrassing position of seeming to have pre-empted the work of a colleague. In effect, he had been manoeuvred into providing the international team with further ammunition to use against him – and, of course, to alienate him further from them. Milik's translation, in fact, did not appear until 1962 – two years after Allegro's, six years after the 'Copper Scroll' had been sliced open in Manchester and ten years after it had been discovered.

In the meantime, *The Dead Sea Scrolls* – Allegro's popular book on the Qumran material, from which all mention of the 'Copper Scroll' had been withheld – had appeared in the late summer of 1956, some five months after the controversy surrounding his radio broadcasts. The controversy, and especially the letter to *The Times*, had, as Allegro predicted, ensured the book's success. The first edition of forty thousand copies sold out in seventeen days, and Edmund Wilson reviewed it enthusiastically on the BBC. *The Dead Sea Scrolls*, now in its second edition and nineteenth printing, continues to be one of the best introductions to the Qumran material. De Vaux did not see it that way, and sent Allegro a lengthy critique. In his reply, dated 16 September 1956, Allegro stated that 'you are unable to treat Christianity any more in an objective light; a pity, but understandable in the circumstances'.[37] In the same letter, he draws attention to a text among the scrolls which refers to the 'son of God':

> You go on to talk blithely about what the first Jewish-Christians thought in Jerusalem, and no one would guess that your only real evidence – if you can call it such – is the New Testament, that body of much worked-over traditions whose 'evidence' would not stand for two minutes in a court of law . . . As for . . . Jesus as a 'son of God' and 'Messiah' – I don't dispute it for a moment; we now know from Qumran that their own Davidic Messiah was reckoned a 'son of God', 'begotten' of God – but that doesn't prove the Church's fantastic claim for Jesus that he was God Himself. There's no 'contrast' in their terminology at all – the contrast is in its interpretation.[38]

Here we have proof of both the deliberate delays and the value of the unpublished Qumran scrolls. The text to which Allegro is alluding, which speaks of the 'son of God', has *still* not been published, despite its importance and despite its early identification and translation. Only in 1990 were excerpts from it to be leaked to *BAR*.[39]

★

After everything that had passed, Allegro would have been extremely naïve to assume that he could still be accepted by his erstwhile colleagues as a member of their team. Nevertheless, that was precisely what he seems to have done. In the summer of 1957, he returned to Jerusalem and spent July, August and September working on his material in the 'Scrollery'. From his letters of the time, it is clear that he did indeed feel himself part of the team again and had no doubt that all was well. In the autumn, he travelled back to London and arranged with the BBC to make a television programme on the scrolls. In October, he returned to Jerusalem with producer and film crew. They immediately went to see Awni Dajani, Jordanian curator of the Rockefeller Museum and one of Allegro's closest friends. The next morning, Dajani took them round 'to get things moving with de Vaux'. In a letter of 31 October to Frank Cross, whom he still assumed to be his ally, Allegro described the ensuing events:

We foregathered . . . and explained what we hoped to do, only to be met with a blank refusal by De V. to collaborate in any way. We stared open-mouthed for some time, and then Dajani and the producer started trying to find out what it was all about. The whole thing was a complete knock-out because, as far as I was aware I had left my dear colleagues on the best of terms – or pretty much so. Certainly no bitterness on my side about anything. But De Vaux said that he had called a meeting of 'his scholars' and that they had agreed to have nothing to do with anything I had anything to do with! My pal the producer then took the old gent outside and explained in words of one syllable that we were avoiding any controversial matter at all in the program on the religious side, but he (de Vaux) was quite adamant. He said that whereas he could not stop us taking pictures of the monastery at Qumran, he would not allow us in the Scrollery or the Museum generally.[40]

Allegro described himself as still flummoxed. Awni Dajani, however, was beginning to get annoyed. He apparently saw the programme as 'a very definite boost for Jordan – antiquities and tourism', and declared a preparedness to assert his authority. He was, after all, an official representative of the Jordanian government, whom not even de Vaux could afford to defy:

> as soon as it became clear to my dear colleagues that even without them the programme was going forward . . . they started putting their cards on the table. It was not the programme they objected to, only Allegro . . . They then called in a taxi at our hotel and made the producer an offer – if he would drop Allegro completely, and have Strugnell as his script writer, or Milik, they would collaborate . . . Then one day, after we had returned from an exhausting day at Qumran, Awni phoned to say that when he had got in it was to find a note (anonymous) waiting for him, offering £150 to him to stop us going to Amman and photographing in the Museum there.[41]

In the same letter, Allegro tried to persuade Cross to appear in the programme. After consulting with de Vaux, Cross refused. By now, the penny had pretty much dropped for Allegro and he knew precisely where he stood in relation to his former colleagues. On the same day that he wrote to Cross, he had also written to another scholar, a man who was not officially a member of the international team but had been allowed to work with the scrolls. Allegro repeated the account of his contretemps and then added that he was 'starting a campaign, very quietly for the moment, to get the scrollery clique broken up and new blood injected, with the idea of getting some of the stuff Milik, Strugnell and Starcky are sitting on, published quickly in provisional form'.[42] Two months later, on 24 December 1957, he wrote to the same scholar saying that he was worried:

> From the way the publication of the fragments is being planned, the non-Catholic members of the team are being removed as quickly as possible . . . In fact, so vast is Milik's, Starcky's and Strugnell's lots of 4Q [Cave 4 material], I believe that they should be split up immediately and new scholars brought in to get the stuff out quickly.
> . . . a dangerous situation is fast developing where the original idea of an international and interdenominational editing group is being bypassed. All fragments are brought first to De V. or Milik,

and, as with cave Eleven, complete secrecy is kept over what they are till long after they have been studied by this group.[43]

This report is extremely disquieting. Scholars outside the international team have suspected that some form of monitoring and selection was taking place. Here, Allegro confirms these suspicions. One can only wonder what might have happened to any fragment that held doctrines opposed to that of the Church.

Allegro then outlined his own plan, part of which involved 'inviting scholars who can spare six months or a year at least to come to Jerusalem and take their place in the team':

I believe that a rule should be laid down that preliminary publications must be made *immediately* the document is collected as far as it seems possible, and that a steady stream of these publications should be made in one journal . . . This business of holding up publication of fragments merely to avoid the 'deflowering' of the final volume seems to me most unscholarly, as is the business of keeping competent scholars away from the fragments . . . There was perhaps good reason . . . when we were in the first stages of collecting the pieces. But now that most of this work is done, anybody can work over a document and publish it in at least provisional form.[44]

One may not immediately sympathise with Allegro as his personality manifests itself through his letters – cavalier, impudent, cheerfully iconoclastic. But it is impossible not to sympathise with the academic integrity of his position. He may indeed have been egocentric in his conviction that his particular interpretation of the Qumran material was valid and important. But the statements quoted above constitute an appeal on behalf of scholarship itself – an appeal for openness, honesty, accessibility, impartiality. Unlike de Vaux and the international team, Allegro displays no propensity for either secrecy or self-aggrandisement. If he is conspiring, he is conspiring only to make the Dead Sea Scrolls available to the world at large, and quickly enough not to betray the trust reposed in academic research. Such an aspiration can only be regarded as honourable and generous.

Allegro's honour and generosity, however, were not to be rewarded, or even recognised. The film, completed by the end of 1957, was not transmitted by the BBC until the summer of 1959, and then only in a late-night slot which attracted a minimal audience. By that time, understandably enough, Allegro was beginning to grow uneasy. On 10 January 1959, after the latest in a long series of postponements, he wrote to Awni Dajani:

> Well, they've done it again. For the fifth time the BBC have put off showing that TV programme on the Scrolls . . . There can be no reasonable doubt now that De Vaux's cronies in London are using their influence to kill the programme, as he wished . . . De Vaux will stop at nothing to control the Scrolls material. Somehow or other he must be removed from his present controlling position. I am convinced that if something does turn up which affects the Roman Catholic dogma, the world will never see it. De Vaux will scrape the money out of some or other barrel and send the lot to the Vatican to be hidden or destroyed . . .[45]

After repeating what he'd come increasingly to see as a viable short-term solution – nationalisation of the Rockefeller Museum, the 'Scrollery' and the scrolls by the Jordanian government – he reveals the sense of punctilio to which he'd previously felt subject: 'I might even let out an instance or two when information has been suppressed – but I'll only do that if De Vaux looks like winning.'[46]

In 1961, King Hussein appointed Allegro honorary adviser on the scrolls to the government of Jordan. The post, however, though prestigious enough, entailed no real authority. It was not until November 1966, five years later, that the Jordanian government finally acted on Allegro's suggestion and nationalised the Rockefeller Museum. By then, as we have seen, it was too late. Within the year, the Six Day War was to erupt, and the museum, the 'Scrollery' and its contents all passed into Israeli hands; and Israel, as we have noted, was too much in need of international support to risk a head-on confrontation with the Vatican and the Catholic hierarchy. Only four years before, Pope John XXIII had officially and doctrinally exculpated the Jews of any responsibility for Jesus' death, and excised all vestiges of anti-Semitism from Roman Catholic Canon Law. No one wished to see this sort of conciliatory work undone.

By that time, too, Allegro was understandably weary and disillusioned with the world of professional scholarship. For some time, he had been anxious to leave academia and sustain himself solely as a writer. He was also eager to return to his original chosen field, philology, and had spent some five years working on a book which derived from what he regarded as a major philological breakthrough. The result of his efforts appeared in 1970 as *The Sacred Mushroom and the Cross* – the work for which Allegro today is most famous, and for which he is almost universally dismissed.

The argument in *The Sacred Mushroom and the Cross* rests on complicated philological premises which we, like many other commentators, find difficult to accept. That, however, is incidental. Scholars tend all the time to expound their theories based on premises of varying validity, and they are usually, at worst, ignored, not publicly disgraced. What turned *The Sacred Mushroom and the Cross* into a scandal were Allegro's conclusions about Jesus. In attempting to establish the source of all religious belief and practice, Allegro asserted that Jesus had never existed in historical reality, was merely an image evoked in the psyche under the influence of an hallucinatory drug, psilocybin, the active ingredient in hallucinogenic mushrooms. In effect, he argued, Christianity, like all other religions, stemmed from a species of psychedelic experience, a ritualistic *rite de passage* promulgated by an orgiastic magic mushroom cult.

Taken separately, and placed in a different context, Allegro's conclusions would probably not have provoked the storm they did. Certainly reputable scholars before Allegro had questioned, and doubted, the existence of an historical Jesus. Some of them, for that matter, still do, though they are in a minority. And there is little dispute today that drugs – psychedelic and of other kinds – were used to at least some extent among the religions, cults, sects and mystery schools of the ancient Middle East – as indeed they were, and continue to be, across the world. It is certainly not inconceivable that such substances were known to, and perhaps employed by, 1st-century Judaism and early Christianity. One must also remember the climate and atmosphere of the late 1960s.

Today, in retrospect, one tends to think in terms of the so-called 'drug culture' – in terms of a facile ersatz mysticism, of Ken Kesey and his 'Merry Pranksters', of Tom Wolfe and *The Electric Kool-Aid Acid Test*, of hippies thronging the streets of San Francisco's Haight-Ashbury, staging 'love-ins' and 'be-ins' in Golden Gate Park. That, however, is only one side of the picture, and tends to eclipse the very real excitement and expectation that psychedelia generated even in more sophisticated and disciplined minds – the conviction, shared by many scientists, neurologists, biochemists, academicians, psychologists, medical practitioners, philosophers and artists, that humanity was indeed on the verge of some genuine epistemological 'breakthrough'.

Books such as Huxley's *The Doors of Perception* enjoyed enormous currency, and not just among the rebellious young. At Harvard, Timothy Leary, with his proclamations of a 'new religion', still possessed in those days a considerable measure of credibility. In *The Teachings of Don Juan*, Castaneda had produced not just a best-selling book, but also an acclaimed academic dissertation for the University of California. Psychedelic substances were routinely used in both medicine and psychotherapy. Divinity students in Boston conducted a service under the influence of LSD, and most of them said afterwards they had indeed experienced an intensified sense of the sacred, a greater rapprochement to the divine. Even the MP Christopher Mayhew, later Minister of Defence, voluntarily appeared stoned on the nation's television screens, beaming beatifically at his interviewer, wearing the seraphically celestial smirk of a man newly promoted to sagehood. One can see why the academic and critical establishment recoiled in alarm from Allegro's book, even though Allegro himself repudiated the mentality of Haight-Ashbury and never himself smoked or drank.

All the same, and even if not for the reasons usually cited, *The Sacred Mushroom and the Cross* was a distinctly unorthodox book, and effectively compromised Allegro's credibility as a scholar. Its reviewer in *The Times*, for example, became personal, embarking on an amateur psychoanalysis of Allegro in order to debunk him.[47] Allegro's own publishers publicly apologised for issuing the book, cravenly admitting it to be 'unnecessarily offensive'.[48] In a letter to

The Times on 26 May 1970, fourteen prominent British scholars repudiated Allegro's conclusions.[49] The signatories included Geza Vermes of Oxford, who'd concurred with much of Allegro's previous work on the Qumran material, and who was soon to echo his complaints about the international team's delays. The signatories also included Professor Godfrey Driver, Allegro's former mentor, who had formulated a more radical interpretation of the Qumran texts than Allegro himself had ever attempted.

Allegro continued to bring the attention of the public to the delays in the publication of the scrolls. In 1987, a year before his death, he declared the international team's delays to be 'pathetic and inexcusable', and added that his former colleagues, for years, 'have been sitting on the material which is not only of outstanding importance, but also quite the most religiously sensitive':

> There is no doubt . . . that the evidence from the scrolls undermines the uniqueness of the Christians as a sect . . . In fact we know damn all about the origins of Christianity. However, these documents do lift the curtain.[50]

By this time, the initiative had passed into the hands of the next generation of scholars and Allegro had left the world of scroll scholarship to pursue his research on the origins of myth and religion. His works subsequent to *The Sacred Mushroom and the Cross* were moderate enough, but for most readers, as well as for the academic establishment, he was to remain an 'exile', the man who, in the sneering words of *The Times*, had 'traced the source of Christianity to an edible fungus'.[51] He died suddenly in 1988, no longer accepted by his colleagues, but still energetic, enthusiastic about his own philological work in progress, and optimistic. It must have been some consolation for him to see, before his death, that his defiance of the international team, and his concern about their delays in releasing material, were already being echoed by others.

In 1956, Edmund Wilson had favourably reviewed Allegro's 'popular' book on the Dead Sea Scrolls. In 1969, when he brought out the new edition of his own book, it had swollen to twice its former length. The situation regarding the scrolls was no longer, for

Wilson, merely a question of 'tension' and 'inhibition'; it had now begun to assume the proportions of a cover-up and a scandal: 'I have been told by a Catholic scholar that at first, in regard to the scrolls, a kind of official policy tended to bias scholarship in the direction of minimising their importance.'[52] By the mid-1970s, biblical scholars were beginning to speak openly of a scandal. Even the most docile began to have their worries, and the international team were alienating men who had no desire to engage in academic controversy. Among the most prominent names in contemporary Semitic scholarship, for example, is that of Dr Geza Vermes, who has, since 1951, been publishing books and articles on the scrolls. Initially, he had no quarrel with the international team and their work. Like many others, however, he gradually began to lose patience with the delays in publication. In 1977, he published a book, *The Dead Sea Scrolls: Qumran in Perspective*, in the first chapter of which he publicly flung down the gauntlet:

> On this thirtieth anniversary of their first coming to light the world is entitled to ask the authorities responsible for the publication of the Qumran scrolls . . . what they intend to do about this lamentable state of affairs. For unless drastic measures are taken at once, the greatest and the most valuable of all Hebrew and Aramaic manuscript discoveries is likely to become the academic scandal *par excellence* of the twentieth century.[53]

True to form, the international team did not deign to take any notice. Nearly a decade later, in 1985, Dr Vermes again called them to account, this time in the *Times Literary Supplement*:

> Eight years ago I defined this situation as 'a lamentable state of affairs' and warned that it was 'likely to become the academic scandal *par excellence* of the twentieth century' unless drastic measures were taken at once. Regrettably, this has not happened and the present chief editor of the fragments has in the meantime gone on the record as one who rejects as unjust and unreasonable any criticism regarding the delay.[54]

In the same statement, Dr Vermes praised Yigael Yadin, who had just died, for the promptitude with which he'd ushered into print the Qumran material in his possession: 'But it is also a reminder to us all, especially to those who have been tardy in responding to the challenge of their privileged task, that time is running out.'[55]

In his desire to avoid undignified controversy, Dr Vermes neglected to pursue the matter further. As before, the international team took no notice whatever of his comments. For Dr Vermes, the situation must be particularly galling. He is a recognised expert in the field. He has published translations of such scrolls as have found their way into the public domain – through Israeli auspices, for example. He is certainly as competent to work on unpublished Qumran material as any member of the international team, and is probably better qualified than most. Yet for the whole of his distinguished academic career, access to that material has been denied him. He has not even been allowed to see it.

In the meantime, valuable evidence continues to remain under wraps. We ourselves can personally testify to vital material which, if it has not exactly been suppressed, has not been made public either. In November 1989, for example, Michael Baigent visited Jerusalem and met with members of the current international team. One of them was Father Emile Puech, the young 'crown prince' of the Ecole Biblique, who 'inherited' the scroll fragments previously assigned to Father Jean Starcky. These included material labelled 'of unknown provenance'. In personal conversation, Father Puech divulged three important discoveries:

1. He had apparently found new overlaps between the scrolls and the Sermon on the Mount, including fresh and significant references to 'the poor in spirit'.[56]
2. In the Epistle of Barnabas, an apocryphal Christian text mentioned as early as the 2nd century AD, Puech had found a quotation hitherto untraced, attributed to an 'unknown prophet'. The quotation, in fact, proved to have come directly from one of the Dead Sea Scrolls, thus establishing that the author of the Epistle of Barnabas was a member of, or had access to, the Qumran community and its teachings. Here was an incontrovertible link between Qumran and Christian tradition.

3. In the work of the 2nd-century Christian writer Justin Martyr, Puech found yet another quotation deriving directly from the Qumran scrolls.

'We are not hiding anything,' Puech insisted adamantly. 'We will publish everything.'[57] To our knowledge, however, none of the revelations confided by Puech in conversation has yet appeared in print, and there seems no immediate likelihood of their doing so. On the other hand, there has been a recent 'leak' which offers some indication of the kind of material still being suppressed. This 'leak' surfaced in 1990, in the pages of *BAR*, and was confided, apparently, by an unnamed scholar whose conscience was troubling him. It consists of a Qumran fragment very similar to a passage in Luke's Gospel. Referring to Jesus' imminent birth, Luke (I:32–5) speaks of a child who will be called 'Son of the Most High' and 'Son of God'. The Qumran fragment from Cave 4 also speaks of the coming of someone who 'by his name shall . . . be hailed [as] the Son of God, and they shall call him Son of the Most High'.[58] This, as *BAR* points out, is an extraordinary discovery, 'the first time that the term "Son of God" has been found in a Palestinian text outside the Bible'.[59] Whatever the circumstances pertaining to the release of this fragment, it derives from the corpus of material hitherto controlled, and rigorously withheld, by the 'elusive' Father Milik.

4

Opposing the Consensus

Edmund Wilson, John Allegro and Geza Vermes all condemned the international team for secrecy, for procrastination and delay in releasing Qumran material and for establishing a scholarly monopoly over the Dead Sea Scrolls. Wilson and Allegro both challenged the team's laboured attempts to distance the Qumran community from so-called 'early Christianity'. In other respects, however, all three scholars concurred with the consensus of interpretation established by the international team. They accepted, for example, the team's dating of the Dead Sea Scrolls as being pre-Christian. They also accepted the team's contention that the members of the Qumran community were Essenes. And they accepted that the supposed Essenes at Qumran were of the traditional kind described by Pliny, Philo and Josephus – ascetic, reclusive, pacifist, divorced from the mainstream of social, political and religious thought. If Christianity were indeed somehow connected with the Qumran community, it therefore emerged as less original than had hitherto been believed. It could be seen to have drawn on Qumran, just as it was acknowledged to have drawn on 'conventional' Old Testament Judaism. Apart from that, there was no particular reason to modify one's image or conception of it.

By the 1960s, however, scholarly opposition to the international team's consensus had begun to arise from another quarter. Its questioning of that consensus was to be much more radical than anything submitted by Wilson, Allegro or Vermes. It was to challenge not only the dating of the Qumran scrolls as established by the international team, but also the allegedly Essene character of the Qumran community. The men responsible for this criticism were Cecil Roth and Godfrey Driver.

Cecil Roth was perhaps the most prominent Jewish historian of his era. After serving with the British Army during the First World War, he had obtained his doctorate from Merton College, Oxford, as an historian. For some years, he was Reader in Jewish Studies at Oxford – the post now occupied by Geza Vermes. He was a prolific writer, with more than six hundred publications to his credit. He was also editor-in-chief of the *Encyclopaedia judaica*. He commanded enormous respect in the academic world, and was recognised especially for his expertise in Judaic history.

Godfrey Driver was a figure of comparable academic stature. He, too, had served with the British Army during the First World War, seeing action particularly in the Middle East. He, too, taught at Oxford, at Magdalen College, becoming, in 1938, Professor of Semitic Philology. Until 1960, he also did three stints as Professor of Hebrew. He was joint director of the team which translated the Old Testament for the New English Bible. As we have noted, he was John Allegro's mentor, and recommended Allegro for the international team.

From the very first discoveries of the Dead Sea Scrolls, Professor Driver had advocated caution about the early, pre-Christian dates ascribed to them. In a letter to *The Times* on 23 August 1949, he warned that the pre-Christian date ascribed to the Qumran scrolls 'seems likely to win general acceptance before being subjected to critical examination'.[1] In the same letter, he stated: 'The external evidence . . . for a pre-Christian date is extremely precarious, while all the internal evidence seems against it.'[2] Driver stressed the risks of attributing too much accuracy to what he called 'external evidence' – to archaeology and palaeography. He advocated, rather, a scrutiny of the 'internal evidence' – the content of the scrolls themselves. On the basis of such evidence, he was eventually to conclude that the scrolls dated from the 1st century of the Christian era.

In the meantime, Cecil Roth had been conducting his own research and, in 1958, published the results in a work entitled *The Historical Background of the Dead Sea Scrolls*. The historical background, he argued, was not pre-Christian, but, on the contrary, dated from the time of the revolt in Judaea, between AD 66 and 74. Like Driver, Roth insisted that the texts of the scrolls themselves were a more accurate guide than archaeology or palaeography. Availing himself of this guide, he developed a number of points that not only ran counter to the international team's consensus, but must also have outraged the Catholics among them. Citing textual references in one of the scrolls, for instance, he demonstrated that the 'invaders' regarded as adversaries by the Qumran community could only be Romans – and, further, could only be Romans of the Empire, of imperial rather than republican times. He also demonstrated that the militant nationalism and messianic fervour in many of the scrolls had less in common with traditional images of the Essenes than with the Zealots described by Josephus. He acknowledged that the original community at Qumran might indeed have been established by Essenes of the traditional kind, but if so, he contended, they would have vacated the site when it was destroyed in 37 BC. Those who occupied it subsequently, after 4 BC, and who deposited the scrolls, would not have been Essenes at all, but Zealots. Pursuing his argument a step further, he then endeavoured to establish links between the Qumran community and the fierce defenders of Masada thirty miles to the south.

Such assertions, needless to say, provoked indignant criticism from Father de Vaux's team. One of de Vaux's associates, Jean Carmignac, in reviewing Roth's book, complained that Roth 'does not miss any occasion to closely link Masada and Qumran, but this is another weakness of his thesis'.[3] Even when, eight years later, Yigael Yadin, in his excavations at Masada, found scrolls identical to some of those discovered at Qumran, the international team refused to consider Roth's thesis. Quite clearly, *some* sort of connection had to exist between Qumran and Masada, yet the team, their logic now creaking painfully at the seams, insisted only one explanation was possible – 'some' of the Essenes from Qumran must have deserted their own community and gone to the defence of Masada, bringing their sacred texts with them!

So far as Masada was concerned, Roth was, then, to be vindicated by Yadin's excavations. But he was also quite capable of fighting his own battles. In an article published in 1959, he focused particularly on de Vaux's assertion, based on supposed 'archaeological evidence', that the scrolls could not have been deposited any later than the summer of AD 68, when Qumran was 'taken by the 10th Legion'.[4] Roth demonstrated conclusively that the 10th Legion, in the summer of AD 68, was nowhere near Qumran.[5]

Roth's arguments may have infuriated de Vaux's international team, but they were shared by his colleague Godfrey Driver. The two worked closely together, and in 1965 Driver published his massive and detailed opus on the Qumran material, *The Judaean Scrolls*. According to Driver, 'arguments to establish a pre-Christian date of the Scrolls are fundamentally unsound'. The sole reasons for establishing such a date were, he pointed out, palaeographical, 'and these cannot stand alone'.[6] Driver agreed with Roth that the scrolls referred to the period of the revolt in Judaea, between AD 66 and 74, and were thus 'more or less' contemporary with the New Testament. He also concurred with Roth that the Qumran community must have consisted of Zealots, not traditional Essenes. He calculated that the scrolls could have been deposited at Qumran any time between then and the end of the second revolt in Judaea, the rebellion of Simeon bar Kochba between AD 132 and 135. He was scathing about the scholarship of the international team, as exemplified especially by de Vaux.

Roth and Driver were both famous, acknowledged, 'heavy-weights' in their respective historical fields, who could not be ignored or cavalierly dismissed. Their prestige and their learning could not be impugned or discredited. Neither could they be isolated. And they were too skilled in academic controversy to put their own necks into a noose, as Allegro had done. They were, however, vulnerable to the kind of patronising condescension that de Vaux and the international team, closing ranks in their consensus, proceeded to adopt. Roth and Driver, august though they might be, were portrayed as out of their element in the field of Qumran scholarship. Thus, de Vaux, reviewing Driver's book in 1967, wrote, 'It is a sad thing to find here once more this conflict of method and mentality between the textual critic and the archaeologist, the man at his desk and the man in the field.'[7] Not, of course, that de Vaux spent so very much time 'in the field' himself. As we have seen, he and most others on the international team were content to remain ensconced in their 'Scrollery', leaving the bulk of the fieldwork to the Bedouin. But the 'Scrollery', it might be argued, was at least closer to Qumran than was Oxford. Moreover, de Vaux and his team could claim first-hand familiarity with the entire corpus of Qumran texts, which Roth and Driver, denied access to those texts, could not. And while Roth and Driver had questioned the international team's historical method, they had not actually confronted its excessive reliance on archaeology and palaeography.

Archaeology and palaeography appeared to be the team's strengths, allowing de Vaux to conclude his review of *The Judaean Scrolls* by stating, confidently and definitively, that 'Driver's theory . . . is impossible'.[8] He could also, by invoking archaeology and palaeography, dazzle other figures in the field and effectively hijack their support. Thus Professor Albright was persuaded to weigh in against Driver, whose thesis, Albright declared, 'has failed completely'. Its failure, Albright went on, derived from 'an obvious scepticism with regard to the methodology of archaeologists, numismatists, and palaeographers. Of course, he [Driver] had the bad luck to run into head-on collision with one of the most brilliant scholars of our day – Roland de Vaux . . .'[9]

Moving on to the offensive, the international team and their colleagues continued to bombard Roth and Driver with increasingly contemptuous criticism. Both, as Eisenman has observed, 'were ridiculed in a manner unbecoming their situation and with such ferocity as to make one wonder'.[10] No one dared support them. No one dared risk the wrath of the now solidly entrenched consensus. 'And the scholarly sheep', as Eisenman says, 'fell into line.'[11] So far as Roth and Driver were concerned, their interests and reputations weren't confined exclusively to Qumran research. In consequence, they simply retired from the arena, not deeming it worthwhile to pursue the matter further. That this should have been allowed to happen testifies to the timidity and docility of other researchers in the field. It remains a black mark in the record of Qumran scholarship.

If the international team had exercised a monopoly before, their position now appeared to be unassailable. They had outmanoeuvred two of their most potentially formidable adversaries, and their triumph seemed to be complete. Roth and Driver had been driven to silence on the subject. Allegro had been discredited. Everyone else who might pose a threat had been intimidated into compliance. By the late 1960s and early 1970s, the hegemony of the international team was virtually absolute.

By the mid-1980s, such opposition as existed to the international team was scattered and disorganised. Most of it found expression in the United States, through a single journal, *Biblical Archaeology Review*. In its issue for September/October 1985, *BAR* reported a conference on the Dead Sea Scrolls held at New York University the previous May. It repeated the statement by Professor Morton Smith made at that conference: 'I thought to speak on the scandals of the Dead Sea documents, but these proved too numerous, too familiar, and too disgusting.'[12] It observed that the international team were 'governed, so far as can be ascertained, largely by convention, tradition, collegiality and inertia'.[13] And it concluded:

> The insiders, the scholars with the text assignments (T.H. Gaster, professor emeritus of Barnard College, Columbia University, calls these insiders 'the charmed circle'), have the goodies – to drip out bit by bit. This gives them status, scholarly power and a wonderful ego trip. Why squander it? Obviously, the existence of this factor is controversial and disputed.[14]

BAR called attention to the residue of frustration and resentment built up among scholars of proven ability who had not been admitted to the 'charmed circle'. It also, by implication, called attention to the benefits reaped by institutions such as Harvard University, where both Cross and Strugnell were stationed and where 'pet' graduate students were granted access to Qumran material while far more experienced and qualified researchers weren't. *BAR* ended its report by calling for 'immediate publication of photographs of the unpublished texts',[15] echoing Morton Smith, who asked his colleagues to 'request the Israeli government, which now has ultimate authority over those scroll materials, immediately to publish photographs of all unpublished texts so that they will then be available to all scholars'.[16]

That Smith's exhortation was ignored again bears witness to academic faint-heartedness. At the same time, it must be mentioned that Smith's exhortation was unfortunate in that it implicitly passed the blame from the international team, the real culprits, to the Israeli government, which had more immediate problems on its hands. The Israelis had kept their side of the bargain, made in 1967, that the international team would be allowed to retain their monopoly, provided they published; the international team had not. Thus, while the Israeli government might have been irresponsible in letting the situation continue, it was not to blame for the situation itself. As Eisenman soon came to realise, most Israelis – scholars and journalists alike, as well as government figures – were appallingly ignorant about the true situation, and, it must be said, indifferent to it. Through this ignorance and indifference, an outdated status quo had been allowed to continue intact.

In 1985, however, the same year as the conference reported by *BAR*, a well-known Israeli MP, Yuval Ne'eman, began to take an interest in the matter, and in the process showed himself to be surprisingly well briefed. Ne'eman was a world-famous physicist, Professor of Physics and head of the Physics Department at Tel Aviv University until 1971, when he became President of the university. Prior to that he had been a military planner, one of those responsible for evolving the basic strategic thinking of the Israeli Army. Between 1961 and 1963, he had been scientific director of the Soreq Research Establishment, the Israeli Atomic Energy Commission. Ne'eman raised the issue of the scrolls in the Knesset, the Israeli Parliament, declaring it a 'scandal' that the Israeli authorities had not reviewed or updated the situation – that the international team had been left with a mandate and monopoly dating from the former Jordanian regime. It was this challenge that finally forced the Israeli Department of Antiquities to investigate how and why an enclave of Catholic-oriented scholars should exercise so complete and exclusive a control over what was, in effect, an Israeli state treasure.

The Department of Antiquities proceeded to confront the international team on the question of publication. What accounted for the procrastination and delays, and what kind of timetable for publication could reasonably be expected? The director of the team at the time was Father Benoit, who on 15 September 1985 wrote to his colleagues.[17] In this letter, a copy of which is in our possession, he reminded them of Morton Smith's call for immediate publication of photographs. He also complained (as if he were the aggrieved party) about the use of the word 'scandal', not just by Morton Smith, but by Ne'eman as well, in the Knesset. He went on to state his intention of recommending John Strugnell as 'chief editor' of future publications. And he requested a timetable for publication from each member of the team.

Compliance with Father Benoit's request was dilatory and patchy. The Department of Antiquities, prodded by Ne'eman, wrote to him again on 26 December 1985, repeating its request for a report and for answers to the questions it had raised.[18] One cannot be sure whether Benoit based his reply on reliable information received from his colleagues, or whether he was simply improvising in order to buy time. But he wrote to the Department of Antiquities promising definitively that everything in the international team's possession would be published within seven years – that is, by 1993.[19] This timetable was submitted, in writing, as a binding undertaking, but of course no one took it seriously, and in personal conversation with us, Ne'eman stated he had heard 'on the grapevine' that the timetable was generally regarded as a joke.[20] It has certainly proved to be so. There is no prospect whatever of all the Qumran material, or even a reasonable part of it, appearing by 1993. Not even the whole of the material from Cave 4 has been published. Following Allegro's volume for *Discoveries in the Judaean Desert* back in 1968, only three more have been issued, in 1977, 1982 and 1990, bringing the total number of volumes to eight.

Nonetheless, the intensifying pressure engendered panic among the international team. Predictably enough, a search began for a scapegoat. Who had brought the Israeli government into the affair? Who had briefed Ne'eman and enabled him to raise the issue in the Knesset? Perhaps because of the repetition of the word 'scandal', the team concluded Geza Vermes to have been responsible. In fact, Vermes had had nothing whatever to do with the matter. It was Robert Eisenman who had briefed Ne'eman.

Eisenman had learned from the omissions of Roth and Driver. He appreciated that the entire edifice of the international team's consensus rested on the supposedly accurate data of archaeology and palaeography. Roth and Driver had correctly dismissed these data as irrelevant, but without confronting them. Eisenman resolved to challenge the international team on their own terrain – by exposing the methodology and demonstrating that the resulting data were irrelevant.

He opened his campaign with the book that first brought him to our attention, *Maccabees, Zadokites, Christians and Qumran*, published by E.J. Brill in Holland in 1983. In this book, he posed the first serious challenge the international team had yet encountered to their archaeology and palaeography. In his introduction, he explicitly flung down the gauntlet to the 'small group of specialists, largely working together' who had 'developed a consensus'.[21] Given the text's limited audience and circulation, of course, the international team could simply ignore the challenge. Indeed, the likelihood is that none of them read it at the time, in all probability dismissing it as a piece of ephemera by an upstart novice.

Eisenman, however, refused to let his efforts be consigned to oblivion. By 1985, his second book, *James the Just in the Habakkuk Pesher*, had appeared in Italy, ironically under the imprint of one of the Vatican presses, Tipographia Gregoriana. It carried an Italian preface, and the next year, with some additions and a revised appendix, was brought out by E.J. Brill. That same year, Eisenman was appointed Fellow-in-Residence at the prestigious Albright Institute in Jerusalem. Here he began working behind the scenes to acquaint the Israeli government with the situation and raise the scrolls on their agenda of priorities.

The international team's stranglehold, he realised, could not be broken solely through decorous or even strident protests in learned journals. It would be necessary to bring external pressure to bear, preferably from above. Accordingly, Eisenman met and briefed Professor Ne'eman, and Ne'eman then forced the issue in the Knesset.

Later that year, Eisenman himself approached Father Benoit, and verbally requested access to the scrolls. Predictably enough, Benoit politely refused, adroitly suggesting that Eisenman should ask the Israeli authorities, and implying that the decision was not his to make. At this point, Eisenman was still unaware of the stratagems employed by the international team to thwart all applicants who wanted access to the scrolls. He was not, however, prepared to be excluded so easily.

All scholars during their tenure on the staff of the Albright Institute give one lecture to the general public. Eisenman's lecture was scheduled for February 1986, and he chose as his subject 'The Jerusalem Community and Qumran', with the provocative subtitle 'Problems in Archaeology, Palaeography, History, and Chronology'. As in the case of his book on James, the title itself was calculated to strike a nerve. In accordance with custom, the Albright Institute sent invitations to all important scholars in the field in Jerusalem, and it was a matter of courtesy for sister institutions, like the French Ecole Biblique, to be represented. Five or six turned up, a higher number than usual.

Since they were unfamiliar with Eisenman and his work, they may not have expected anything out of the ordinary. Gradually, however, their complacency began to crumble, and they listened to his arguments in silence.* They declined to ask any questions at the end of the lecture, leaving without extending the usual courtesy of congratulations. For the first time, it had become apparent to them that in Eisenman they faced a serious challenge. True to form, they ignored it, in the hope, presumably, that it would go away.

The following spring, one of Eisenman's friends and colleagues, Professor Philip Davies of Sheffield University, arrived in Jerusalem for a short stay. He and Eisenman went to discuss with Magen Broshi, director of the Shrine of the Book, their desire to see the unpublished scroll fragments still sequestered by the inter-

---

*For an outline of Eisenman's remarks, see Chapter 10, Science in the Service of Faith.

national team. Broshi laughed at what apparently struck him as a vain hope: 'You will not see these things in your lifetime,' he said.[22] In June, towards the end of his stay in Jerusalem, Eisenman was invited to tea at the house of a colleague, a professor at the Hebrew University who would later become a member of the Israeli 'Scroll Oversight Committee'. Again he took Davies with him. A number of other academics, including Joseph Baumgarten of Baltimore Hebrew College, were present, and early in the evening John Strugnell – Allegro's old adversary and subsequently the head of the international team – made his appearance. Boisterous and apparently intent on confrontation, he began to complain about 'unqualified people' importunately demanding access to the Qumran material. Eisenman responded on cue. How did Strugnell define 'qualified'? Was he himself 'qualified'? Aside from his supposed skills in analysing handwriting, did he know anything about history? Ostensibly, it was all a half-joking, more or less 'civilised' debate, but it was growing ominously personal.

The next year, 1986–7, Eisenman spent at Oxford, as Senior Scholar at the Oxford Centre for Postgraduate Hebrew Studies and visiting Member of Linacre College. Through contacts in Jerusalem, he had been given two secret documents. One was a copy of a scroll on which Strugnell was working, part of his 'private fiefdom'. This text, written apparently by a leader of the ancient Qumran community and outlining a number of the community's governing precepts, is known by those in the field as the '*MMT*' document. Strugnell had shown it around at the 1985 conference, but had not published it.[23] (Nor has he yet, though the entire text comes to a mere 121 lines.)

The second document was of more contemporary significance. It comprised a computer print-out, or list, of *all* Qumran texts in the hands of the international team.[24] What made it particularly important was that the international team had repeatedly denied that any such print-out or list existed. Here was definitive proof that vast quantities of material had not yet been published and were being suppressed.

Eisenman had no hesitation about what to do:

Since I had decided that one of the main problems between scholars, which had created this whole situation in the first place, was over-protectiveness and jealously guarded secrecy, I decided to circulate anything that came into my hands without conditions. This was the service I could render; plus, it would undermine the international cartel or monopoly of such documents.[25]

Eisenman accordingly made available a copy of the 'MMT' document to anyone who expressed a desire to see it. These copies apparently circulated like wildfire, so much so that a year and a half later he received one back again from a third party who asked if he had seen it. He could tell by certain notations that this was one of the copies that he had originally allowed to circulate.

The print-out, like the 'MMT' document, was duly circulated, producing precisely the effect Eisenman had anticipated. He made a particular point of sending a copy of it to Hershel Shanks of *BAR*, thus providing the journal with ammunition to renew its campaign.

By this time, needless to say, Eisenman's relations with the international team were deteriorating. On the surface, of course, each maintained with the other a respectable academic demeanour of frosty civility. They could not, after all, publicly attack him for his actions, which had been manifestly disinterested, manifestly in the name of scholarship. But the rift was widening between them; and it wasn't long before a calculated attempt was made to freeze him out.

In January 1989, Eisenman visited Amir Drori, the newly appointed director of the Israeli Department of Antiquities. Drori inadvertently reported to Eisenman that he was about to sign an agreement with the team's new chief editor, John Strugnell. According to this agreement, the team's monopoly would be retained. The previous deadline for publication, accepted by Father Benoit, Strugnell's predecessor, was to be abrogated. All remaining Qumran material was to be published not by 1993, but by 1996.[26]

Eisenman was naturally appalled. Attempts to dissuade Drori, however, proved futile. Eisenman left the meeting determined to employ a new and more drastic stratagem. The only means of bringing pressure to bear on both the international team and on

the Department of Antiquities, and perhaps stop Drori from proceeding with the contract, would be Israel's High Court of Justice,
which dealt with miscarriages of justice and private appeals from
individuals.

Eisenman explored the question with lawyers. Yes, they concluded, the High Court might be persuaded to intervene. In order
for it to do so, however, Eisenman would have to present it with
proof of a miscarriage of justice; he would have to show, preferably
in writing, that access to the scrolls by a legitimate scholar had been
refused. At the time, no such record existed – not, at least, in the
legalistic sense the Court would require. Other scholars had, of
course, been refused access to the scrolls; but some of them were
dead, others were scattered across the world, and there was none
of the required documentation. Strugnell would therefore have to
be approached with a series of new requests for access to specific
materials – which, as a foregone conclusion, he would refuse. Now
that Eisenman had the catalogue numbers, his task would be easier.

Not wishing to make this request alone, Eisenman felt it would
be more impressive if he enlisted the support of others. He
approached Philip Davies of Sheffield, who agreed to support
him in what both recognised would be only the first shot of
a prolonged engagement fought through the Israeli High Court.
On 16 March 1989, the two professors submitted a formal letter to
John Strugnell. They requested access to certain original fragments,
and photographs of fragments, found at the Qumran site designated
Cave 4, and listed in the computer print-out which Eisenman had
leaked into circulation. In order to preclude any misunderstanding,
they cited the reference numbers assigned by the print-out to the
photographic negatives. They also requested access to a number
of scroll commentaries, or commentary fragments, related to the
primary text. They offered to pay all costs involved and promised
not to publish any definitive transcription or translation of the
material, which would be used only in their own research. They
promised, too, to abide by all the normal procedures of copyright
law.

In their letter, Eisenman and Davies acknowledged the time and
energy expended over the years by the international team – but, they

said, they felt the team had 'already been adequately compensated' by enjoying such long and exclusive access to the Qumran material. They stated that thirty-five to forty years was long enough for other scholars to have waited for similar access, without which 'we can no longer make meaningful progress in our endeavours'. The letter continued:

> Surely your original commission was to publish these materials as quickly as possible for the benefit of the scholarly community as a whole, not to control them. It would have been different, perhaps, if you and your scholars had discovered these materials in the first place. But you did not; they were simply assigned to you . . .
>
> . . . The situation as it now stands is abnormal in the extreme. Therefore, as mature scholars at the height of our powers and abilities, we feel it is an imposition upon us and a hardship to ask us to wait any longer for the research availability of and access to these materials forty years after their discovery.[27]

Eisenman and Davies expected Strugnell to refuse their requests. Strugnell, however, did not bother to reply at all. On 2 May, therefore, Eisenman wrote to Amir Drori – who earlier that year had renewed the international team's monopoly with the publication deadline of 1996. Eisenman enclosed a copy of the letter to Strugnell, mentioning that it had been posted to both of Strugnell's addresses, at Harvard and in Jerusalem. Of Strugnell's failure to reply, he wrote: 'Frankly, we are tired of being treated contemptuously. This kind of cavalier treatment is not really a new phenomenon, but is part and parcel of the process that has been going on for 20–30 years or more . . .'[28]

Since Strugnell would not grant access to the Qumran material, Eisenman requested that Drori, exercising a higher authority, should do so. He then made two particularly important points. As long as the international team continued to control the Qumran texts, it would not be sufficient merely to speed up the publication schedule. Nothing short of free scholarly access would be satisfactory – to check the international team's conclusions, to allow for variations in translation and interpretation, to discern connections the team themselves might perhaps have overlooked:

> We cannot be sure . . . that they have exhausted all possible fragments in relation to a given document or that they are putting fragments together in proper sequence. Nor can we be sure if the inventories are in fact complete and that fragments may not have been lost, destroyed or overlooked in some manner or for some reason. Only the whole of the interested scholarly community working together can assure this.[29]

The second point would appear, at least with hindsight, to be self-evident. The international team insisted on the importance of archaeology and palaeography. It was on the basis of their supposedly accurate archaeological and palaeographical studies, as Eisenman had explained, that dates for the Qumran texts had been posited – and accepted. Yet the texts themselves had been subject only to carbon-dating tests in use at around the time of the scrolls' discovery – tests which were very clumsy and consumed much manuscript material. Lest too much text be lost, therefore, only some of the wrappings found in the jars had been tested. These confirmed a date of around the beginning of the Christian era. None of the texts had been tested by the more recent techniques of Carbon-14 dating, even though Carbon-14 dating had now been refined by the newer AMS (Accelerator Mass Spectroscopy) technique. Little material would now be lost in the process and greater accuracy could be achieved. Eisenman therefore suggested that Drori exercise his authority and perform new, up-to-date tests. He also recommended that outsiders be brought into the process to keep it fair. He concluded his letter with a passionate appeal: 'Please act to release these materials to interested scholars who need them to proceed with professional research without prejudice and without distinction immediately.'[30]

No doubt prompted by Drori, Strugnell, in Jerusalem at the time, at last replied on 15 May. Despite the fact that Eisenman's letter to him had been posted to his address at both Harvard and Jerusalem, he blamed the delay on its having been sent to 'the wrong country'.[31]

According to *BAR*, 'Strugnell's imperious reply to Eisenman's request for access displays extraordinary intellectual hauteur and academic condescension.'[32] In it, he declares himself 'puzzled' as to why Eisenman and Davies showed their letter to 'half the *Who's Who* of Israel'. He accuses them of not having followed 'acceptable norms' and refers to them as 'lotus-eaters', which, in Strugnell's Mandarin, presumably denotes Californians, though why this term should apply to Philip Davies at Sheffield is an open question. Strugnell contrives not just to deny Eisenman's and Davies's request for access, but also to dodge each of the salient points they had raised. He advises them to take as their example the way 'such requests have been handled in the past' and go through established channels – ignoring the fact that all such requests 'in the past' had been denied. He also complains that the print-out Eisenman and Davies had used to cite reference numbers of photographic negatives was old and out of date. He neglects to mention that this print-out, not to mention any new one, had been unavailable to non-members of the international team until Eisenman put it into circulation.[33]

Eisenman responded to Strugnell's brush-off by going as public as he possibly could. By the middle of 1989, the issue had become a *cause célèbre* in American and Israeli newspapers, and, to a lesser degree, was picked up by the British press as well. Eisenman was extensively and repeatedly quoted by the *New York Times*, the *Washington Post*, the *Los Angeles Times*, the *Chicago Tribune*, *Time Magazine* and Canada's *Maclean's Magazine*. He stressed five major points:

1. That all research on the Dead Sea Scrolls was being unfairly monopolised by a small enclave of scholars with vested interests and a biased orientation.
2. That only a small percentage of the Qumran material was finding its way into print and that most of it was still being withheld.
3. That it was misleading to claim that the bulk of the so-called 'biblical' texts had been released, because the most important material consisted of the so-called 'sectarian' texts – *new* texts,

never seen before, with a great bearing on the history and religious life of the 1st century.

4. That after forty years, access to the scrolls should be made available to all interested scholars.

5. That AMS Carbon-14 tests, monitored by independent laboratories and researchers, should immediately be conducted on the Qumran documents.

As was perhaps inevitable, once the media had begun to sensationalise it, the affair quickly degenerated, with Eisenman being misquoted on two separate occasions, and a barrage of invective coming from both sides. But behind the clash of egos, the central issue remained unresolved. As Philip Davies had written in 1988:

Any archaeologist or scholar who digs or finds a text but does not pass on what has been found deserves to be locked up as an enemy of science. After forty years we have neither a full and definitive report on the dig nor a full publication of the scrolls.[34]

5
Academic Politics and Bureaucratic Inertia

Early in 1989, Eisenman had been invited to present a paper at a conference on the scrolls to be held at the University of Groningen that summer. The organiser and chairman of the conference was the secretary of the journal *Revue de Qumran*, the official organ of the Ecole Biblique, the French–Dominican archaeological school in Jerusalem of which most of the international team were members or associates. According to the arrangement, all papers presented at the conference would subsequently be published in the journal. By the time of the conference, however, Eisenman's conflict with the international team, and the ensuing controversy, had become public. It was not, of course, feasible to retract Eisenman's invitation. He was therefore allowed to present his paper, but its publication in *Revue de Qumran* was blocked.*

The chairman of the conference was deeply embarrassed, apologising to Eisenman and explaining there was nothing he could do – his superiors, the editors of the journal, had insisted on excluding Eisenman's paper.[1] *Revue de Qumran* had thus effectively revealed itself, not as a non-partisan forum for the spectrum of scholarly opinion, but as a species of mouthpiece for the international team.

---

*The paper has since been published. See Eisenman, 'Interpreting "Abeit-Galuto" in the Habakkuk *Pesher*', *Folia orientalia*, vol. xxvii (1990).

The balance was, however, slowly beginning to tilt in Eisenman's favour. The *New York Times*, for example, had monitored the dispute throughout, and had assessed the arguments of the opposing factions. On 9 July 1989, it pronounced its judgment in an editorial entitled 'The Vanity of Scholars':

Some works of scholarship, like the compilation of dictionaries, legitimately take a lifetime. But with others, the reasons for delay can be less lofty: greed for glory, pride, or just plain old sloth.

Consider the sorry saga of the Dead Sea Scrolls, documents that might cast spectacular new light on the early history of Christianity and the doctrinal evolution of Judaism.

The scrolls were discovered in 1947, but many that are in fragments remain unpublished. More than 40 years later, a coterie of dawdling scholars is still spinning out the work while the world waits and the precious pieces lapse into dust.

Naturally, they refuse to let others see the material until it is safely published under their names. The publication schedule of J.T. Milik, a Frenchman responsible for more than 50 documents, is a source of particular frustration to other scholars . . .

Archaeology is particularly vulnerable to scholars who gain control of materials and then refuse to publish them.[2]

Despite the unseemly squabbling, the clack and crack of ruptured *amour propre*, the fustian and umbrage and general high dudgeon, Eisenman's arguments were now beginning to carry weight, to convince people. And there was also another development, of comparable importance. The 'outsiders' – the adversaries of the international team – were beginning to organise, to consolidate their efforts and conduct conferences of their own. In the months following the editorial in the *New York Times*, there were to be two such conferences.

The first of these was arranged by Professor Kapera of Kraków, with the aid of Philip Davies, and took place at Mogilany, Poland. It produced what became known as the 'Mogilany Resolution', with two main demands: that 'the relevant authorities' in Israel should obtain photographic plates of all unpublished scrolls, and that these should be supplied to Oxford University Press for immediate publication; and that the data obtained from de Vaux's excavations at Qumran between 1951 and 1956, much of which had not yet appeared, should now be issued in definitive published form.

Seven and a half months later, a second conference was convened, on Eisenman's home territory, California State University at Long Beach. Papers were presented by a number of academics, including Eisenman himself, Professor Ludwig Koenen and Professor David Noel Freedman from the University of Michigan, Professor Norman Golb from the University of Chicago and Professor James M. Robinson from Claremont University, who had headed the team responsible for publishing the Nag Hammadi Scrolls. Two resolutions were produced: first, that a facsimile edition of all hitherto unpublished Qumran fragments should be issued immediately – a necessary 'first step in throwing the field open to scholars irrespective of point of view or approach'; and second, that a data bank of AMS Carbon-14 results on known manuscripts should be established, to facilitate the future dating of all previously undated texts and manuscripts, whether on papyrus, parchment, codex or any other material.

None of these resolutions, of course, either from Mogilany or from Long Beach, was in any sense legally binding. In the academic community, however, and in the media, they carried considerable weight. Increasingly, the international team were finding themselves on the defensive; furthermore, they were beginning, albeit slowly, to give way. Thus, for example, Milik, while the public battle raged, quietly passed over one text – the very text Eisenman and Davies had requested to see in their letter to Strugnell – to Professor Joseph Baumgarten of Hebrew College in Baltimore. Baumgarten, of course, who was now a member of the international team, characteristically refused to let anyone else see the text in question. Neither did Strugnell – who as head of the team was supposed to authorise and supervise such transactions – bother to inform Eisenman or Davies what had occurred. But the mere fact that Milik was handing over material at all reflected some progress, some sense that he felt sufficiently pressured to relinquish at least part of his private fiefdom – and with it, some of the onus of responsibility.

86

More promising still, Milik, in 1990, surrendered a second text, this time to Professor James VanderKamm of North Carolina State University. VanderKamm, in a break with the international team's tradition, promptly offered access to other scholars. 'I will show the photographs to anyone who is interested in seeing them', he announced.[3] Milik, not surprisingly, described VanderKamm's behaviour as 'irresponsible'.[4] VanderKamm then withdrew his offer.

An important role in the campaign to obtain open access to the Dead Sea Scrolls was, as we have already indicated, played by Hershel Shank's journal, *Biblical Archaeology Review*. It was *BAR* that fired the opening salvo of the current media campaign, when in 1985 it published a long and hard-hitting article on the delays in releasing Qumran material. And when Eisenman obtained a copy of the computer print-out listing all the fragments in the international team's possession, he leaked this document to *BAR*. He thus furnished *BAR* with invaluable ammunition. In return, *BAR* was only too eager to provide publicity and an open forum.

As we have also noted, however, *BAR*'s attack, at least in part, was directed at the Israeli government, whom it held as responsible for the delays as the international team themselves.[5] Eisenman was careful to distance himself from *BAR*'s position in this respect. To attack the Israeli government, he felt, was simply to divert attention from the real problem – the withholding of information.

Despite this initial difference of approach, however, *BAR*'s contribution has been immense. Since the spring of 1989, in particular, the magazine has sustained a relentless, non-stop barrage of articles directed at the delays and deficiencies of Qumran scholarship and research. *BAR*'s basic position is that, 'in the end the Dead Sea Scrolls are public treasures'.[6] As for the international team: 'The team of editors has now become more an obstacle to publication than a source of information.'[7] *BAR* has in general pulled very few punches and, indeed, often comes very close to the legal limits of what can be printed. And while Eisenman may not have shared *BAR*'s eagerness to attack the Israeli government, there is no question that those attacks have helped to produce at least some results.

Thus, for example, the Israeli authorities were persuaded to assume some measure of authority over the unpublished Qumran material. In April 1989 the Israeli Archaeological Council appointed a 'Scroll Oversight Committee' to supervise the publication of all Qumran texts and ensure that the members of the international team were indeed fulfilling their assigned tasks. In the beginning, the creation of this committee may have been something of a cosmetic exercise, intended merely to convey the impression that something constructive was being done. In practice, however, as the international team have continued to drag their feet, the committee has assumed more and more power.

As we have noted, Father Benoit's timetable, according to which the whole of the Qumran material would be published by 1993, was superseded by Strugnell's new and (theoretically at least) more realistic timetable, with a deadline of 1996. Eisenman had remained profoundly sceptical of the team's intentions. *BAR* was more vociferous. The 'suggested Timetable', the magazine proclaimed, was 'a hoax and a fraud'.[8] It was not signed, *BAR* pointed out; it technically bound no one to anything; it made no provision whatever for progress reports or proof that the international team were actually doing their jobs. What would happen, *BAR* asked the Israeli Department of Antiquities, if the stipulated deadlines were not met?

The Department of Antiquities did not reply directly to this query, but on 1 July 1989, in an interview with the *Los Angeles Times*, Amir Drori, the department's director, issued what might be construed as a nebulous threat: 'For the first time, we have a plan, and if someone does not complete his work on time we have the right to deliver the scrolls to someone else.'[9] Strugnell himself, however, in an interview with the *International Herald Tribune*, made clear how lightly he took such threats. 'We are not running a railroad',[10] he said. And in an interview with ABC Television, he was even more explicit: 'If I don't meet [the deadline] by one or two years, I won't worry at all.'[11] Milik, in the meantime, remained, as *Time Magazine* put it, 'elusive', although the magazine did manage to extract one characteristically arrogant statement from him: 'The world will see the manuscripts when I have done the necessary work.'[12]

Justifiably unappeased, *BAR* continued its campaign. In the ABC Television interview, Strugnell, with somewhat lumbering humour, and manifest contempt, had complained of the recent attacks to which he and his colleagues had been subjected. 'It seems we've acquired a bunch of fleas', he said, 'who are in the business of annoying us.'[13] *BAR* promptly ran a signally unflattering photograph of Professor Strugnell surrounded by 'named fleas'. In addition to Eisenman and Davies, the 'named fleas' included Professors Joseph Fitzmyer of Catholic University, David Noel Freedman of the University of Michigan, Dieter Georgi of the University of Frankfurt, Norman Golb of the University of Chicago, Z.J. Kapera of Kraków, Philip King of Boston College, T.H. Gaster and Morton Smith of Columbia, and Geza Vermes of Oxford University. *BAR* invited all other biblical scholars who wished to be named publicly as 'fleas' to write in. This invitation elicited a stream of letters, including one from Professor Jacob Neusner of the Institute for Advanced Study at Princeton, author of a number of important works on the origins of Judaism and the formative years of Christianity. Speaking of the international team's work, Professor Neusner described the history of the Dead Sea Scrolls scholarship as 'a monumental failure', which he attributed to 'arrogance and self-importance'.[14]

By the autumn of 1989, we had already begun to research this book and, in the process, to become embroiled, albeit quietly, in the controversy. On a trip to Israel to gather material and interview a number of scholars, Michael Baigent decided to check on the so-called 'Oversight Committee', recently formed to supervise the work of the international team. In theory, the committee might be anything. On the one hand, it might be a 'paper tiger', a means of formally institutionalising official inaction. On the other, it might offer a real possibility of power being taken from the international team and placed in more assiduous hands. Would the committee merely serve to cosmeticise further delays? Or did it possess both the authority and the will to do something constructive about the existing situation?

Among the individuals making up the committee were two members of the Israeli Department of Antiquities – Amir Drori, the department's head, and Mrs Ayala Sussman. Baigent had arranged initially to speak with Drori. On his arrival at the Department of

Antiquities, however, he was urged to speak instead with Mrs Sussman, who presided over the sub-department in charge of the Qumran texts themselves. Drori, in other words, had a number of matters on his plate. Mrs Sussman's activities were focused more specifically on the scrolls.

The meeting with Mrs Sussman took place on 7 November 1989. She clearly, and perhaps understandably, regarded it as an unwelcome intrusion on her already busy schedule. While being scrupulously polite, she was also therefore impatient, dismissive and vague, vouchsafing few details, endeavouring to get the conversation over with as soon as possible. Baigent was also, of course, polite; but it proved necessary for him to become tiresomely insistent, conveying the impression that he was prepared to wait in the office all day unless some answers to his queries were forthcoming. Eventually, Mrs Sussman capitulated.

Baigent's first questions concerned the formation and purposes of the 'Oversight Committee'. Mrs Sussman, at that point, apparently regarding her interviewer not as a researcher with some background in the subject, but as a casual journalist skating on the surface of a story, imprudently confided that the committee had been formed to deflect criticism from the Department of Antiquities. In effect, Baigent was given the impression that the committee had no real interest in the scrolls themselves, but was merely a species of bureaucratic screen.

What was its nominally official role, Baigent asked, and how much actual authority did it exercise? Mrs Sussman remained vague. The committee's job, she said, was to 'advise' Amir Drori, Director of the Department of Antiquities, in his dealings with Professor Strugnell, chief editor for any publication of Qumran material. The committee intended, she added, to work closely with Strugnell, Cross and other members of the international team, towards whom the Department of Antiquities felt an obligation. 'Some,' she declared, 'have gone very far with their work, and we do not want to take it away from them.'[15]

What about *BAR*'s suggestion, Baigent asked, and the resolution adopted by the convention at Mogilany two months before – of making facsimiles or photographs available to all interested scholars? Mrs Sussman's gesture was that of a woman dropping an irrelevant letter into a wastepaper basket. 'No one discussed it seriously,' she said. On the other hand, and somewhat more reassuringly, she stated that the new timetable, according to which all Qumran documents would be published by 1996, was correct. 'We can reassign,' she stressed, 'if, for example, Milik doesn't meet the dates.'[16] Every text in Milik's possession, she emphasised, had been allocated a publication date in the schedule. At the same time, she acknowledged her sympathy for Strugnell's position. Her husband, she revealed, a professor of Talmudic studies, was helping Strugnell on the translation – all 121 lines of it – of the long-delayed '*MMT*' document.

So far as Mrs Sussman was concerned, everything on the whole seemed to be in order and proceeding acceptably. Her chief preoccupation, however, seemed to be less the Qumran material itself than the adverse publicity directed at the Department of Antiquities. This profoundly disturbed her. The scrolls, after all, were 'not our job'. 'Why is it causing trouble?' she asked, almost plaintively. 'We have other, more important things to do.'[17]

Baigent, needless to say, left the meeting disquieted. It is accepted wisdom in Israel that if one wishes to bury a subject, one creates a committee to study it. And as a matter of historical fact, every previous official attempt to oversee the work of the international team had been circumvented by de Vaux and Benoit. Was there any reason to suppose the situation would change?

The following day, Baigent met with Professor Shemaryahu Talmon, one of two scholars at Hebrew University who were also members of the 'Oversight Committee'. Professor Talmon proved to be congenial company indeed – wry, witty, well-travelled, sophisticated. Unlike Mrs Sussman, moreover, he seemed to have not only an overview of the problem, but a familiarity with its minutiae and details – and a manifest sympathy for independent scholars seeking access to the Qumran material. Indeed, he said, he had had difficulties himself in the past, had been unable to obtain access to original texts, had been obliged to work with transcriptions and secondary sources – whose accuracy, in some instances, had subsequently proved to be questionable.

'Controversy is the lifeblood of scholarship,' Professor Talmon declared at the very beginning of Baigent's meeting with him.[18] He made it clear that he regarded his membership of the 'Oversight Committee' as a welcome opportunity to help change the situation. 'If it is only a watch-dog committee,' he said, 'then I shall resign.'[19] The committee, he stressed, had to be able to achieve some concrete results if it was to justify its existence. He acknowledged the problems confronted by the international team: 'Scholars are always under pressure and always take on too much. A deadline is always dead.'[20] But, he added, if a particular researcher had more texts in his possession than he could effectively handle, he must pass some of them on. The committee would 'encourage' researchers to do precisely this. In passing, Talmon also mentioned that, according to rumour, there were still large fragments in the archives, hitherto unknown and yet to be assigned. This rumour was subsequently to prove correct.

Baigent asked Professor Talmon about the fuss resulting from Eisenman and Davies's requesting to see certain documents. Talmon said he was wholly in favour of access being granted them. There was, he stated, a 'need to help people in utilising unpublished information. This is a legitimate demand.'[21] The scrolls, he concluded, should be made available to all interested and qualified researchers. At the same time, he acknowledged that certain technical difficulties had to be sorted out. These difficulties, which were now being taken in hand, fell under three headings: first, the now out-of-date and superseded catalogue needed revision and updating; second, there was still no full inventory of all the scrolls and scroll fragments, some of which were still unassigned ('the only person who knows what is where is Strugnell'); and finally, there was an urgent need for a general concordance encompassing all the known texts.

As for the timetable according to which everything would be published by 1996, Talmon was honestly doubtful. Quite apart from whether or not the international team met their deadlines, he queried whether Oxford University Press would be able to produce so many volumes in so short a time. Looking at the schedule, he observed that no fewer than nine volumes were due to appear between 1990 and 1993. Could OUP cope with this? And could Strugnell handle the editing of so much while still pursuing his own research?

If they arose, however, these obstacles would at least be legitimate obstacles, not attributable to obstruction or deliberate withholding of material. They were, in effect, the only obstacles Talmon was prepared to tolerate. This was genuinely reassuring. In Talmon, the 'Oversight Committee' appeared to have a serious and responsible scholar who understood the problems, was determined to confront them and would not be deflected by obfuscation.

Baigent had learned that the 'Oversight Committee' was scheduled to meet the following day, at ten in the morning. He had therefore arranged a meeting for nine o'clock with Professor Jonas Greenfield, another member of the committee who was on the staff at Hebrew University. He put to Greenfield what had now become a routine question – would the 'Oversight Committee' 'have teeth'? 'We would like it to have teeth,' Greenfield replied, 'but they will have to grow.'[22] Having nothing to lose, Baigent decided to put the cat among the pigeons. He repeated to Professor Greenfield what Ayala Sussman had said to him – that the committee had been formed primarily to deflect criticism from the Department of Antiquities. Perhaps this would elicit some reaction.

It most certainly did. The next morning, Mrs Sussman telephoned Baigent. Sounding somewhat rattled at first, she stated she was annoyed with him for telling Professor Greenfield she had made so dismissive a remark. It wasn't true, she protested. She couldn't possibly have said anything like that. 'We are very keen,' she stressed, 'for this committee to do things.'[23] Baigent asked if she wished him to read back to her his notes; when she said yes, he did so. No, Mrs Sussman insisted: 'The committee was formed to advise the Department [of Antiquities] on sensitive matters.'[24] As for her dismissive remarks, she had thought she was speaking 'off the record'. Baigent replied that he had originally arranged his interview with Amir Drori, the department's director, in order to obtain, precisely *for* the record, a statement of official policy on the matter. Drori had passed him on to Mrs Sussman, whom he had no reason to suppose was expressing anything other than the 'official line'. The interview, therefore, had been very much 'on the record'.

Baigent then became somewhat more conciliatory, explaining the grounds for his concern. The 'Oversight Committee', he said, was potentially the best thing that had happened in the whole sorry saga of Dead Sea Scroll research. It offered, for the first time, a genuine possibility of breaking the log-jam, of transcending academic squabbles and ensuring the release of texts which should have been made public forty years ago. It had thus been profoundly disconcerting to hear that this unique opportunity might be squandered, and that the committee might be no more than a bureaucratic mechanism for maintaining the status quo. On the other hand, Baigent concluded, he had been reassured by his conversations with Professors Talmon and Greenfield, both of whom had expressed an unimpugnably sincere desire for the committee to be both active and effective. Mrs Sussman now hastened to concur with her colleagues. 'We are very keen to get this moving,' she affirmed. 'We are searching for ways to do it. We want to get the whole project moving as fast as possible.'[25]

Partly through the determination of Professors Talmon and Greenfield, partly through Mrs Sussman's embarrassment, the 'Oversight Committee' had been galvanised into some sort of resolve. There remained, however, the disquieting question raised by Professor Talmon – whether it was technically and mechanically possible for Oxford University Press to produce the stipulated volumes in accordance with Strugnell's timetable. Had the timetable perhaps been drawn up in full knowledge that it couldn't conceivably be met? Might it perhaps have been just another tactic for delaying things, while at the same time absolving the international team of any blame?

On his return to the United Kingdom, Baigent telephoned Strugnell's editor at Oxford University Press. Was the schedule, he asked, feasible? Could eighteen volumes of *Discoveries in the Judaean Desert* be produced between 1989 and 1996? If a blanch could be audible over the telephone, Baigent would have heard one. The prospect, Strugnell's editor replied, 'seems highly unlikely'. She reported that she'd just had a meeting with Strugnell. She'd also just had a fax on the matter from the Israeli Department of Antiquities. It was generally accepted, she said, that 'the dates were very vague. Each

94

date was taken with a pinch of salt. We couldn't cope with more than two or three a year at the most.'[26]

Baigent reported that both the Department of Antiquities and the 'Oversight Committee' were worried about whether the timetable could be met. 'They are right to be worried about the dates,' the editor at OUP replied.[27] She then expressed what sounded disturbingly like a desire to fob off the entire project. OUP, she said, felt no need to demand that the series be reserved wholly for themselves. Perhaps some other press – university or otherwise – might be interested in co-publication? She wasn't even sure that OUP covered its costs on each volume.

During the last four months of 1990, developments pertaining to the international team and their monopoly began to occur with accelerating momentum. Criticism by scholars denied access to the Qumran material received increasing publicity and currency, and the Israeli government, it seems, was susceptible to the mounting pressure. This pressure was intensified by an article which appeared in November in *Scientific American*, fiercely castigating the delays and the general situation, and according independent scholars space in which to voice their grievances.

In mid-November, news broke that the Israeli government had appointed a Dead Sea Scroll scholar, Emmanuel Tov, to act as 'joint editor-in-chief' of the project to translate and publish the entire corpus of Qumran material. This appointment was apparently made without consulting the existing editor-in-chief, John Strugnell, who was reported to have opposed it. By that time, however, Strugnell was ill in hospital and not available for comment – or, it would seem, for any serious opposition. By that time, too, even his former colleagues, such as Frank Cross, were beginning to distance themselves from him and to criticise him publicly.

There were also other reasons for this sequence of events. Earlier in November, Strugnell, from his quarters at the Ecole Biblique, had given an interview to a journalist for *Ha aretz*, a leading Tel Aviv newspaper. The precise context of his remarks is not, at the moment, altogether clear; but the remarks themselves, as reported by the world's press, were hardly calculated to endear him to the Israeli authorities – and display, for a man in his position, what can only be described as a flamboyant lack of tact. According to the *New York Times* of 12 December 1990, Strugnell – a Protestant convert to Catholicism – said of Judaism: 'It's a horrible religion. It's a Christian heresy, and we deal with our heretics in different ways.' Two days later, the *Times* contained more of Strugnell's statement: 'I think Judaism is a racist religion, something very primitive. What bothers me about Judaism is the very existence of Jews as a group . . .' According to London's *Independent*, Strugnell also said that the 'solution' – an ominous word – for Judaism was 'mass conversion to Christianity'.

In themselves, of course, these comments had no direct relevance to the question of Dead Sea Scroll scholarship, to the withholding of Qumran material from other researchers and the procrastination in its release. But such comments could hardly have been expected to enhance the credibility of a man responsible for the translation and publication of ancient Judaic texts. Not surprisingly, a major scandal ensued. It was covered by British newspapers. It was a front-page item for newspapers in Israel, France and the United States. Strugnell's former colleagues, as gracefully but as hastily as possible, endeavoured to disown him. By the middle of December, it was announced that he had been dismissed from his post – a decision in which, apparently, his former colleagues and the Israeli authorities had concurred. Delays in publication and problems of health were cited as factors contributing to his dismissal.

II
THE VATICAN'S
REPRESENTATIVES

6
The Onslaught of Science

Until now, this book has referred to the 'villains of the piece' as 'the international team'. In our conversations with them, however, Robert Eisenman and others would often allude to the Ecole Biblique, the French–Dominican archaeological school in Jerusalem. Indeed, the 'international team' and the Ecole Biblique were frequently used interchangeably; and Allegro, too, in his letters, would refer to the international team as the 'Ecole Biblique gang'. We wondered why this association should constantly be made. Why were the international team and the Ecole Biblique treated as though they were the same thing? What was the relationship between them? Was it formally defined and delineated? Was the international team 'officially' an adjunct of the Ecole Biblique? Or was the overlap between them so great as to render any distinction superfluous? With some advice and pointers from Eisenman, we endeavoured to clarify the matter.

As we have noted, the international team, from its very beginnings, was dominated by Father de Vaux, then director of the Ecole Biblique, and by his close friend and disciple, the then Father Milik. As Allegro complained, both men would constantly arrogate first claim to all incoming texts: 'All fragments are brought first to De V. or Milik, and . . . complete secrecy is kept over what they are till long after they have been studied by this group.'[1] Even Strugnell stated that when fresh material came in, Milik would invariably

99

pounce on it, claiming it fell within the parameters of his own particular assignment.[2]

Not surprisingly, then, Milik ended up with the lion's share of the most important material – and particularly of the controversial 'sectarian' material. The creation of his monopoly was facilitated by the fact that he was permanently resident in Jerusalem at the time, along with two of his staunchest supporters, de Vaux and Father Jean Starcky. Father Skehan, though not permanently resident in Jerusalem, threw his weight behind this triumvirate. So did Professor Cross – who had been assigned 'biblical' rather than 'sectarian' material anyway. Allegro, of course, cast himself in the role of rebel, but his opposition was hampered by the fact that he was in Jerusalem only intermittently. Of those residing in Jerusalem during the crucial period of excavation, purchase of material, allocation of texts and collation of fragments, only the young John Strugnell (who would hardly have challenged de Vaux anyway) was not Catholic – and he subsequently converted. All the others were, in fact, Roman Catholic priests, attached to, and residing at, the Ecole Biblique. Among the other current members of the team or writers in the area of Qumran studies working at the Ecole are Father Emile Puech and Father Jerome Murphy-O'Connor.

It was not just by virtue of being on the spot that this Catholic conclave came to dominate Qumran scholarship. Neither, certainly, was it by virtue of any outstanding pre-eminence in the field. Indeed, there was no shortage of no less competent or qualified scholars who, as we have noted, were excluded. A major determining factor was the Ecole Biblique itself, which systematically undertook to establish for itself, as an institution, a position of unrivalled pre-eminence. The Ecole had its own journal, for example, *Revue biblique*, edited by de Vaux, who published in its pages some of the most consequential and influential early articles on Qumran – articles bearing the stamp of first-hand authority. And in 1958, the Ecole launched a second journal, *Revue de Qumran*, devoted exclusively to the Dead Sea Scrolls and related matters. Thus the Ecole officially controlled the two most prominent and prestigious forums for discussion of Qumran material. The Ecole's editors could accept or reject articles as they saw fit, and were thereby enabled to exert a decisive influence on the entire course of Qumran scholarship. This situation was inaugurated at the very inception of Qumran studies.

In addition to its publications, the Ecole created a special research library oriented specifically towards Qumran studies. A card index was compiled, which documented every book, every scholarly article, every newspaper or magazine report published on the Dead Sea Scrolls anywhere in the world. All publications on the subject were collected and filed in the library – which was not open to the general public. Although some of the secret, unclassified and still unassigned scroll material was kept at the Ecole, most of it was housed at the Rockefeller Museum. Nevertheless, the Rockefeller was reduced to the status of a mere 'workshop'. The Ecole became the 'headquarters', the 'offices', the 'school' and the 'nerve centre'. Thus the Ecole contrived to establish itself as the *de facto* and generally recognised centre of all Qumran scholarship, the focus of all legitimate and academically respectable research in the field. The Ecole's 'stamp of approval' could, in effect, underwrite, certify and guarantee a scholar's reputation. Withholding such endorsement was tantamount to destroying a man's credibility.

Officially, of course, the studies over which the Ecole presided were supposed to be non-denominational, non-partisan, impartial, unbiased. The Ecole presented to the world a façade of 'scientific objectivity'. But could such 'objectivity' in fact be expected on the part of a Dominican institution, with vested Catholic interests to protect? 'My faith has nothing to fear from my scholarship', de Vaux once stated to Edmund Wilson.[3] No doubt it didn't, but that was never in fact the real question. The real question was whether his scholarship, and its reliability, had anything to fear from his faith.

As we ourselves became *au fait* with the situation, we began to wonder if the correct questions were indeed being asked, if blame was indeed being correctly apportioned. *Biblical Archaeology Review*, for example, had focused on the Israeli government as a primary culprit. But if the Israeli government was guilty of anything, it was guilty only of an understandable sin of omission. By virtue of John Allegro's success in persuading the Jordanian government to nationalise the Rockefeller Museum,[4] and political and military circumstance – the Six Day War and its aftermath – Israel suddenly found itself, as a *fait accompli*, in possession of Arab East Jerusalem, where the Rockefeller Museum and the Ecole Biblique were situated. As 'spoils of war', the Dead Sea Scrolls thus became *de facto* Israeli. But Israel was fighting for its own survival at the time. In the turmoil of the moment, there were more urgent matters to deal with than the sorting out of scholarly disputes or the rectifying of academic inequities. Neither could Israel afford to isolate itself further on the international scene by antagonising a body of prestigious researchers and thereby provoking a reaction from the intellectual community – as well, quite possibly, as from the Vatican. In consequence, the Israeli government had taken the expedient course of doing nothing, of implicitly sanctioning the status quo. The international team had simply been asked to get on with their business.

It was, of course, more accurate to assign responsibility to the international team themselves – as, indeed, a number of commentators had not hesitated to do. But were the motives ascribed to the team wholly accurate? Was it simply a matter of what the *New York Times* called 'the vanity of scholars', and Professor Neusner in *BAR* 'arrogance and self-importance'?[5] These factors undoubtedly played a part. But the real question was one of accountability. To whom, ultimately, *were* the international team accountable? In theory, they should have been accountable to their peers, to other scholars. But was that indeed the case? In reality, the international team seemed to recognise no accountability whatever, except to the Ecole Biblique. And to whom was the Ecole Biblique accountable? Although he'd not investigated the matter himself, Eisenman prompted us, when we probed him, to explore the connection between the Ecole and the Vatican.

We approached other scholars in the field, some of whom had gone publicly on record to condemn the 'scandal'. Not one of them, it transpired, had thought to look into the Ecole Biblique's background and official allegiances. They had, of course, recognised that the Ecole was Catholic, but they did not know whether it had any direct or formal connection with the Vatican. Professor Davies at Sheffield, for example, confessed that he found the question intriguing. Now that he thought about it, he said, he found it striking how criticism was so often and so assiduously deflected away from the Ecole.[6] According to Professor Golb at the University of Chicago, 'people hint . . . that there are connections' between the Ecole and the Vatican. 'A lot of events,' he said, 'fit the theory [of connection].'[7] Like his colleagues, however, he had not explored the matter any further.

Given the Ecole's undisputed dominance of Qumran scholarship, it seemed to us particularly important to ascertain the institution's official orientation, attitudes, allegiances and accountability. Here, we decided, was something we ourselves could undertake to investigate in detail. The results were to prove a major revelation, not just to us, but to other independent researchers in the field as well.

Today, in the late 20th century, one takes the procedures and methodology of historical and archaeological research more or less for granted. Until the mid-19th century, however, historical and archaeological research, as we understand such things today, simply didn't exist at all. There were no accepted methods or procedures; there was no coherent discipline or training; there was no real awareness that such research in any sense constituted a form of 'science', requiring the rigour, the 'objectivity', the systematic approach that any science does. The 'field', such as it was, existed not as a sphere of formal academic study but as a happy hunting-ground for learned – and often not so learned – amateurs. The territory was as yet too uncharted to accommodate anything that might be called 'professionalism'.

Thus, for example, in the early 19th century, wealthy Europeans, on their 'grand tour', might rummage about at random for Greek or Roman artefacts to ship back to the château, schloss or country house at home. In their search for antiquities, a few ventured further afield, digging holes all over the fertile terrain of the vast and moribund Ottoman Empire. Such enterprises amounted, in effect, not to anything that might pass for archaeology, but to treasure-hunting. Knowledge of the past was deemed less important than whatever booty it might provide; and funds for the plundering of such booty were supplied by, or for, various museums in quest of large and dramatic statues to place on display. Public demand for relics of

103

this sort was considerable. Crowds would flock to museums to see the latest trophies, and the popular press would have a field day. But the trophies themselves were more an inspiration to the imagination, and to imaginative speculation, than to any form of scientific method. Flaubert's *Salammbô*, for example, published in 1862, represents an extraordinary feat of 'literary archaeology', a grandiose imaginative attempt to reconstruct, with meticulous scientific precision, the splendour of ancient Carthage. But science itself had not yet caught up with Flaubert's aesthetic objectives. Certainly no historian had ever attempted to use scientific or archaeological data to bring ancient Carthage so vividly back to life.

Until the mid-19th century, what passed for archaeology was, more often than not, a sorry business indeed. Wall paintings, carvings and other artefacts would visibly disintegrate before the bemused eyes of their discoverers – who, of course, had no real concept of conservation. Priceless statues would be demolished in the search for some supposed treasure concealed within them. Or they might be hacked into fragments to make transportation easier – and then lost, when the barges transporting them sank. To the extent that any systematic form of excavation was practised at all, it had not yet been yoked to history – to the principle of illuminating the past. The excavators themselves lacked the knowledge, the skill and the technology to turn their discoveries to account.

The acknowledged 'father of modern archaeology' was the German-born Heinrich Schliemann (1822–90), naturalised as an American citizen in 1850. From his boyhood, Schliemann had been a passionate admirer of Homer's *Iliad* and *Odyssey*. He was firmly convinced that these epics were not 'mere fables', but mythologised history, chronicles inflated to legendary status, perhaps, but still referring to events, people and places which had once actually existed. The Trojan War, Schliemann insisted, to the mockery and scepticism of his contemporaries, was an event in historical fact. Troy was not just a figment of a poet's imagination. On the contrary, it had once been a 'real' city. One could use Homer's work as a species of map. One could identify certain recognisable geographical and topographical features. One could compute approximate speeds of travel at the time, and thereby estimate the distance between one point and another cited by Homer. By such means, Schliemann concluded, one could retrace the itinerary of the Greek fleet in the *Iliad* and locate the actual historical site of Troy. After performing the requisite calculations, Schliemann was firmly convinced he had found 'the X that marked the spot'.

Having amassed a fortune in commerce, Schliemann embarked on what his contemporaries regarded as a quixotic enterprise – to undertake a full-scale excavation of the 'X' he had located. In 1868, he went to Greece and proceeded, using a poem that was two and a half millennia old as his guide, to retrace the alleged route of the Greek fleet. At what he believed to be the relevant site in Turkey, he began to dig. And to the world's consternation, astonishment and admiration, Schliemann there found Troy – or, at any rate, a city that conformed to Homer's account of Troy. As a matter of fact, Schliemann found a number of cities. In four campaigns of excavation, he uncovered no fewer than nine, each superimposed on the ruins of what had been its predecessor. Nor, after this initial spectacular success, did he confine himself to Troy. A few years later, between 1874 and 1876, he excavated at Mycenae in Greece, where his discoveries were deemed to be perhaps even more important than those made in Turkey.

Schliemann demonstrated triumphantly that archaeology could do more than just prove or disprove the historical validity underlying archaic legends. He also demonstrated that it could add flesh and substance to the often bald, stark chronicles of the past – could provide a recognisably human and social context for them, could provide a matrix of daily life and practices that enabled one to understand the mentality and milieu from which they had issued. What was more, he demonstrated the applicability of strict scientific method and procedures, the careful observation and recording of data. In addressing himself to the nine superimposed cities at Troy, Schliemann employed the same techniques that had only recently come into favour in geological studies. These enabled him to conclude what to the modern mind appears self-evident – that one stratum of deposits can be distinguished from others on the basic premise that the lowest is the earliest in time. Schliemann thus became the pioneer of the archaeological discipline known as 'stratigraphy'. Almost single-handed, he revolutionised archaeological thought and methodology.

It was quickly recognised, of course, that Schliemann's scientific approach could readily be brought to bear on the field of biblical archaeology. In 1864, four years before the discovery of Troy, Sir Charles Wilson, then a captain in the Royal Engineers, had been sent to Jerusalem, to survey the city and produce a definitive map. In the course of his work, Wilson became the first modern researcher to excavate and explore beneath the Temple, where he discovered what were believed to have been Solomon's stables. His endeavours inspired him to help co-found the Palestine Exploration Fund, the chief patron of which was no less a person than Queen Victoria herself. At first, the work of this organisation proceeded in a characteristically uncoordinated fashion. At the 1886 annual meeting, however, Wilson announced that 'some of the wealthy men of England would follow Dr. Schliemann's example' and apply his scientific approach to a specific biblical site.[8] The enterprise was entrusted to the charge of a prominent archaeologist then active in Egypt, William Matthew Flinders Petrie. Adopting Schliemann's methods, Flinders Petrie, after two false starts, discovered a mound containing the ruins of eleven superimposed cities.

During his work in Egypt, Flinders Petrie had evolved another technique for the dating of ancient ruins, based on a pattern of gradual development and change in the shape, design and embellishment of household pottery. This enabled him to establish a chronological sequence not just for the artefacts themselves, but for the rubble surrounding them as well. Although certainly not foolproof, Petrie's approach brought another manifestation of scientific methodology and observation to bear on archaeological research. It became one of the standard procedures employed by his team in Palestine – a team which, in 1926, was joined by the young Gerald Lankester Harding. As we have noted, Harding, eventually head of Jordan's Department of Antiquities, was to play a crucial role in the early excavation and compilation of the Dead Sea Scrolls.

While British archaeologists in Egypt and Palestine followed in Schliemann's footsteps, the Germans refined and elaborated his procedures. German archaeology endeavoured to do, in fact, what

106

Flaubert, in *Salammbô*, had done in fiction – to re-create, down to the most minute detail, the entire milieu and society from which specific archaeological artefacts had issued. This, needless to say, was a slow, painstaking process, requiring much care and inexhaustible patience. It did not just involve the excavation of 'treasures', or of monumental structures. It also involved the excavation and reconstruction of administrative, commercial and residential buildings. Using this approach, Robert Koldeway, between 1899 and 1913, excavated the ruins of Babylon. From his work, there evolved a coherent and comprehensively detailed picture of what had previously, to all intents and purposes, been a 'lost civilisation'.

The archaeological advances of the 19th century stemmed in large part from Schliemann's critical scrutiny of Homer's epics, his methodical scientific insistence on disengaging fact from fiction. It was, needless to say, only a matter of time before scripture itself was subjected to the same sort of rigorous scrutiny. The man most responsible for this process was the French theologian and historian Ernest Renan. Born in 1823, Renan embarked on a career in the priesthood, enrolling in the seminary of St Sulpice. In 1845, however, he renounced his intended vocation, having been led by Germanic biblical scholarship to question the literal truth of Christian teaching. In 1860, Renan embarked on an archaeological journey to Palestine and Syria. Three years later, he published his famous (or notorious) *La vie de Jésus*, (*The Life of Jesus*), which was translated into English the following year. Renan's book sought to demystify Christianity. It portrayed Jesus as 'an incomparable man', but still a man – an eminently mortal and non-divine personage – and formulated a hierarchy of values which today would be called a form of 'secular humanism'. Renan was no obscure academic or fly-by-night sensationalist. On the contrary, he was one of the most esteemed and prestigious intellectual figures of his age. As a result, *The Life of Jesus* created one of the greatest upsets in the history of 19th-century thought. It became one of the half-dozen or so best-selling books of the entire century, and has never subsequently been out of print. For the 'educated classes' of the time, Renan became as much a household name as Freud or Jung might be today; and, in the absence of television, he was probably much more widely read. At a single stroke, *The Life of Jesus* transformed attitudes towards biblical scholarship almost beyond recognition. And for the next thirty years of his life, Renan was to remain a thorn in the Church's side, publishing subsequent works on the Apostles, on Paul and on early Christianity in the context of imperial Roman thought and culture. He produced two epic series of texts, *Histoire des origines du christianisme* (1863–83) and *Histoire du peuple d'Israël* (1887–93). It is no exaggeration to say that Renan released from its bottle a genie which Christianity has never since managed to recapture or tame.

At the same time, of course, Rome was being buffeted from other quarters as well. Four years before *The Life of Jesus*, Charles Darwin had published *The Origin of Species*, and followed it in 1871 with *The Descent of Man*, a more theologically oriented work which questioned scriptural accounts of the creation. In Darwin's wake, there followed the great age of English agnosticism, exemplified by Thomas Huxley and Herbert Spencer. Influential and widely read philosophers – Schopenhauer, for example, and particularly Nietzsche – were also challenging, even blasphemously demolishing, conventional Christian ethical and theological assumptions. Under the doctrine of '*l'art pour l'art*', the arts were becoming established as a self-contained religion of their own, moving into sacred territory which organised religion seemed increasingly to have abdicated. Bayreuth became, in effect, the temple of a new cult, a new creed; and well-educated Europeans deemed it quite as acceptable to be 'a Wagnerian' as to be a Christian.

The Church was under sustained political attack as well. In 1870–72, Prussia's shattering victory in her war with France, and the creation of the new German Empire, produced, for the first time in modern history, a supreme military power in Europe which owed no allegiance whatever to Rome. To the extent that the new empire was Christian at all, it was Lutheran; but the Lutheran Church, to all intents and purposes, was little more than an adjunct of the War Office. Most traumatic of all, Garibaldi's partisan army, by 1870, had finally effected the unification of Italy – had captured Rome, had wrested the Papal States and all other territory from the Church, and reduced Catholicism to the status of a non-secular power.

16   Father Jean Starcky celebrating Mass at the ruins of Qumran prior to
the day's archaeological excavations.

17 Members of the international team at the Rockefeller Museum, Jerusalem, working on the scrolls from Cave 4. Centre, bearded, is Father de Vaux, with Father Milik to his right and Father Starcky to his left. John Allegro is seated to the right of the illustration.

20   John Allegro and John Strugnell working in the 'Scrollery'.

18 Members of the international team working on scroll fragments in the 'Scrollery': (left to right) Father Patrick Skehan, John Strugnell, John Allegro.

19 (left to right) John Strugnell, Frank Cross, Father Milik, John Allegro and Father Starcky.

21   (left to right) John Strugnell, John Allegro, Father Skehan,
Dr Claus–Hunno Hunzinger and Father Milik.

22   John Allegro working on the 'Nahum Commentary' in the 'Scrollery'.

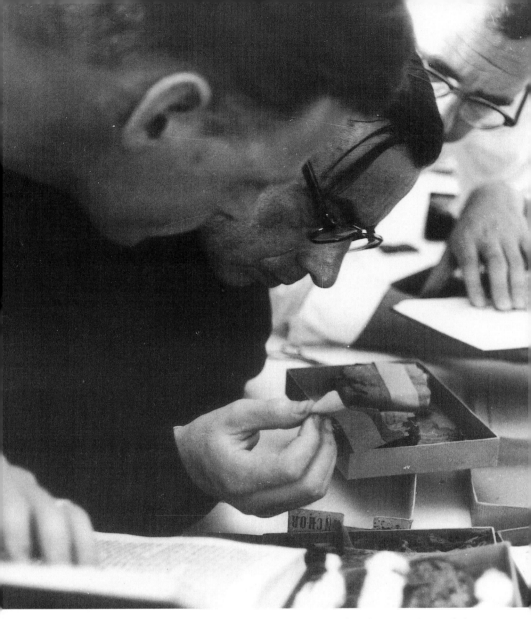

23   Father Milik, flanked by Dr Hunzinger and Father Benoit, studying some newly purchased scroll fragments in January 1956. The fragments probably came from Cave II.

24   Dr Hunzinger in January 1956 holding the 'Psalms Scroll' from Qumran, Cave II. This scroll was not to be published until 1965.

25   Scroll fragments as they were brought in by the Bedouin who discovered them in January 1956.

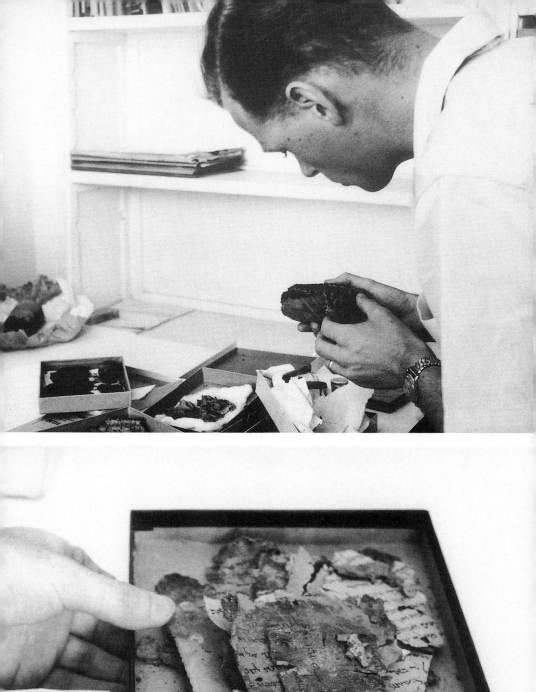
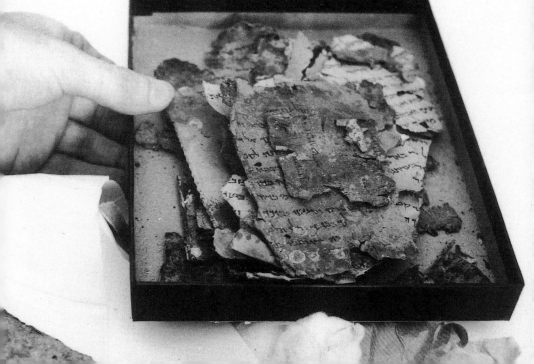

26 The 'Psalms Scroll' from Cave 11 before it was unrolled.

27 A seal found at the Qumran ruins with, curiously, the owner's name, 'Josephus', written in Greek rather than Hebrew or Aramaic.

Beleaguered by onslaughts from science, from philosophy, from the arts and from secular political powers, Rome was more shaken than she had been at any time since the beginning of the Lutheran Reformation three and a half centuries before. She responded with a number of desperate defensive measures. She sought – vainly, it transpired – political allegiances with Catholic, or nominally Catholic, powers, such as the Habsburg Empire. On 18 July 1870, after a vote by the First Vatican Council, Pope Pius IX – characterised by Metternich as 'warm of heart, weak of head and lacking utterly in common sense'[9] – promulgated the dogma of Papal Infallibility.[10] And to counter the depredations being wrought on scripture by Renan and German biblical scholarship, the Church began equipping her own cadres of meticulous scholars – élite intellectual 'shock troops' who were supposed to confront Catholicism's adversaries on their own ground. Thus arose the Catholic Modernist Movement.

The Modernists were originally intended to deploy the rigour and precision of Germanic methodology not to challenge scripture, but to support it. A generation of clerical scholars was painstakingly trained and groomed to provide the Church with a kind of academic strike force, a corps specifically formed to defend the literal truth of scripture with all the heavy ordnance of the most up-to-date critical scholarship. To Rome's chagrin and mortification, however, the programme backfired. The more it sought to arm younger clerics with the requisite tools for combat in the modern polemical arena, the more those same clerics began to desert the cause for which they had been recruited. Critical scrutiny of the Bible revealed a multitude of inconsistencies, discrepancies and implications that were positively inimical to Roman dogma. The Modernists themselves quickly began to question and subvert what they were supposed to be defending.

Thus, for example, Alfred Loisy, one of the most prominent and prestigious Modernists, wondered publicly how, in the light of recent biblical history and archaeology, many of the Church's doctrines could still be justified. 'Jesus proclaimed the coming of the Kingdom', Loisy declared, 'but what came was the Church.'[11] Loisy argued that many points of dogma had crystallised as historically conditioned reactions to specific events, at specific places and times. In consequence, they were not to be regarded as fixed and immutable truths, but as – at best – symbols. According to Loisy, such basic tenets of Christian teaching as the Virgin Birth and Jesus' divinity were no longer tenable.

Rome, in trying to play Frankenstein, had created a monster in her own laboratory. In 1903, shortly before his death, Pope Leo XIII created the Pontifical Biblical Commission, to supervise and monitor the work of Catholic scriptural scholarship. Later that year, Leo's successor, Pius X, placed Loisy's works on the Inquisition's Index of forbidden books. In 1904, the new Pope issued two encyclicals opposing all scholarship which questioned the origins and early history of Christianity. All Catholic teachers suspected of 'Modernist tendencies' were summarily dismissed from their posts.

The Modernists, of course, comprising the best-educated, most erudite and articulate enclave in the Church, did not hesitate to fight back. They were supported by prominent thinkers, by distinguished cultural and literary figures. In Italy, one such was Antonio Fogazzaro. In 1896, Fogazzaro had become a senator. He was also regarded as 'the leading Catholic layman of his day' and, by his contemporaries at least, as the greatest novelist Italy had produced since Manzoni. In *The Saint*, published in 1905, Fogazzaro wrote: 'The Catholic Church, calling herself the fountain of truth, today opposes the search after truth when her foundations, the sacred books, the formulae of her dogmas, her alleged infallibility, become objects of research. To us, this signifies that she no longer has faith in herself.'[12]

Fogazzaro's work, needless to say, was itself promptly placed on the Index. And the Church's campaign against the movement it had fostered and nurtured proceeded to intensify. In July 1907, the Holy Office published a decree officially condemning Modernist attempts to question Church doctrine, papal authority and the historical veracity of biblical texts. Less than two months later, in September, Modernism was effectively declared to be a heresy and the entire movement was formally banned. The number of books on the Index suddenly and dramatically increased. A new, much more stringent censorship was instituted. Clerical commissars monitored teaching with a doctrinal rigidity unknown since the Middle Ages. At last, in 1910, a decree was issued requiring all Catholics involved in teaching or preaching to take an oath renouncing 'all the errors of Modernism'. A number of Modernist writers were excommunicated. Students at seminaries and theological colleges were even forbidden to read newspapers.

In the 1880s, however, all of this still lay in the future. Among the young Modernist clerics of the 1880s, there was a naive credulity and optimism, a fervent conviction that methodical historical and archaeological research would confirm, rather than contradict, the literal truth of scripture. The Ecole Biblique et Archéologique Française de Jérusalem – which subsequently came to dominate Dead Sea Scroll scholarship – was rooted in the first generation of Modernism, before the Church realised how close it had come to subverting itself. It originated in 1882, when a French Dominican monk on pilgrimage in Jerusalem resolved to establish a Dominican house there, consisting of a church and a monastery. He chose a site on the Nablus Road, where excavations had revealed the remains of an earlier church. According to tradition, it was precisely here that St Stephen, supposedly the first Christian martyr, had been stoned to death.

Rome not only approved the idea, but embellished and expanded it. Pope Leo XIII suggested that a biblical school also be established. This school was founded in 1890 by Father Albert Lagrange and opened in 1892, with living quarters for fifteen resident students. The installation was one of a number of institutions created at the time, to equip Catholic scholars with the academic expertise necessary to defend their faith against the threat posed by developments in historical and archaeological research.

Father Lagrange had been born in 1855. After studying law, he had gained his doctorate in 1878, then entered the seminary of St Sulpice, the centre of Modernist studies at the time. In 1879, he had become a Dominican. On 6 October 1880, however, under the Third French Republic, all religious orders were banished from France. The 25-year-old Lagrange had accordingly gone to Salamanca, in Spain, where he studied Hebrew and taught Church history and philosophy. It was at Salamanca that he was ordained a priest, on St Dagobert's Day (23 December), 1883. In 1888, he was sent to the University of Vienna to study Oriental languages. Two years later, on 10 March 1890, at the age of thirty-five, he arrived at the fledgling Dominican house of St Stephen in Jerusalem, and there, on 15 November, established a biblical school. The school was called initially the 'Ecole Practique d'Etudes Bibliques'. Lagrange created for it its own journal, *Revue biblique*, which began publication in 1892 and continues today. Through this organ, as well, of course, as through the programme of studies, he sought to imbue the new institution with an attitude towards historical and archaeological research which can best be summed up in his own words. According to Father Lagrange, 'the various stages in the religious history of mankind form a *récit*, a history that is directly and supernaturally guided by God to lead to the ultimate and definitive stage – the messianic age inaugurated by Jesus Christ'.[13] The Old Testament was 'a group of books indicating a register of the various stages of an oral tradition that God used and guided . . . in the preparation for the definitive New Testament era'.[14] The orientation was clear enough. To the extent that Lagrange employed modern methodology at all, he would employ it to 'prove' what he had already, *a priori*, decided to be true – that is, the literal veracity of scripture. And the 'definitive' nature of the New Testament and the events it chronicled rendered it effectively off limits to scholarly scrutiny.

In 1890, when Lagrange established the Ecole Biblique, Modernism had not yet come under a cloud. By 1902, however, it had fallen into serious official disrepute. In that year, as we have noted, Pope Leo XIII created the Pontifical Biblical Commission, to supervise and monitor the work of Catholic scriptural scholarship. In the same year, Lagrange returned to France to lecture at Toulouse – where he was accused of being a Modernist, and met with furious opposition. By that time, the mere suggestion of historical and archaeological research was sufficient to get one stigmatised.

The Pope himself, however, recognised that Lagrange's faith was still intact, and that his heart, so far as the Church was concerned, was in the right place. And indeed, much of Lagrange's work comprised a systematic rebuttal of Alfred Loisy and other Modernists.

Lagrange was accordingly made a member, or 'consultant', of the Pontifical Biblical Commission, and his journal, *Revue biblique*, became the Commission's official organ. This arrangement obtained until 1908, when the Commission launched a journal of its own, the *Acta apostolicae sedis*.

From lower down in the ecclesiastical hierarchy, accusations of Modernism continued. So demoralising were these accusations that Lagrange, in 1907, temporarily renounced his work in Old Testament studies. In 1912, he resolved to abandon biblical studies altogether and leave Jerusalem. He was duly recalled to France. But the Pope again rallied to his support, dispatched him back to his post in Jerusalem and ordered him to continue his work. The Ecole Biblique, originally created as a forum for Modernism, had now become a bulwark against it.

Among the original team of international scholars assembled by Father de Vaux in 1953 was the late Monsignor Patrick Skehan. Father Skehan was head of the Department of Semitic and Egyptian Languages and Literatures at the Catholic University in Washington. He was also, later, a member of the Pontifical Biblical Commission. And in 1955, he was director of the Albright Institute in Jerusalem. In this capacity, he was instrumental in the political manoeuvrings which established the Ecole Biblique's dominance of Dead Sea Scroll research. In 1956, he played a key role in organising the letter to *The Times* that was intended to isolate and discredit John Allegro.[15]

Father Skehan was among the few scholars to be entrusted with access to the scrolls themselves. His attitudes offer some indication of the orientation of the Catholic scholars associated with the Ecole Biblique. Writing in 1966, Father Skehan declared that the Old Testament was not 'a thumbnail sketch of the history and prehistory of the human race . . . In the fullness of time, Our Lord came; and a proper part of the duty of every Old Testament scholar is to trace in sacred history the development of the readiness to be aware of Christ when he would come . . .'[16] In other words, the primary responsibility of every biblical scholar is to ferret out from the Old Testament supposed anticipations of accepted Christian doctrine. Viewed any other way, the Old Testament presumably has scant value and relevance. This is a curious definition of 'dispassionate scholarship'. But Father Skehan was even more explicit:

> it would seem that in our day it is incumbent upon biblical scholars . . . to indicate . . . as best they can the general lines of the progress by which God steadily led, as he surely did, stone age, Chalcolithic, and ancient pagan man to the capability of measuring up, in some degree, to the social fact which is the Christian Church.[17]

Father Skehan, of course, made no real pretence to 'dispassionate scholarship'. In fact, he regarded it as positively dangerous – considering that 'studies carried out from a perspective that puts literary and historico-critical considerations in the foreground can, usually in the hands of popularizers, result in oversimplification, exaggeration, or neglect of more profound matters'.[18] Ultimately, the biblical scholar's work should be guided and determined by Church doctrine and 'be subject always to the sovereign right of Holy Mother Church to witness definitively what is in fact concordant with the teaching she has received from Christ'.[19]

The implications of all this are staggering. All enquiry and investigation, regardless of what it might turn up or reveal, *must* be subordinated and accommodated to the existing corpus of official Catholic teaching. In other words, it must be edited or adjusted or distorted until it conforms to the requisite criteria. And what if something comes to light which can't be made thus to conform? From Father Skehan's statements, the answer to that question would seem clear. Anything that can't be subordinated or accommodated to existing doctrine *must*, of necessity, be suppressed.

Father Skehan's position, of course, was not unique. It was effectively echoed by Pope Pius XII himself, who maintained 'that the biblical exegete has a function and a responsibility to perform in matters of importance to the church'.[20] As for the Ecole Biblique and its research on the Dead Sea Scrolls, Skehan says:

Are there not . . . providential elements also in the curious fact that the Holy Land is the place on earth best suited to be a kind of laboratory for the study of human life continuously, with no major periods missing . . . I believe that there are . . .

. . . Therefore, it seems to me that there is an ultimate religious value which we cannot yet measure, but which has Providence behind it, in the fact that Père Lagrange established upon Palestinian soil an institute . . .[21]

For years, most independent scholars were quite unaware of any such divine mandate having been possessed by the Ecole Biblique, or of the Vatican's wishful thinking on the matter. On the contrary, the Ecole appeared to be an impartial scholarly institution dedicated, among other things, to collecting, collating, researching, translating and elucidating the Dead Sea Scrolls, not for suppressing them or transforming them into Christian propaganda. Thus, for example, a scholar or graduate student in Britain, or the States, or anywhere else, having established some academic credibility with a thesis or publication in one or another sphere of biblical study, would apply for access to the Qumran material. He'd have no reason to expect a rebuff – would assume the scrolls were available for study by anyone who had acquired legitimate academic credentials. In every case known to us, however, requests for access have been summarily refused, without apology or explanation – and with the inevitable concurrent implication that the applicant himself was somehow inadequate.

Such, to take but one example, was the case for Professor Norman Golb of the University of Chicago. Professor Golb had done his doctoral dissertation on Qumran and on Qumran-related material found in Cairo. Having amassed years of experience in the field, he embarked on a research project to check the palaeographical dating of the scrolls, which had been established by Professor Cross of the international team and which Golb felt could be improved. To confirm his thesis, Golb of course needed to see certain original texts – photographic facsimiles would obviously not have sufficed. In 1970, he was in Jerusalem and accordingly wrote to de Vaux, then head of the Ecole Biblique and the international team, requesting access and explaining that he needed it to validate a research project which had already occupied years of his life. Three days later, de Vaux replied, stating that no access could be granted without 'the explicit permission of the scholar who is in charge of their edition'.[22] The scholar in question was the then Father Milik, who, as de Vaux knew only too well, wasn't prepared to let anyone see anything. After all the time and effort he had invested in it, Golb was obliged to abandon his project. 'Since then,' he told us, 'I have had good reason to doubt all Cross's datings of texts by palaeography.'[23]

On the other hand, fragments of Qumran material *will* be made available to researchers affiliated with the Ecole itself, to young scholars and protégés of the international team, to graduate students under the tutelage of one or another team member, who can be assured of toeing the official 'party line'. Thus, for instance, Eugene Ulrich of Notre Dame, a student of Cross's, 'inherited' the scroll material originally assigned to Father Patrick Skehan. He also appears to have inherited something of Skehan's attitude to other scholars. When asked why facsimile photographic editions couldn't be produced, he replied that 'the vast majority of people who will use these editions – including average university professors – are barely able to judge competently difficult readings'.[24]

Independent scholars from Britain, the States and elsewhere have thus found it impossible to get access to unpublished scroll material. For Israeli scholars, such access has been inconceivable. As we have noted, Father de Vaux, a former member of the notorious Action Française, was a fairly outspoken anti-Semite. To this day, members of the Ecole Biblique seem to remain hostile to Israel, even though it is supposed in theory to be a neutral enclave for impartial scholarship, a refuge from the political and religious divisions rending modern-day Jerusalem. When asked why no scholars from Tel Aviv University were involved in editing the scrolls, Strugnell replied: 'We are looking for quality in Qumran studies, and you don't get it there.'[25] With his characteristic, and self-incriminating, eloquence, the late Father Skehan effectively articulated his and his colleagues' anti-Israeli bias in a letter quoted in *Jerusalem Post Magazine*:

I feel obliged to tell you . . . that I should not under any circumstances grant through any Israeli functionary, any permission to dispense, for any purpose, or to any extent, of anything whatsoever that is lawfully housed in the Palestine Archaeological Museum. I regard the State of Israel and all of its personnel as having no legal standing whatsoever with respect to the Museum and its contents.[26]

As we have noted, this attitude is shared by the former Father Milik. Neither he nor another of his colleagues, the late Father Starcky, ever returned to Jerusalem after the 1967 war, when the scrolls passed into Israeli hands. Then again, of course, their position only echoes that of the Vatican itself, which, even today, does not recognise the State of Israel. But one is prompted to ask whether their prejudice simply coincided with official Church policy, or whether it was formally dictated by the ecclesiastical hierarchy.

7

The Inquisition Today

As an antidote to the spreading 'infection' of Modernism, Pope Leo XIII, in 1903, had created the Pontifical Biblical Commission to supervise and monitor the progress (or lack thereof) of Catholic scriptural scholarship. It consisted originally of a dozen or more cardinals appointed by the Pope and a number of 'consultants', all deemed to be experts in their fields of research and study. According to the *New Catholic Encyclopaedia*, the Commission's official function was (and still is) 'to strive . . . with all possible care that God's words . . . will be shielded not only from every breath of error but even from every rash opinion'.[1] The Commission would further undertake to ensure that scholars 'endeavour to safeguard the authority of the scriptures and to promote their right interpretation'.[2]

As we have noted, Father Lagrange, founder of the Ecole Biblique, was one of the earliest members of the Pontifical Biblical Commission. The Ecole Biblique's journal, *Revue biblique*, was also, until 1908, the Commission's official organ. Given the close affiliation between the two institutions, it is clear that the original Ecole Biblique was an adjunct of the Commission's propaganda machine – an instrument for promulgating Catholic doctrine under the guise of historical and archaeological research, or for enforcing the adherence of historical and archaeological research to the tenets of Catholic doctrine.

One might expect this situation to have changed during the

last half-century, and especially in the years since the Second Vatican Council of the early 1960s. In fact, it has not. The Ecole Biblique today retains as close an association with the Pontifical Biblical Commission as it did in the past. Degrees at the Ecole, for example, are conferred specifically by the Commission. Most graduates of the Ecole are placed by the Commission as professors in seminaries and other Catholic institutions. Of the Commission's nineteen official 'consultants' today, a number are influential in determining what the general public learns of the Dead Sea Scrolls. Thus, for instance, Father Jean-Luc Vesco, the current head of the Ecole Biblique and a member of the *Revue biblique*'s editorial board, is also a member of the Pontifical Biblical Commission. So, too, is at least one other member of the journal's editorial board, José Loza. So, too, is a prominent writer on the scrolls, a Jesuit named Joseph Fitzmyer, who has compiled the official concordance for much of the Qumran material.[3]

In 1956, the name of Father Roland de Vaux, Director of the Ecole Biblique, appeared for the first time on the list of the Commission's 'consultants'.[4] He would have been appointed the year before, in 1955, and he continued as a 'consultant' until his death in 1971. The timing of de Vaux's appointment is interesting. In 1955, it must be remembered, much of the crucial and controversial 'sectarian' material from Cave 4 was still being purchased and collated. In December of that year, indeed, the Vatican laid out money for a number of important fragments. In 1955, too, the 'Copper Scroll' was unrolled in Manchester, under John Allegro's auspices, and Allegro himself was beginning to go public in a potentially embarrassing fashion. The Vatican thus became aware, for the first time, of the kind of problems it might have to face in connection with the Qumran material then coming to light. The ecclesiastical hierarchy almost certainly felt the need of some sort of 'chain of command', or, at least, 'chain of accountability', whereby some measure of control could be exercised over Qumran scholarship. In any case, it is significant, if not particularly surprising, that from 1956 on, every director of the Ecole Biblique has also been a member of the Pontifical Biblical Commission. When de Vaux died in 1971, the Commission's list of 'consultants' was updated to include the name of his successor at the Ecole, Father Pierre Benoit.[5] When Benoit died in 1987, the new director, Jean-Luc Vesco, became a 'consultant' to the Commission in turn.[6]

Even today, the Pontifical Biblical Commission continues to supervise and monitor all biblical studies conducted under the auspices of the Catholic Church. It also publishes official decrees on 'the right way to teach . . . scripture'.[7] In 1907, adherence to these decrees was made obligatory by Pope Pius X. Thus, for example, the Commission 'established', by decree, that Moses was the literal author of the Pentateuch. In 1909, a similar decree affirmed the literal and historical accuracy of the first three chapters of Genesis. More recently, on 21 April 1964, the Commission issued a decree governing biblical scholarship in general and, more specifically, the 'historical truth of the Gospels'. The decree was quite unequivocal, stating that 'at all times the interpreter must cherish a spirit of ready obedience to the Church's teaching authority'.[8] It further declared that those in charge of any 'biblical associations' are obliged to 'observe inviolably the laws already laid down by the Pontifical Biblical Commission'.[9] Any scholar working under the Commission's aegis – and this, of course, includes those at the Ecole Biblique – is thus in effect constrained by the Commission's decrees. Whatever conclusions he might reach, whatever the revelations to which his research might lead him, he must not, in his writing or his teaching, contradict the Commission's doctrinal authority.

The head of the Pontifical Biblical Commission today is Cardinal Joseph Ratzinger. Cardinal Ratzinger is also head of another Catholic institution, the Congregation for the Doctrine of the Faith. This designation is fairly new, dating from 1965, and probably unfamiliar to most laymen; but the institution itself is one of long-established pedigree. It has, in fact, a unique and resonant history behind it, extending back to the 13th century. In 1542, it had become known officially as the Holy Office. Prior to that, it was called the Holy Inquisition. Cardinal Ratzinger is, in effect, the Church's modern-day Grand Inquisitor.

The official head of the Congregation for the Doctrine of the Faith is always the reigning Pope, and the executive head of the

Congregation is today called its secretary, although in earlier times he was known as the Grand Inquisitor. Of all the departments of the Curia, that of the Congregation for the Doctrine of the Faith is the most powerful. Ratzinger is perhaps the closest to the Pope of all the Curia cardinals. Certainly they have many attitudes in common. Both wish to restore many pre-Vatican II values. Both dislike theologians. Ratzinger sees theologians as having opened the Church up to corrosive secular influences. A deeply pessimistic man, he feels that the Church is 'collapsing', and only the suppression of all dissent can assure its survival as a unified faith. He regards those who do not share his pessimism as 'blind or deluded'.[10]

Like the Inquisition of the past, the Congregation for the Doctrine of the Faith is in large part a tribunal. It has its own judges, the chief of whom is called the 'Assessor'. The 'Assessor' is aided by a 'Commissar' and two Dominican monks. These individuals have the specific task of preparing whatever 'investigations' the Congregation chooses to undertake. Such investigations generally pertain to breaches of doctrine on the part of clerics, or anything else that might threaten Church unity. As in the Middle Ages, all investigations are conducted and pursued under conditions of total secrecy.

Until 1971, the Pontifical Biblical Commission and the Congregation for the Doctrine of the Faith were supposed to be separate organisations. In reality, however, the separation between them was little more than nominal. The two organisations overlapped one another in a multitude of respects, ranging from their functions to the membership of their governing bodies. In 1969, for example, eight of the twelve cardinals presiding over the Congregation also presided over the Commission.[11] A number of individuals acted as 'consultants' for both. At last, on 27 June 1971, Pope Paul VI, in an attempt to streamline bureaucracy, amalgamated the Commission and the Congregation in virtually everything but name. Both were housed in the same offices, at the same address – the Palace of the Congregation at Holy Office Square in Rome. Both were placed under the directorship of the same cardinal. On 29 November 1981, that cardinal became Joseph Ratzinger.

Numerous contemporary priests, preachers, teachers and writers have been muzzled, expelled or deprived of their posts by the body over which Ratzinger now presides. The victims have included certain of the most distinguished and intelligent theologians in the Church today. One such was Father Edward Schillebeeckx, of the University of Nigmegen in Holland. In 1974, Schillebeeckx had published a book, *Jesus: An Experiment in Christology*. In this work, he appeared, in the eyes of his adversaries, to be questioning the literal truth of certain dogma, such as the Resurrection and the Virgin Birth. In December 1979, Schillebeeckx was hauled before a tribunal of the Congregation for the Doctrine of the Faith, where one of his judges publicly accused him of heresy. He survived his investigation by the tribunal, but in 1983 he was again summoned to a tribunal of the Congregation, this time for his latest book, *Ministry: A Case for Change*.

What were Schillebeeckx's transgressions? If only tentatively, he had questioned the Church's position on celibacy. He had sympathised with arguments for the ordination of women. Most seriously of all, he had suggested the Church should 'change with the times' rather than remaining fettered to immutably fixed doctrines.[12] The Church, he contended, should respond to, and evolve with, the needs of its faithful, instead of imposing draconian codes upon them. He had argued, in short, for a dynamic pastoral approach, as opposed to the static one favoured by Pope John Paul II and Cardinal Ratzinger. Once again, Schillebeeckx survived the Congregation's investigation and interrogation. To this day, however, he remains under close scrutiny, and his every word, written or spoken, is carefully monitored. It goes without saying that such assiduously vigilant surveillance will exert a profoundly inhibiting influence.

A more telling case is that of the eminent Swiss theologian Dr Hans Küng, formerly head of the Department of Theology at the University of Tübingen. Küng was generally acknowledged to be among the most brilliant, most influential, most topically relevant Catholic writers of our age – a man who, following in the footsteps of Pope John XXIII, seemed to offer a new direction for the Church, a new humanity, a new flexibility and adaptability. But Küng was also controversial. In his book *Infallible?*, first published in German in 1970 and in English the following year, he challenged the doctrine of papal infallibility – which, one must remember, had never existed in the Church until 1870 and had only then been established by a vote. 'No one is infallible', Küng wrote, 'but God himself.'[13] Further, 'the traditional doctrine of infallibility in the Church . . . rests on foundations that cannot be regarded as secure'.[14] Küng also recognised the distinction between theology and history, and the former's propensity to parade itself as the latter. He attacked the sophistry of such Church 'scholars' as Cardinal Jean Danielou, who, in 1957, had published *The Dead Sea Scrolls and Primitive Christianity*, a work primarily of theological propaganda: 'Theologians such as Danielou . . . now bring an aura of pseudo-learning to the rôle of Grand Inquisitor, are appointed Cardinals of the Holy Roman Church and fulfil its expectations.'[15]

After the election of John Paul II, Küng was critical of the new pontiff's rigidity in morals and dogma. 'Is the Catholic theologian', he asked, 'going to be allowed . . . to ask critical questions . . . ?'[16] Was John Paul II really free, Küng wondered, of the personality cult which had bedevilled earlier popes; and was he not perhaps excessively preoccupied with doctrine, at the expense of 'the liberating message of Christ'?

> Can the Pope and the Church credibly speak to the conscience of today's people if a self-critical examination of conscience on the part of the Church and its leadership does not also simultaneously occur . . . ?[17]

Küng's outspokenness made him, of course, an irresistible target for the inquisitional tribunals of the Congregation for the Doctrine of the Faith. Having evaluated his statements, the tribunal accordingly passed judgment. On 18 December 1979, the Pope, acting on the formal recommendation of the Congregation, stripped Küng of his post and pronounced him no longer qualified to teach Roman Catholic doctrine. He was informed that he was no longer a Catholic theologian, and was forbidden to write or publish further. Küng himself effectively summarised what had befallen him: 'I have been condemned by a pontiff who has rejected my theology without ever having read one of my books and who always has refused to

123

see me. The truth is that Rome is not waiting for dialogue but for submission.'[18]

Under the directorship of Cardinal Ratzinger, the Congregation, during the last decade, has become increasingly entrenched, intransigent and reactionary. Ratzinger is vehemently critical of all changes in the Church since the Second Vatican Council of 1962–5. The Church's teachings, he maintains, are being 'tarnished' by doubt and questioning. According to one commentator, Ratzinger seeks 'a return to Catholic fundamentalism . . . and reasserting the literal truth of papally-defined dogma'.[19] Through the Congregation for the Doctrine of the Faith, Ratzinger's attitudes determine the attitudes of the Pontifical Biblical Commission, of which he is also head, and filter down from there into the Ecole Biblique.

During the course of 1990, these attitudes served to place the Congregation prominently in the news. In May, the Congregation issued a preliminary draft of the new, revised and updated 'Universal Catechism of the Catholic Church' – the official formulation of tenets in which all Catholics are obliged formally to believe. Allowing no flexibility whatever, the new 'Catechism' definitively condemns, along with a catalogue of other things, divorce, homosexuality, masturbation and sexual relations before or outside marriage. It lays down, as basic tenets of the Catholic faith, papal infallibility, the Immaculate Conception and the Assumption of the Virgin Mary, as well as the 'Universal Authority of the Catholic Church'. In one particularly dogmatic passage, the new 'Catechism' declares that 'the task of giving an authentic interpretation of the Word of God . . . has been entrusted to the living teaching office of the Church alone'.[20]

In June, there appeared a second document, published by the Congregation for the Doctrine of the Faith and written by Cardinal Ratzinger himself. This document addresses itself specifically to the functions and obligations of the theologian, a term intended to encompass the biblical historian and archaeologist as well. According to this document, approved and endorsed by the Pope, Catholic theologians have no right to dissent from the established teachings of the Church. Indeed, dissent is itself promoted (or demoted) to the status of an actual 'sin': 'To succumb to the temptation of dissent . . . [allows] infidelity to the Holy Spirit . . .'[21] If a theologian begins to question Church doctrine, he is thus, by skilful psychological manipulation, made to feel morally tainted for doing so. Any propensity to question is effectively turned back on the questioner and transformed into guilt – something in which the Church has always trafficked most profitably.

In the same document, Cardinal Ratzinger states:

> The freedom of the act of faith cannot justify a right to dissent. This freedom does not indicate freedom with regard to the truth, but signifies the free determination of the person in conformity with his moral obligations to accept the truth.[22]

In other words, one is perfectly free to accept the teachings of the Church, but not to question or reject them. Freedom cannot be manifested or expressed except through submission. It is a curious definition of freedom.

Such restrictions are monstrous enough when imposed on Catholics alone – monstrous in the psychological and emotional damage they will cause, the guilt, intolerance and bigotry they will foster, the horizons of knowledge and understanding they will curtail. When confined to a creed, however, they apply only to those who voluntarily submit to them, and the non-Catholic population of the world is free to ignore them. The Dead Sea Scrolls, however, are not articles of faith, but documents of historical and archaeological importance which belong properly not to the Catholic Church, but to humanity as a whole. It is a sobering and profoundly disturbing thought that, if Cardinal Ratzinger has his way, everything we ever learn about the Qumran texts will be subject to the censorship machinery of the Congregation for the Doctrine of the Faith – will be, in effect, filtered and edited for us by the Inquisition.

Given its obligatory allegiance to the Congregation, one is justified in wondering whether, quite simply, the Ecole Biblique can be trusted. Even if the Israeli government clamped down and ordered the immediate release of all Qumran material, how could we be sure that items potentially compromising to the Church would ever see the light of day? We personally, in this book, should like to pose publicly certain basic questions to Father Jean-Luc Vesco, the Ecole Biblique's current director.

- ●If the Ecole Biblique is accountable to the Pontifical Biblical Commission and the Congregation for the Doctrine of the Faith, what are its responsibilities to scholarship?
- ●How can any reputable academic institution function under the strain of such potentially divided, even mutually hostile, loyalties?
- ●And what exactly would the Ecole Biblique do if, among the unpublished or perhaps as yet undiscovered Qumran material, something inimical to Church doctrine turned up?

III
THE DEAD SEA
SCROLLS

8
The Dilemma for Christian Orthodoxy

There is virtually unanimous agreement among all the concerned parties – apart, of course, from the international team themselves and the Ecole Biblique – that the history of Dead Sea Scroll scholarship does constitute a 'scandal'. And there would seem to be little doubt that something irregular – licit, perhaps, but without moral or academic sanction – lurks behind the delays, the procrastinations, the equivocation, the restrictions on material. To some extent, of course, this irregularity may indeed stem simply from venal motives – from academic jealousy and rivalry, and from the protection of vested interests. Reputations do, after all, stand to be made or broken, and there is no higher currency in the academic world than reputation. The stakes, therefore, at least for those 'on the inside', are high.

They would be high, however, in any sphere where a lack of reliable first-hand testimony had to be redressed by historical and archaeological research. They would be high if, for example, a corpus of documents pertaining to Arthurian Britain were suddenly to come to light. But would there be the same suppression of material as there is in connection with the Dead Sea Scrolls? And would one find, looming as a supreme arbiter in the background, the shadowy presence of an ecclesiastical institution such as the Congregation for the Doctrine of the Faith? The Nag Hammadi Scrolls are a case in point. Certainly, they afforded ample opportunity for venal motives to come into play. Such motives, to one or another degree, may indeed have done so. But the Church had no opportunity to establish control over the texts found at Nag Hammadi. And, venal motives notwithstanding, the entire corpus of Nag Hammadi material found its way quickly into print and the public domain.

The Church's high-level involvement in Dead Sea Scrolls scholarship must inevitably foster a grave element of suspicion. Can one ignore the possibility of a causal connection between that involvement and the shambles that Qumran research has become? One is compelled to ask (as, indeed, many informed 'outsiders' have) whether some other vested interest may be at stake, a vested interest larger than the reputations of individual scholars – the vested interest of Christianity as a whole, for example, and of Christian doctrine, at least as propounded by the Church and its traditions. Ever since the Dead Sea Scrolls were first discovered, one single, all-pervasive question has haunted the imagination, generating excitement, anxiety and, perhaps, dread. Might these texts, issuing from so close to 'the source', and (unlike the New Testament) never having been edited or tampered with, shed some significant new light on the origins of Christianity, on the so-called 'early Church' in Jerusalem and perhaps on Jesus himself? Might they contain something compromising, something that challenges, possibly even refutes, established traditions?

Certainly official interpretation ensured that they did not. There is, of course, nothing to suggest any deliberate or systematic falsification of evidence on the part of the international team. But for Father de Vaux, his most intensely personal convictions were deeply engaged and were bound to have exerted some influence. The key factor in determining the significance of the scrolls, and their relation, or lack of it, to Christianity, consisted, of course, in their dating. Were they pre- or post-Christian? How closely did they coincide with Jesus' activities, around AD 30? With the travels and letters of Paul, roughly between AD 40 and 65? With the composition of the Gospels, between AD 70 and 95? Whatever the date ascribed to them, they might be a source of possible embarrassment to Christendom, but the degree of embarrassment would be variable. If, for example, the scrolls could be dated from well before the Christian era, they might threaten to compromise Jesus' originality and uniqueness – might show some of his words and concepts to have been not wholly his own, but to have derived from a current of thought, teaching and tradition already established and 'in the air'. If the scrolls dated from Jesus' lifetime, however, or from shortly thereafter, they might prove more embarrassing still. They might be used to argue that the 'Teacher of Righteousness' who figures in them was Jesus himself, and that Jesus was not therefore perceived as divine by his contemporaries. Moreover, the scrolls contained or implied certain premises inimical to subsequent images of 'early Christianity'. There were, for example, statements of a militant messianic nationalism associated previously only with the Zealots – when Jesus was supposed to be non-political, rendering unto Caesar what was Caesar's. It might even emerge that Jesus had never dreamed of founding a new religion or of contravening Judaic law.

The evidence can be interpreted in a number of plausible ways, some of which are less compromising to Christendom than others. It is hardly surprising, in the circumstances, that de Vaux should have inclined towards and promulgated the less compromising interpretations. Thus, while it was never stated explicitly, a necessity prevailed to read or interpret the evidence in accordance with certain governing principles. So far as possible, for example, the scrolls and their authors had to be kept as dissociated as possible from 'early Christianity' – as depicted in the New Testament – and from the mainstream of 1st-century Judaism, whence 'early Christianity' sprang. It was in adherence to such tenets that the orthodoxy of interpretation established itself and a scholarly consensus originated.

Thus, the conclusions to which Father de Vaux's team came in their interpretation of the scrolls conformed to certain general tenets, the more important of which can be summarised as follows:

1. The Qumran texts were seen as dating from long prior to the Christian era.
2. The scrolls were regarded as the work of a single reclusive community, an unorthodox 'sect' on the periphery of Judaism, divorced from the epoch's main currents of social, political and

131

religious thought. In particular, they were divorced from militant revolutionary and messianic nationalism, as exemplified by the defenders of Masada.

3. The Qumran community must have been destroyed during the general uprising in Judaea in AD 66–73, leaving all their documents behind, hidden for safety in nearby caves.

4. The beliefs of the Qumran community were presented as entirely different from Christianity; and the 'Teacher of Righteousness', because he was not portrayed as divine, could not be equated with Jesus.

5. Because John the Baptist was altogether too close to the teachings of the Qumran community, it was argued that he wasn't really 'Christian' in any true sense of the word, 'merely' a precursor.

There are, however, numerous points at which the Qumran texts, and the community from which they issued, paralleled early Christian texts and the so-called 'early Church'. A number of such parallels are immediately apparent.

First, a similar ritual to that of baptism, one of the central sacraments of Christianity, obtained for the Qumran community. According to the Dead Sea text known as the 'Community Rule', the new adherent 'shall be cleansed from all his sins by the spirit of holiness uniting him to its truth . . . And when his flesh is sprinkled with purifying water and sanctified by cleansing water, it shall be made clean by the humble submission of his soul to all the precepts of God.'[1]

Secondly, in the Acts of the Apostles, the members of the 'early Church' are said to hold all things in common: 'The faithful all lived together and owned everything in common; they sold their goods and possessions and shared out the proceeds among themselves according to what each one needed. They went as a body to the Temple every day . . .'[2] The very first statute of the 'Community Rule' for Qumran states that 'All . . . shall bring all their knowledge, powers and possessions into the Community . . .'[3] According to another statute, 'They shall eat in common and pray in common . . .'[4] And another declares of the new adherent that 'his property

132

shall be merged and he shall offer his counsel and judgment to the Community'.[5]

Acts 5:1–11 recounts the story of one Ananias and his wife, who hold back some of the assets they are supposed to have donated to the 'early Church' in Jerusalem. Both are struck dead by a vindictive divine power. In Qumran, the penalty for such a transgression was rather less severe, consisting, according to the 'Community Rule', of six months' penance.

Thirdly, according to Acts, the leadership of the 'early Church' in Jerusalem consists of the twelve Apostles. Among these, according to Galatians, three – James ('the Lord's Brother'), John and Peter – exercise a particular authority. According to the 'Community Rule', Qumran was governed by a 'Council' composed of twelve individuals. Three 'priests' are also stressed, though the text does not clarify whether these three are included in the twelve of the 'Council' or separate from them.[6]

Fourthly, and most important of all, both the Qumran community and the 'early Church' were specifically messianic in orientation, dominated by the imminent advent of at least one new 'Messiah'. Both postulated a vivid and charismatic central figure, whose personality galvanised them and whose teachings formed the foundation of their beliefs. In the 'early Church', this figure was, of course, Jesus. In the Qumran texts, the figure is known as the 'Teacher of Righteousness'. At times, in their portrayal of the 'Teacher of Righteousness', the Qumran texts might almost seem to be referring to Jesus; indeed, several scholars suggested as much. Granted, the 'Teacher of Righteousness' is not depicted as divine; but neither, until some time after his death, was Jesus.

If the Qumran texts and those of the 'early Church' have certain ideas, concepts or principles in common, they are also strikingly similar in imagery and phraseology. 'Blessed are the meek', Jesus says, for example, in perhaps the most famous line of the Sermon on the Mount, 'for they shall inherit the earth' (Matt. 5:5). This assertion derives from Psalm 37:11: 'But the meek shall possess the land, and delight themselves in abundant prosperity.' The same psalm was of particular interest to the Qumran community. In the Dead Sea Scrolls, there is a commentary on its meaning: 'Interpreted,

133

this concerns the congregation of the Poor . . .'7 The 'Congregation of the Poor' (or the 'meek') was one of the names by which the Qumran community referred to themselves. Nor is this the only such parallel: 'Blessed are the poor in spirit: for theirs is the kingdom of heaven', preaches Jesus (Matt. 5:3); the 'War Scroll' from Cave 1 states: 'Among the poor in spirit there is a power . . .'8 Indeed, the whole of the Gospel of Matthew, and especially Chapters 10 and 18, contains metaphors and terminology at times almost interchangeable with those of the 'Community Rule'. In Matthew 5:48, for instance, Jesus stresses the concept of perfection: 'You must therefore be perfect just as your heavenly Father is perfect.' The 'Community Rule' speaks of those 'who walk in the way of perfection as commanded by God'.9 There will be, the text affirms, 'no pity on all who depart from the way . . . no comfort . . . until their way becomes perfect'.10 In Matthew 21:42, Jesus invokes Isaiah 28:16 and echoes Psalm 118:22: 'Have you never read in the scriptures: It was the stone rejected by the builders that became the keystone.' The 'Community Rule' invokes the same reference, stating that 'the Council of the Community . . . shall be that tried wall, that precious corner-stone'.11

If the Qumran scrolls and the Gospels echo each other, such echoes are even more apparent between the scrolls and the Pauline texts – the Acts of the Apostles and Paul's letters. The concept of 'sainthood', for example, and, indeed, the very word 'saint', are common enough in later Christianity, but striking in the context of the Dead Sea Scrolls. According to the opening line of the 'Community Rule', however, 'The Master shall teach the saints to live according to the Book of the Community Rule . . .'12 Paul, in his letter to the Romans (15:25–7), uses the same terminology of the 'early Church': 'I must take a present of money to the saints in Jerusalem.'

Indeed, Paul is particularly lavish in his use of Qumran terms and images. One of the Qumran texts, for example, speaks of 'all those who observe the Law in the House of Judah, whom God will deliver . . . because of their suffering and because of their faith in the Teacher of Righteousness'.13 Paul, of course, ascribes a similar redemptive power to faith in Jesus. Deliverance, he says in his epistle to the Romans (3:21–3), 'comes through faith to everyone . . . who believes in Jesus Christ'. To the Galatians (2:16–17), he declares that 'what makes a man righteous is not obedience to the Law, but faith in Jesus Christ'. It is clear that Paul is familiar with the metaphors, the figures of speech, the turns of phrase, the rhetoric used by the Qumran community in their interpretation of Old Testament texts. As we shall see, however, he presses this familiarity to the service of a very different purpose.

In the above quote from his letter to the Galatians, Paul ascribes no inordinate significance to the Law. In the Qumran texts, however, the Law is of paramount importance. The 'Community Rule' begins: 'The Master shall teach the saints to live according to the Book of the Community Rule, that they may seek God . . . and do what is good and right before Him, as He commanded by the hand of Moses and all His servants the Prophets . . .'[14] Later, the 'Community Rule' states that anyone who 'transgresses one word of the Law of Moses, on any point whatever, shall be expelled'[15] and that the Law will endure 'for as long as the domain of Satan endures'.[16] In his rigorous adherence to the Law, Jesus, strikingly enough, is much closer to the Qumran texts than he is to Paul. In the Sermon on the Mount (Matt. 5:17–19), Jesus makes his position unequivocally clear – a position that Paul was subsequently to betray:

Do not imagine that I have come to abolish the Law or the Prophets. I have come not to abolish but to complete them. I tell you solemnly . . . not one dot, not one little stroke, shall disappear from the Law until its purpose is achieved. Therefore, the man who infringes even one of the least of these commandments and teaches others to do the same will be considered the least in the kingdom of heaven . . .

If Jesus' adherence to the Law concurs with that of the Qumran community, so, too, does his timing of the Last Supper. For centuries, biblical commentators have been confused by apparently conflicting accounts in the Gospels. In Matthew (26:17–19), the Last Supper is depicted as a Passover meal, and Jesus is crucified the next day. In the Fourth Gospel (13:1 and 18:28), however, it is said to occur *before* the Passover. Some scholars have sought to reconcile

135

the contradiction by acknowledging the Last Supper as indeed a Passover feast, but a Passover feast conducted in accordance with a different calendar. The Qumran community used precisely such a calendar – a solar calendar, in contrast to the lunar calendar used by the priesthood of the Temple.[17] In each calendar, the Passover fell on a different date; and Jesus, it is clear, was using the same calendar as that of the Qumran community.

Certainly the Qumran community observed a feast which sounds very similar in its ritual characteristics to the Last Supper as it is described in the Gospels. The 'Community Rule' states that 'when the table has been prepared . . . the Priest shall be the first to stretch out his hand to bless the first-fruits of the bread and new wine'.[18] And another Qumran text, the 'Messianic Rule', adds: 'they shall gather for the common table, to eat and to drink new wine . . . let no man extend his hand over the first fruits of bread and wine before the Priest . . . thereafter, the Messiah of Israel shall extend his hand over the bread'.[19]

This text was sufficient to convince even Rome. According to Cardinal Jean Danielou, writing with a 'Nihil Obstat' from the Vatican: 'Christ must have celebrated the last supper on the eve of Easter according to the Essenian calendar.'[20]

One can only imagine the reaction of Father de Vaux and his team on first discovering the seemingly extraordinary parallels between the Qumran texts and what was known of 'early Christianity'. It had hitherto been believed that Jesus' teachings were unique – that he admittedly drew on Old Testament sources, but wove his references into a message, a gospel, a statement of 'good news' which had never been enunciated in the world before. Now, however, echoes of that message, and perhaps even of Jesus' drama itself, had come to light among a collection of ancient parchments preserved in the Judaean desert.

To an agnostic historian, or even to an undogmatic Christian, such a discovery would have been exciting indeed. It probably would have been with a certain sacred awe that one handled documents actually dating from the days when Jesus and his followers walked the sands of ancient Palestine, trudging between Galilee and

Judaea. One would undoubtedly, and with something of a frisson, have felt closer to Jesus himself. The sketchy details of Jesus' drama and milieu would have broken free from the print to which they had been confined for twenty centuries – would have assumed density, texture, solidity. The Dead Sea Scrolls were not like a modern book expounding a controversial thesis; they would comprise first-hand evidence, buttressed by the sturdy struts of 20th-century science and scholarship. Even for a non-believer, however, some question of moral responsibility would have arisen. Whatever his own scepticism, could he, casually and at a single stroke, undermine the faith to which millions clung for solace and consolation? For de Vaux and his colleagues, working as representatives of the Roman Catholic Church, it must have seemed as though they were handling the spiritual and religious equivalent of dynamite – something that might just conceivably demolish the entire edifice of Christian teaching and belief.

9
The Scrolls

I t is not feasible or relevant in this book to list all the texts
known to have been found at Qumran, or even to have been
translated and published. Many of them are of interest solely to
specialists. Many of them consist of nothing more than small fragments, whose context and significance cannot now be reconstructed.
A substantial number of them are commentaries on various books
of the Old Testament, as well as on other Judaic works known as
apocrypha and pseudepigrapha. But it is worth at this point noting
a few of the Qumran documents which contain material of special
relevance – and two in particular which will prove not only most
illuminating, but most controversial indeed.

The 'Copper Scroll'

Found in the Qumran cave designated number 3, the 'Copper Scroll'
simply lists, in the dry fashion of an inventory, sixty-four sites where
a treasure of gold, silver and precious religious vessels is alleged to
have been hidden. Many of the sites are in Jerusalem proper, some of
them under or adjacent to the Temple. Others are in the surrounding
countryside, perhaps as far afield as Qumran itself. If the figures
in the scroll are accurate, the total weight of the various scattered
caches amounts to sixty-five tons of silver and twenty-six tons of
gold, which would be worth some £30 million at today's prices. It
is not a particularly staggering sum as such things go – a sunken
Spanish treasure galleon, for example, would fetch far more – but

not many people would turn their noses up at it; and the religious and symbolic import of such a treasure would place it, of course, beyond all monetary value. Although this was not publicised when the contents of the scroll were originally revealed, the text clearly establishes that the treasure derived from the Temple – whence it was removed and secreted, presumably to protect it from the invading Romans. One can therefore conclude that the 'Copper Scroll' dates from the time of the Roman invasion in AD 68. As we have noted, certain members of the international team, such as Professor Cross and the former Father Milik, deemed the treasure to be wholly fictitious. Most independent scholars now concur, however, that it did exist. Nevertheless, the depositories have proved impossible to find. The directions, sites and landmarks involved are indicated by local names long since lost; and the general configuration and layout of the area has, in the course of two thousand years and endless wars, changed beyond all recognition.

In 1988, however, a discovery was made just to the north of the cave in which the 'Copper Scroll' was found. Here, in another cave, three feet or so below the present surface, a small jug was exhumed, dating from the time of Herod and his immediate successors. The jug had clearly been regarded as very valuable, and had been concealed with extreme care, wrapped in a protective cover of palm fibres. It proved to contain a thick red oil which, according to chemical analysis, is unlike any oil known today. This oil is generally believed to be balsam oil – a precious commodity reported to have been produced nearby, at Jericho, and traditionally used to anoint Israel's rightful kings.[1] The matter cannot be definitively established, however, because the balsam tree has been extinct for some fifteen hundred years.

If the oil is indeed balsam oil, it may well be part of the treasure stipulated in the 'Copper Scroll'. In any case, it is an incongruously costly commodity to have been used by a community of supposedly isolated ascetics in the desert. As we have noted, however, one of the most important features of the 'Copper Scroll' is that it shows Qumran not to have been so isolated after all. On the contrary, it would seem to establish links between the Qumran community and factions associated with the Temple in Jerusalem.

The 'Community Rule'

Found in Cave 1 at Qumran, the 'Community Rule', as we have seen, adumbrates the rituals and regulations governing life in the desert community. It establishes a hierarchy of authority for the community. It lays down instructions for the 'Master' of the community and for the various officers subordinate to him. It also specifies the principles of behaviour and the punishment for violation of these principles. Thus, for instance, 'Whoever has deliberately lied shall do penance for six months.'[2] The text opens by enunciating the basis on which the community define and distinguish themselves. All members must enter into a 'Covenant before God to obey all His commandments';[3] and he who practises such obedience will be 'cleansed from all his sins'.[4] Adherence to the Law is accorded a paramount position. Among the various terms by which the community's members are designated, one finds 'Keepers of the Covenant'[5] and those who have 'zeal for the Law'.[6]

Among the rituals stipulated, there is cleansing and purification by baptism – not just once, but, apparently, every day. Daily prayers are also specified, at dawn and at sunset, involving recitations of the Law. And there is a ritually purified 'Meal of the Congregation'[7] – a meal very similar, as other scrolls attest, to the 'Last Supper' of the so-called 'early Church'.

The 'Community Rule' speaks, too, of the 'Council' of the Community, made up of twelve men and, possibly, a further three priests. We have already discussed the interesting echoes of the 'cornerstone' or 'keystone' image in relation to the Council of the Community. But the scroll also states that the Council 'shall preserve the faith in the Land with steadfastness and meekness and shall atone for sin by the practice of justice and by suffering the sorrows of affliction'.[8]

In their eagerness to distance the Qumran community from Jesus and his entourage, scholars promoting the consensus of the international team stress that the concept of atonement does not figure in Qumran teachings – that Jesus is to be distinguished from Qumran's 'Teacher of Righteousness' in large part by virtue of his doctrine of atonement. The 'Community Rule', however, demonstrates that atonement figured as prominently in Qumran as it did with Jesus and his followers in the so-called 'early Church'.

Finally, the 'Community Rule' introduces the Messiah – or perhaps Messiahs, in the plural. Members of the Community, 'walking in the way of perfection', are obliged to adhere zealously to the Law 'until there shall come the prophet and the Messiahs of Aaron and Israel'.[9] This reference is usually interpreted as meaning two distinct Messiahs, two equally regal figures, one descended from the line of Aaron, one from the established line of Israel – i.e. the line of David and Solomon. But the reference may also be to a dynasty of single Messiahs descended from, and uniting, both lines. In the context of the time, of course, 'Messiah' does not signify what it later comes to signify in Christian tradition. It simply means 'the Anointed One', which denotes consecration by oil. In Israelite tradition, it would seem, both kings and priests – in fact, any claimant to high office – were anointed, and hence Messiahs.

The 'War Scroll'

Copies of the 'War Scroll' were found in Caves 1 and 4 at Qumran. On one level, the 'War Scroll' is a very specific manual of strategy and tactics, obviously intended for specific circumstances, at a specific place and time. Thus, for example: 'Seven troops of horsemen shall also station themselves to right and to left of the formation; their troops shall stand on this side . . .'[10] On another level, however, the text constitutes exhortation and prophetic propaganda, intended to galvanise morale against the invading foe, the 'Kittim', or Romans. The supreme leader of Israel against the 'Kittim' is called, quite unequivocally, the 'Messiah' – though certain commentators have sought to disguise or dissemble this nomenclature by referring to him as 'Thine anointed'.[11] The advent of the 'Messiah' is stated as having been prophesied in Numbers 24:17, where it is said that 'a star from Jacob takes the leadership, a sceptre arises from Israel'. The 'Star' thus becomes a sobriquet for the 'Messiah', the regal warrior priest-king who will lead the forces of Israel to triumph. As Robert Eisenman has stressed, this prophecy linking the Messiah figure with the image of the star occurs elsewhere in the Qumran literature, and is of crucial importance. It is also significant that the same prophecy is cited by sources quite independent of both Qumran and the New Testament – by historians and chroniclers of 1st-century Rome, for example, such as Josephus, Tacitus and Suetonius. And Simeon bar Kochba, instigator of the second revolt against the Romans between AD 132 and 135, called himself the 'Son of the Star'.

The 'War Scroll' imparts a metaphysical and theological dimension to the struggle against the 'Kittim' by depicting it as a clash between the 'Sons of Light' and the 'Sons of Darkness'. More importantly still, however, the scroll contains a vital clue to its own dating and chronology. When speaking of the 'Kittim', the text refers quite explicitly to their 'king'. The 'Kittim' concerned cannot, therefore, be the soldiers of republican Rome, who invaded Palestine in 63 BC and who had no monarch. On the contrary, they would have to be the soldiers of imperial Rome, who invaded in the wake of the revolt of AD 66 – although, of course, occupying troops had been present in Palestine since the imposition of imperial Roman prefects or procurators in AD 6. It is thus clear that the 'War Scroll' must be seen in the context not of pre-Christian times, but of the 1st century. As we shall see, this internal evidence of chronology – which advocates of the 'consensus' contrive to ignore – will be even more persuasively developed in one of the other, and most crucial, of the Qumran texts, the 'Commentary on Habakkuk'.

The 'Temple Scroll'

The 'Temple Scroll' is believed to have been found in Cave 11 at Qumran, though this has never been definitively established. As its name suggests, the scroll deals, at least in part, with the Temple of Jerusalem, with the design, furnishings, fixtures and fittings of the structure. It also outlines specific details of rituals practised in the Temple. At the same time, however, the name conferred on the scroll, by Yigael Yadin, is somewhat misleading.

In effect, the 'Temple Scroll' is a species of Torah, or Book of the Law – a kind of alternative Torah used by the Qumran community and other factions elsewhere in Palestine. The 'official'

Torah of Judaism comprises the first five books of the Old Testament – Genesis, Exodus, Leviticus, Numbers and Deuteronomy. These are deemed to be the books of laws which Moses received on Mount Sinai, and their authorship is traditionally ascribed to Moses himself. The 'Temple Scroll' constitutes, in a sense, a sixth Book of the Law.

The laws it contains are not confined to rites of worship and observance in the Temple. There are also laws pertaining to more general matters, such as ritual purification, marriage and sexual practices. Most important and interesting of all, there are laws governing the institution of kingship in Israel – the character, comportment, behaviour and obligations of the king. The king, for example, is strictly forbidden to be a foreigner. He is forbidden to have more than one wife. And like all other Jews, he is forbidden to marry his sister, his aunt, his brother's wife or his niece.[12]

There is nothing new or startling about most of these taboos. They can be found in Leviticus 18–20 in the Old Testament. But one of them – that forbidding the king's marriage to his niece – is new. It is found elsewhere in only one other place, another of the Dead Sea Scrolls, the 'Damascus Document'. As Eisenman has pointed out, this stricture provides an important clue to the dating of both the 'Temple Scroll' and the 'Damascus Document' – and, by extension, of course, to the other Dead Sea Scrolls as well. As we have noted, the consensus of the international team regards the Dead Sea Scrolls as pre-Christian, dating from the era of Israel's Maccabean kings. But there is no evidence that the Maccabean kings – or any Israelite kings before them – ever married their nieces or ever incurred criticism for doing so.[13] The issue seems to have been utterly irrelevant. Either marriage to one's niece was accepted, or it was never practised at all. In either case, it was not forbidden.

The situation changed dramatically, however, with the accession of Herod and his descendants. In the first place, Herod was, by Judaic standards at the time, a foreigner, of Arabian stock from Idumaea – the region to the south of Judaea. In the second place, the Herodian kings made a regular practice of marrying their nieces. And Herodian princesses regularly married their uncles.

Bernice, sister of King Agrippa II (AD 48–53), married her uncle, for example. Herodias, sister of Agrippa I (AD 37–44), went even further, marrying two uncles in succession. The strictures in the 'Temple Scroll' are thus of particular relevance to a very specific period, and constitute a direct criticism of the Herodian dynasty – a dynasty of foreign puppet kings, imposed on Israel forcibly and sustained in power by imperial Rome.

Taken in sum, the evidence of the 'Temple Scroll' runs counter to the consensus of the international team in three salient respects:

1. According to the consensus, the Qumran community had no connection with, or interest in, either the Temple or the 'official' Judaism of the time. Like the 'Copper Scroll', however, the 'Temple Scroll' establishes that the Qumran community were indeed preoccupied with Temple affairs and with the governing theocracy.
2. According to the consensus, the supposed 'Essenes' of Qumran were on cordial terms with Herod. The 'Temple Scroll', however, goes out of its way to include certain specific strictures – strictures intended to damn Herod and his dynasty.[14] These strictures would be meaningless in any other context.
3. According to the consensus, the 'Temple Scroll' itself, like all the other Qumran texts, dates from pre-Christian times. Yet the internal evidence of the scroll points to issues that would have become relevant only during the Herodian period – that is, during the 1st century of the Christian era.

The 'Damascus Document'

The 'Damascus Document' was known to the world long before the discovery of the Dead Sea Scrolls at Qumran. In the absence of a context, however, scholars were not sure what to make of it. Towards the end of the last century, the loft of an ancient synagogue in Cairo was found to contain a '*geniza*' – a depository for the disposal of worn-out or redundant religious texts – dating from the 9th century AD. In 1896, a few fragments from this '*geniza*' were confided to one Solomon Schecter, a lecturer at Cambridge

University who happened to be in Cairo at the time. One fragment proved to contain the original Hebrew version of a text which, for a thousand years, had been known only in secondary translations. This prompted Schecter to investigate further. In December 1896, he collected the entire contents of the *'geniza'* – 164 boxes of manuscripts housing some 100,000 pieces – and brought them back to Cambridge. From this welter of material, two Hebrew versions emerged of what came to be known as the 'Damascus Document'. The versions from the Cairo *'geniza'* were obviously later copies of a much earlier work. The texts were incomplete, lacking endings and probably large sections in the middle; the order of the texts was scrambled and the logical development of their themes confused. Even in this muddled form, however, the 'Damascus Document' was provocative, potentially explosive. Schecter published it for the first time in 1910. In 1913, R.H. Charles reprinted it in his compilation *The Apocrypha and Pseudepigrapha of the Old Testament*.

When Eisenman was given, and passed on to *Biblical Archaeology Review*, the computer print-out which inventoried all the Qumran material in the hands of the international team, there were listed, among the items, additional versions and/or fragments of the 'Damascus Document'. Having been found at Qumran, they were obviously much earlier than those of the Cairo *'geniza'*, and probably more complete. It was the Qumran parallels and the fragments of the 'Damascus Document' that Eisenman and Philip Davies of Sheffield requested to see in their formal letter to John Strugnell, thereby precipitating the bitter and vindictive controversy of 1989. Why should this document be such a bone of contention?

The 'Damascus Document' speaks firstly of a remnant of Jews who, unlike their co-religionists, remained true to the Law. A 'Teacher of Righteousness' appeared among them. Like Moses, he took them into the wilderness, to a place called 'Damascus', where they entered into a renewed 'Covenant' with God. Numerous textual references make it clear that this Covenant is the same as the one cited by the 'Community Rule' for Qumran. And it is obvious enough – no scholar disputes it – that the 'Damascus Document' is speaking of the same community as the other Qumran scrolls. Yet the location of the community is said to be 'Damascus'.

It is clear from the document's context that the place in the desert called 'Damascus' cannot possibly be the Romanised city in Syria. Could the site for 'Damascus' have been in fact Qumran? Why the name of the location should have been thus masked remains uncertain – though simple self-preservation, dictated by the turmoil following the revolt of AD 66, would seem to be explanation enough, and Qumran had no name of its own at the time. In any case, it can hardly be coincidental that, according to the international team's computer print-out, no fewer than ten copies or fragments of the 'Damascus Document' were found in Qumran's caves.[15]

Like the 'Community Rule', the 'Damascus Document' includes a list of regulations. Some of these are identical to those in the 'Community Rule'. But there are some additional regulations as well, two of which are worth noting. One pertains to marriage and children – which establishes that the Qumran community were not, as Father de Vaux maintained, celibate 'Essenes'. A second refers – quite in passing, as if it were common knowledge – to affiliated communities scattered throughout Palestine. In other words, Qumran was not as isolated from the world of its time as de Vaux contended.

The 'Damascus Document' fulminates against three crimes in particular, crimes alleged to be rampant among the enemies of the 'Righteous', those who have embraced the 'New Covenant'. These crimes are specified as wealth, profanation of the Temple (a charge levelled by the 'Temple Scroll' as well) and a fairly limited definition of fornication – taking more than one wife, or marrying one's niece. As Eisenman has shown, the 'Damascus Document' thus echoes the 'Temple Scroll' in referring to issues of unique relevance to the period of the Herodian dynasty.[16] And it echoes, as we shall see, a dispute in the community which figures more prominently in another of the Dead Sea Scrolls, the 'Habakkuk Commentary'. This dispute involves an individual designated as 'the Liar', who defects from the community and becomes its enemy. The 'Damascus Document' condemns those 'who enter the New Covenant in the land of Damascus, and who again betray it and depart'.[17] Shortly thereafter, the document speaks of those 'who deserted to the Liar'.[18]

The 'Damascus Document' also echoes the 'Community Rule' and the 'War Scroll' by speaking of a Messianic figure (or perhaps two such figures) who will come to 'Damascus' – a prophet or 'Interpreter of the Law' called 'the Star' and a prince of the line of David called 'the Sceptre'.[19] On five subsequent occasions in the text, there is a focus on a single figure, 'the Messiah of Aaron and Israel'.[20]

The significance of this Messiah figure will be explored later. For the moment, it is worth considering the implications of 'Damascus' as a designation for Qumran. To most Christians, of course, 'Damascus' is familiar from Chapter 9 of the Acts of the Apostles, where it is taken to denote the Romanised city in Syria, that country's modern-day capital. It is on the road to Damascus that Saul of Tarsus, in one of the best-known and most crucial passages of the entire New Testament, undergoes his conversion into Paul.[21]

According to Acts 9, Saul is a kind of inquisitor-cum-'enforcer', dispatched by the high priest in the Temple of Jerusalem to suppress the community of heretical Jews – i.e. 'early Christians' – residing in Damascus. The priesthood are collaborators with the occupying Romans, and Saul is one of their instruments. In Jerusalem, he is already said to have participated actively in attacks on the 'early Church'. Indeed, if Acts is to be believed, he is personally involved in the events surrounding the stoning to death of the individual identified as Stephen, acclaimed by later tradition as the first Christian martyr. He himself freely admits that he has persecuted his victims 'to death'.

Prompted by his fanatical fervour, Saul then embarks for Damascus, to ferret out fugitive members of the 'early Church' established there. He is accompanied by a band of men, presumably armed; and he carries with him arrest warrants from the high priest in Jerusalem.

Syria, at the time, was not a part of Israel, but a separate Roman province, governed by a Roman legate, with neither an administrative nor a political connection with Palestine. How, then, could the high priest's writ conceivably run there? The Roman Empire would hardly have sanctioned self-appointed 'hit-squads' moving from one territory to another within its domains, serving arrests, perpetrating assassinations and threatening the precarious stability of civic order. According to official policy, every religion was to be tolerated, provided it posed no challenge to secular authority or the social structure. A Jerusalem-based 'hit-squad' operating in Syria would have elicited some swift and fairly gruesome reprisals from the Roman administration – reprisals such as no high priest, whose position depended on Roman favour, would dare to incur. Given these circumstances, how could Saul of Tarsus, armed with warrants from the high priest, possibly have undertaken his punitive expedition to Damascus – if, that is, 'Damascus' is indeed taken to be the city in Syria?

If 'Damascus' is understood to be Qumran, however, Saul's expedition suddenly makes perfect historical sense. Unlike Syria, Qumran *did* lie in territory where the high priest's writ legitimately ran. It would have been entirely feasible for the high priest in Jerusalem to dispatch his 'enforcers' to extirpate heretical Jews at Qumran, a mere twenty miles away, near Jericho. Such action would have thoroughly conformed to Roman policy, which made a point of not meddling in purely internal affairs. Jews, in other words, were quite free to harry and persecute other Jews within their own domains, so long as such activities did not encroach on the Roman administration. And since the high priest was a Roman puppet, his efforts to extirpate rebellious co-religionists would have been all the more welcome.

This explanation, however, despite its historical plausibility, raises some extremely awkward questions. According to the consensus of the international team, the community at Qumran consisted of Judaic sectarians – the so-called 'Essenes', a pacifist ascetic sect having no connection either with early Christianity or with the 'mainstream' of Judaism at the time. Yet Saul, according to Acts, embarks for Damascus to persecute members of the 'early Church'. Here, then, is a provocative challenge both to Christian tradition and to adherents of the consensus, who have studiously avoided looking at the matter altogether. Either members of the 'early Church' were sheltering with the Qumran community – or the 'early Church' and the Qumran community were one and the same. In either case, the 'Damascus Document' indicates that the Dead Sea Scrolls cannot be distanced from the origins of Christianity.

The 'Habakkuk Commentary'

Found in Cave 1 at Qumran, the 'Habakkuk *Pesher*', or 'Habakkuk Commentary', represents perhaps the closest approximation, in the entire corpus of known Dead Sea Scrolls, to a chronicle of the community – or, at any rate, of certain major developments in its history. It focuses in particular on the same dispute cited by the 'Damascus Document'. This dispute, verging on incipient schism, seems to have been a traumatic event in the life of the Qumran community. It figures not just in the 'Damascus Document' and the 'Habakkuk Commentary', but in four other Qumran texts as well; and there seem to be references to it in four further texts.[22]

Like the 'Damascus Document', the 'Habakkuk Commentary' recounts how certain members of the community, under the iniquitous instigation of a figure identified as 'the Liar', secede, break the New Covenant and cease to adhere to the Law. This precipitates a conflict between them and the community's leader, 'the Teacher of Righteousness'. There is mention, too, of a villainous adversary known as 'the Wicked Priest'. Adherents of the consensus have generally tended to regard 'the Liar' and 'the Wicked Priest' as two different sobriquets for the same individual. More recently, however, Eisenman has effectively demonstrated that 'the Liar' and 'the Wicked Priest' are two quite separate and distinct personages.[23] He has made it clear that 'the Liar', unlike 'the Wicked Priest', emerges from *within* the Qumran community. Having been taken in by the community and accepted as a member in more or less good standing, he then defects. He is not just an adversary, therefore, but a traitor as well. In contrast, 'the Wicked Priest' is an outsider, a representative of the priestly establishment of the Temple. Although an adversary, he is not therefore a traitor. What makes him important for our purposes is the clue he provides to the dating of the events recounted in the 'Habakkuk Commentary'. If 'the Wicked Priest' is a member of the Temple establishment, it means the Temple is still standing

149

and the establishment intact. In other words, the activities of 'the Wicked Priest' *pre-date* the destruction of the Temple by Roman troops.

As in the 'War Scroll', but even more explicitly, there are references that can only be to imperial, not republican, Rome – to Rome, that is, in the 1st century AD. The 'Habakkuk Commentary', for example, alludes to a specific practice – victorious Roman troops making sacrificial offerings to their standards. Josephus provides written evidence for this practice at the time of the fall of the Temple in AD 70.[24] And it is, in fact, a practice that would make no sense under the republic, when victorious troops would have offered sacrifices to their gods. Only with the creation of the empire, when the emperor himself was accorded the status of divinity, becoming the supreme god for his subjects, would his image, or token, or monogram, be emblazoned on the standards of his soldiers. The 'Habakkuk Commentary', therefore, like the 'War Scroll', the 'Temple Scroll' and the 'Damascus Document', points specifically to the Herodian epoch.

10

Science in the
Service of Faith

According to the consensus of the international team, the historical events reflected in *all* the relevant Dead Sea Scrolls occurred in Maccabean times – between the mid-2nd and mid-1st centuries BC. The 'Wicked Priest', who pursues, persecutes and perhaps kills the 'Teacher of Righteousness', is generally identified by them as Jonathan Maccabaeus, or perhaps his brother Simon, both of whom enjoyed positions of prominence during that epoch; and the invasion of a foreign army is taken to be that launched by the Romans under Pompey in 63 BC.[1] The historical backdrop of the scrolls is thus set safely back in pre-Christian times, where it becomes disarmed of any possible challenge to New Testament teaching and tradition.

But while some of the Dead Sea Scrolls undoubtedly do refer to pre-Christian times, it is a grievous mistake – for some, perhaps, deliberate obfuscation – to conclude that all of them do so. Pompey, who invaded the Holy Land in 63 BC, was, of course, a contemporary of Julius Caesar. At the time of Pompey and Caesar, Rome was still a republic, becoming an empire only in 27 BC, under Caesar's son, Octavian, who took the imperial title of Augustus. If the Roman invasion referred to in the scrolls was that of Pompey, it would have involved the armies of republican Rome. Yet the 'War Rule' speaks of a 'king' or 'monarch' of the invaders. And the 'Habakkuk Commentary' is even more explicit in its reference to victorious invaders sacrificing to their standards.

It would therefore seem clear that the invasion in question was that of imperial Rome – the invasion provoked by the revolt of AD 66.

Professor Godfrey Driver of Oxford found numerous textual references within the scrolls that provide clues to their dating. Focusing in particular on the 'Habakkuk Commentary', he concluded that the invaders could only be 'the Roman legions at the time of the revolt in AD 66'. This conclusion, he added, 'is put beyond doubt by the reference to their sacrificing to their military standards'.[2] His statements, however, elicited a vicious attack from Father de Vaux, who recognised that they led inexorably to the conclusion that 'the historical background of the scrolls therefore is the war against Rome'.[3] This, of course, de Vaux could not possibly accept. At the same time, however, he could not refute such precise evidence. In consequence, he contrived to dismiss the evidence and attack only Driver's general thesis: 'Driver has started from the pre-conceived idea that all scrolls were post-Christian, and that this idea was based on the fallacious witness of orthography, language and vocabulary.'[4] It was, he declared, for professional historians 'to decide whether [Driver's] motley history . . . has sufficient foundation in the texts'.[5] It is interesting that de Vaux, who taught biblical history at the Ecole Biblique, should suddenly (at least when he had to answer Professor Driver) don a cloak of false modesty and shrink from considering himself an historian, taking refuge instead behind the supposed bulwarks of archaeology and palaeography.[6] In fact, archaeological data reinforce the indications of chronology provided by the internal data of the scrolls themselves. External evidence concurs with internal evidence – evidence of which the consensus would seem to remain oblivious. At times, this has led to an embarrassing *faux pas*.

De Vaux, it will be remembered, embarked on a preliminary excavation of the Qumran ruins in 1951. His findings were sufficiently consequential to justify a more ambitious enterprise. A characteristic lassitude set in, however, and no full-scale excavation was undertaken until 1953. Annual excavations then continued until 1956; and in 1958, an associated site at Ein Feshka, less than a mile to the south, was also excavated. In his eagerness to distance the Qumran community from any connection with early Christianity, de Vaux rushed his conclusions about dating into print. In some instances, he did not even wait for archaeological evidence to support him. As early as 1954, the Jesuit professor Robert North noted no fewer than four cases in which de Vaux had been forced to retract on his dating. North also found it distressing that, even on so crucial a matter, no specialists 'independently of de Vaux's influence' were asked to contribute their conclusions.[7] But it was not de Vaux's style to invite opinions that might conflict with his own and shed a more controversial light on the material. Nor was he eager to announce his errors when they occurred. Although quick to publish and publicise conclusions that confirmed his thesis, he was markedly more dilatory in retracting them when they proved erroneous.

One important element for de Vaux was a thick layer of ash found to be blanketing the surroundings of the ruins. This layer of ash patently attested to a fire of some sort, which had obviously caused considerable destruction. Indeed, it had led to Qumran's being partially, if not wholly, abandoned for some years. A study of the coins found at the site revealed that the fire had occurred at some time towards the beginning of the reign of Herod the Great, who occupied the throne from 37 BC until 4 BC. The same data indicated that rebuilding had commenced under the regime of Herod's son, Archelaus, who ruled (not as king, but as ethnarch) from 4 BC until AD 6.

According to de Vaux's thesis, the Qumran community consisted of supposedly placid, peace-loving and ascetic 'Essenes', on good terms with Herod as with everyone else. If this were the case, the fire which destroyed the community should have resulted not from any deliberate human intention – from an act of war, for example – but from an accident, or a natural disaster. Fortunately for de Vaux, a large crack was found running through a cistern. Although independent researchers found no indication that the crack extended any further, de Vaux claimed to have traced it through the whole of the ruins, the whole of the Qumran community.[8] Even if it did, a number of experts concluded, it could probably be ascribed to erosion.[9] For de Vaux, however, the crack, such as it was, seemed the result of one of the many earthquakes the region has suffered over the centuries. Instead of trying to identify the cause of the crack, in other words, de Vaux went rummaging for an earthquake that might have been responsible. As it happened, there was a more or less convenient earthquake on record. Josephus speaks of one that occurred towards the beginning of Herod's reign, in 31 BC. This, de Vaux concluded, had caused the fire which led to the abandoning of the community. He did not bother to explain why rebuilding did not commence for a quarter of a century before, suddenly, proceeding with noticeable rapidity.

Robert Eisenman points to the strikingly precise timing of the delay in rebuilding. It coincides perfectly with Herod's reign. No sooner had he died than reconstruction promptly began – and part of this reconstruction consisted of strengthening the defensive towers, as well as creating a rampart. It would thus seem clear, for some reason which de Vaux chose to ignore, that no one dared to rebuild Qumran while Herod remained on the throne. But why should that be the case if the community were on as congenial a footing with Herod as de Vaux maintained, and if the destruction of the community resulted from an earthquake? It would appear much more likely that the community was destroyed deliberately, on Herod's orders, and that no reconstruction *could* begin until after his death. But why should Herod order the destruction of a community so placid, so universally loved, so divorced from political activity?

Whether wilfully or through negligence, de Vaux remained oblivious of such questions. Eventually, however, the logic he mustered to support his hypothetical earthquake became too strained even for the closest of his supporters, the then Father Milik. In 1957, Milik wrote of the fire and the alleged earthquake that:

> the archaeological evidence from Qumran is not unambiguous as to the order of these two events . . . the thick layers of ashes suggests a very violent conflagration, better to be explained as a result of a conscious attempt to burn down the whole building; so the ashes may show the traces of an intentional destruction of Qumran.[10]

Whether the fire was caused by earthquake or by deliberate human agency cannot be definitively established. Certainly the evidence offers less support to de Vaux than it does to Milik and Eisenman, who, on this unique occasion, are in accord. Nevertheless, many adherents of the consensus still invoke the earthquake, and it still figures with metronomic regularity in their texts.

In another instance, however, de Vaux's misinterpretation of the evidence – or, to put the matter charitably, wishful thinking – was much more conclusively exposed. Very early in his excavations, he found a heavily oxidised coin on which, he said, he 'believed' he could discern the insignia of the Roman 10th Legion.[11] Purporting to cite Josephus, he also said that the 10th Legion had conquered Jericho, eight miles away, in June of AD 68. Everything seemed to fit nicely. On the basis of his coin, de Vaux argued that Qumran must have been destroyed by the 10th Legion in AD 68. 'No manuscript of the caves', he later declared, waxing dogmatic on the basis of questionable data, 'can be later than June, AD 68.'[12]

De Vaux had first described his discovery of the coin in 1954, in *Revue biblique*. He repeated his account five years later, in 1959, in the same journal.[13] The 'fact' of the coin, and de Vaux's emphatic dating on the basis of it, thus became enshrined in the established corpus of evidence routinely invoked by adherents of the consensus. Thus, for example, Frank Cross would write that the coin stamped with the insignia of the 10th Legion constituted 'grim confirmation'.[14]

De Vaux, however, had made two bizarre errors. In the first place, he had somehow contrived to misread Josephus, ascribing to Josephus precisely the opposite of what Josephus in fact said. Josephus most emphatically did *not* assert that the 10th Legion captured Jericho in AD 68. As Professor Cecil Roth demonstrated, of the three Roman legions in the vicinity, only the 10th was not engaged in the conquest of Jericho.[15] The 10th Legion had remained a considerable distance to the north, guarding the top of the Jordan Valley. In the second place, the coin de Vaux had found proved not to be from the 10th Legion at all, or, for that matter, from any other. Although badly damaged and oxidised, the coin, when subjected to expert scrutiny, proved to have come from Ashkelon and to date from AD 72 or 73.

Here was a blunder that could not be equivocated away.

De Vaux had no choice but to publish a formal retraction. This retraction, however, appeared only as a footnote in his opus *L'archéologie et les manuscrits de la mer morte*, published in French in 1961 and in English translation in 1973. 'Mention of this was unfortunate', de Vaux says laconically, 'for this coin does not exist.'[16]

On the whole, de Vaux tended to be shamelessly cavalier in his conclusions about coins. When he found any that did not conform to his theories, he simply dismissed them. Thus, for example, he found one dating from the period between AD 138 and 161. He shrugged off its possible relevance with the comment that it 'must have been lost by a passer-by'.[17] By the same token, of course, an earlier coin, on which he attempted to establish his dating and chronology for Qumran, could also have been lost by a passer-by; but de Vaux seems not to have considered this possibility.

Of the archaeological evidence found at Qumran, coins have been particularly important to the international team and the adherents of their consensus. Indeed, it was on the basis of this evidence that they deduced the timespan of the community; and it was through their interpretation of this evidence that they established their dating and chronology. Prior to Eisenman, however, no one had bothered to question their misinterpretation. Roth and Driver, as we have seen, endeavoured to establish a chronology on the basis of the *internal* evidence of the scrolls themselves. De Vaux and the international team were able to discredit them simply by invoking the external evidence supposedly provided by the coins. That this evidence had been spuriously interpreted went unnoticed. Eisenman recognised that Roth and Driver, arguing on the basis of internal evidence, had in fact been correct. But in order to prove this, he had first to expose the erroneous interpretation of the external evidence. He began with the coin distribution, pointing out that they revealed two periods of peak activity.

Some 450 bronze coins were discovered at Qumran in the course of excavation. They encompassed a span of some two and a half centuries, from 135 BC to AD 136. The following table groups them according to the reigns in which they were minted:

1 coin	from	135–104 BC
1 coin	from	104 BC
143 coins	from	103–76 BC
1 coin	from	76–67 BC
5 coins	from	67–40 BC
4 coins	from	40–37 BC
10 coins	from	37–4 BC
16 coins	from	4 BC–6 AD
91 coins	from	6–41 AD (time of the procurators)
78 coins	from	37–44 AD (reign of Agrippa I)
2 Roman coins	from	54–68 AD
83 coins	from	67 AD (2nd year of the revolt)
5 coins	from	68 AD (3rd year of the revolt)
6 additional coins from the revolt, too oxidised to identify more precisely		
13 Roman coins	from	67–8 AD
1 Roman coin	from	69–79 AD
2 coins	from	72–3 AD
4 coins	from	72–81 AD
1 Roman coin	from	87 AD
3 Roman coins	from	98–117 AD
6 coins	from	132–6 AD (revolt of Simeon bar Kochba)[18]

The distribution of coins would appear to indicate two periods when the community at Qumran was most active – that between 103 and 76 BC, and that between AD 6 and 67. There are a total of 143 coins from the former period, 254 from the latter. For adherents of the consensus, this did not mesh as neatly as they would have liked with their theories. According to their reading of the scrolls, the 'Wicked Priest' was most likely to be identified as the high priest Jonathan, who lived between 160 and 142 BC – half a century *before* the first concentration of coins. In order to support his thesis, Father de Vaux needed a very early date for the founding

157

of the Qumran community. He was thus forced to argue that the solitary coin dating from between 135 and 104 BC served to prove the thesis correct – even though common sense suggests that the community dates from between 103 and 76 BC, the period from which there is a concentration of 143 coins. The earlier coin, on which de Vaux rests his argument is much more likely to have been merely one that remained in circulation for some years after it was minted.

De Vaux ascribed particular significance to the disappearance of Judaic coins after AD 68 and the nineteen Roman coins subsequent to that year. This, he maintained, 'proves' that Qumran was destroyed in AD 68; the Roman coins, he argued, indicated that the ruins were 'occupied' by a detachment of Roman troops. On this basis, he proceeded to assign a definitive date to the deposition of the scrolls themselves: 'our conclusion: none of the manuscripts belonging to the community is later than the ruin of Khirbet Qumran in AD 68.'[19]

The spuriousness of this reasoning is self-evident. In the first place, Judaic coins have been found which date from Simeon bar Kochba's revolt between AD 132 and 136. In the second place, the coins indicate only that people were wandering around Qumran and dropping them; they indicate nothing, one way or the other, about the deposition of manuscripts, which could have been buried at Qumran as late as bar Kochba's time. And finally, it is hardly surprising that the coins subsequent to AD 68 should be Roman. In the years following the revolt, Roman coins were the *only* currency in Judaea. This being the case, they need hardly have been dropped solely by Romans.

Eisenman is emphatic about the conclusions to be drawn from de Vaux's archaeology. If it proves anything, he states, it proves precisely the opposite of what de Vaux concludes – proves that the latest date for the scrolls having been deposited at Qumran is not AD 68 but AD 136. Any time up to that date would be perfectly consistent with the archaeological evidence.[20] Nor, Eisenman adds, is the consensus correct in assuming that the destruction of the main buildings at Qumran necessarily meant the destruction of the site.[21] There are, in fact, indications that at least some cursory or rudimentary rebuilding occurred, including a 'crude canal' to feed water into a cistern. Rather unconvincingly, de Vaux claimed this to have been the work of the Roman garrison supposed, on the basis of the coins, to have occupied the site.[22] But Professor Driver pointed out that the sheer crudeness of the reconstruction does not suggest Roman work.[23] De Vaux maintained that his theory, conforming as it did to the alleged destruction of Qumran in AD 68, was in accord with '*les données d'histoire*', the 'accepted givens of history' – 'having forgotten', as Professor Driver observed drily, 'that the historical records say nothing of the destruction of Qumran in AD 68 by the Romans'. In short, Driver concluded, 'the "*données d'histoire*" are historical fiction'.[24]

There is another crucial piece of archaeological evidence which runs diametrically counter to the interpretation of the consensus. De Vaux himself studiously, and justifiably, avoided referring to the ruins at Qumran as a 'monastery'. As he explained, he 'never used the word when writing about the excavations at Qumran, precisely because it represents an inference which archaeology, taken alone, could not warrant'.[25] It is clear, however, that he nevertheless thought of Qumran as a species of monastery. This is reflected by his uninhibited use of such monastic terms as 'scriptorium' and 'refectory' to describe certain of the structures. And if de Vaux himself had some reservations about dubbing Qumran a 'monastery', other adherents of the consensus did not. In his book on the Dead Sea Scrolls, for example, Cardinal Danielou babbled happily about the 'monks of Qumran', even going so far as to state that 'the monasticism of Qumran can be considered as the source of Christian monasticism'.[26]

What de Vaux, his colleagues and adherents of the consensus chose consistently to overlook was the distinctly and unmistakably military character of some of the ruins. When one visits Qumran today, one will inevitably be struck initially by the remains of a substantial defensive tower, with walls of some feet in thickness and an entrance only on the second storey. Less obvious, but just across a small passageway from the tower, there is another structure whose function may not be immediately apparent. In fact, it is what remains of a well-built forge – complete with its own water

159

supply for tempering the tools and weapons crafted within it. Not surprisingly, the forge is something of an embarrassment to the scholars of the international team, clinging to their image of placid, pacifist 'Essenes'. Thus de Vaux scuttled away from the issue as fast as tongue and pen could carry him:

> there was a workshop comprising a furnace above which was a plastered area with a drainage conduit. The installation implies that the kind of work carried on there required a large fire as well as an abundant supply of water. I do not venture to define its purpose any more precisely than that.[27]

Which is rather like not venturing to define the purpose of empty cartridge cases and spent projectiles of lead scattered around the OK Corral in Tombstone, Arizona. Professor Cross, following in de Vaux's footsteps but incapable of the same disingenuousness, grudgingly alludes to 'what appears to have been a forge'.[28]

In fact, arrows were found *inside* the ruins of Qumran; and while one could argue that these were loosed by attacking Romans, they are, as Professor Driver asserted, 'as likely to have belonged to the occupants'[29] – if not, indeed, more likely. On the whole, the military character of the ruins is so flagrant that another independent scholar, Professor Golb of the University of Chicago, has gone so far as to see in them an *entirely* martial installation.[30] According to Golb, the scrolls were never composed or copied at Qumran at all, but were brought there, from Jerusalem, specifically for protection. 'No fragment of parchment or papyrus', Golb has pointed out, 'was ever found in the debris . . . nor any tools of scribes . . .'[31]

Apart from coins and the physical ruins, the most important body of external evidence used by the international team for dating the Dead Sea Scrolls derived from the tenuous science of palaeography. Palaeography is the comparative study of ancient calligraphy. Assuming a strictly chronological and linear progression in the evolution of handwriting, it endeavours to chart developments in the specific shape and form of letters, and thus to assign dates to an entire manuscript. One might find, for example, an old charter or some other document in one's attic. On the basis not of its content, but of its script alone,

one might guess it to date from the 17th as opposed to the 18th century. To that extent, one would be practising a species of amateur palaeography. The procedure, needless to say, even when employed with the most scientific rigour, is far from conclusive. When applied to the texts found at Qumran, it becomes feeble indeed – and sometimes tips over into the ludicrous. Nevertheless, de Vaux invoked palaeography as another corpus of external evidence to discredit the conclusions, based on internal evidence, of Roth and Driver. It was, therefore, the alleged palaeographical evidence pertaining to Qumran that Eisenman had next to demolish.

Palaeography, according to Frank Cross of the international team, 'is perhaps the most precise and objective means of determining the age of a manuscript'. He goes on to explain:

> we must approach the problems relating to the historical interpretation of our texts by first determining the time period set by archaeological data, by paleographical evidence, and by other more objective methods before applying the more subjective techniques of internal criticism.[32]

Why internal evidence should necessarily be more 'subjective' than that of archaeology and palaeography Cross does not bother to clarify. In fact, this statement inadvertently reveals why palaeography should be deemed so important by adherents of the consensus: it can be used to counter the internal evidence of the documents – evidence which makes sense only in the context of the 1st century AD.

The most prominent palaeographical work on the Dead Sea Scrolls was done by Professor Solomon Birnbaum of the University of London's School of Oriental Studies. Birnbaum's endeavours received fulsome endorsement from Professor Cross, who hailed them as 'a monumental attempt to deal with all periods of Hebrew writing'.[33] Attempting to parry the copious criticism to which Birnbaum's exegesis was subjected, Cross asked his readers to remember 'that it was written by a professional paleographer tried to the limit by the Lilliputian attacks of non-specialists'.[34] Such is the intensity of academic vituperation generated by the question of palaeographical evidence.

Birnbaum's method is bizarre to say the least, reminiscent less of the modern scientific method with which he purports to dignify it than of, say, the nether reaches of numerology. Thus, for example, he presupposes – and the whole of his subsequent procedure rests on nothing more than this unconfirmed presupposition – that the entire spectrum of the texts found at Qumran extends precisely from 300 BC to AD 68. Thus, in one instance, he takes a text of Samuel found in Cave 4 at Qumran. Having methodically combed this text, he cites forty-five specimens of a particular calligraphic feature, eleven specimens of another. '*Mit der Dummheit*', Schiller observed, '*kämpfen Götter selbst vergeben.*' For reasons the gods themselves must find mind-boggling, Birnbaum then proceeds to set up an equation: the proportion of 56 to 11 equals 368 to x (368 being the number of years the texts span, and x being the date he hopes to assign to the text in question). The value of x – calculated, legitimately enough, in purely mathematical terms – is 72, which should then be subtracted from 300 BC, Birnbaum's hypothetical starting point. He arrives at 228 BC; 'the result', he claims triumphantly, 'will be something like the absolute date' for the Samuel manuscript.[35] To speak of 'something like' an 'absolute date' is rather like speaking of 'a relatively absolute date'. But quite apart from such stylistic solecisms, Birnbaum's method, as Eisenman says, 'is, of course, preposterous'.[36] Nevertheless, Birnbaum employed his technique, such as it was, to establish 'absolute dates' for all the texts discovered at Qumran. The most alarming fact of all is that adherents of the consensus still accept these 'absolute dates' as unimpugnable.

Professor Philip Davies of Sheffield states that 'most people who take time to study the issue agree that the use of paleography in Qumran research is unscientific', adding that 'attempts have been made to offer a precision of dating that is ludicrous'.[37] Eisenman is rather more scathing, describing Birnbaum's endeavours as 'what in any other field would be the most pseudo-scientific and infantile methods'.[38] To illustrate this, he provides the following example.[39]

Suppose two scribes of different ages are copying the same text at the same time, and the younger scribe were trained more recently in a more up-to-date 'scribal school'? Suppose the older scribe were deliberately using a stylised calligraphy which he'd learned in his

youth? Suppose either or both scribes, in deference to tradition
or the hallowed character of their activity, sought deliberately to
replicate a style dating from some centuries before – as certain
documents today, such as diplomas or certificates of award, may
be produced in archaic copper-plate? What date could possibly be
assigned definitively to their transcriptions?

In his palaeographic assumptions, Birnbaum overlooked one particularly important fact. If a document is produced merely to convey
information, it will, in all probability, reflect the most up-to-date
techniques. Such, for example, are the techniques employed by
modern newspapers (except, until recently, in England). But everything suggests that the Dead Sea Scrolls weren't produced merely
to convey information. Everything suggests they had a ritual or
semi-ritual function as well, and were lovingly produced so as to
preserve an element of tradition. It is therefore highly probable that
later scribes would deliberately attempt to reproduce the style of
their predecessors. And, indeed, all through recorded history, scribes
have consistently been conservative. Thus, for example, illuminated
manuscripts of the Middle Ages contrived to reflect a sacred quality
of antiquity, not the latest technological progress. Thus many modern Bibles are reproduced in 'old-fashioned' print. Thus one would
not expect to find a modern Jewish Torah employing the style or
technique used to imprint a slogan on a T-shirt.

Of the calligraphy in the Dead Sea Scrolls, Eisenman concludes
that 'they simply represent a multitude of different handwriting
styles of people working more or less at the same time within
the same framework, and tell us nothing about chronology at
all'.[40] Cecil Roth of Oxford was, if anything, even more emphatic:
'In connection for example with the English records, although a
vast mass of dated manuscript material exists covering the entire
Middle Ages, it is impossible to fix precisely within the range of
a generation the date of any document *on the basis of palaeography
alone.*' He warned that 'a new dogmatism' had arisen in the field
of palaeography, and that 'without any fixed point to serve as a
basis, we are already expected to accept as an historical criterion
a precise dating of these hitherto unknown Hebrew scripts'. He
even, in his exasperation at the complacency and intransigence of

the international team, had recourse to the unscholarly expedient of capital letters:

IT MUST BE STATED HERE ONCE AND FOR ALL THAT THE SO-CALLED PALAEOGRAPHICAL EVIDENCE IS WHOLLY INADMISSIBLE IN THIS DISCUSSION.[41]

11
The Essenes

The reader by now will be familiar with the conclusions of the consensus view of the international team and, as expressed through its journals, the Ecole Biblique, as well as with the processes by which those conclusions were reached. It is now time to return to the evidence and see whether any alternative conclusions are possible. In order to do so, certain basic questions must again be posed. Who, precisely, *were* the elusive and mysterious denizens of Qumran, who established their community, transcribed and deposited their sacred texts, then apparently vanished from the stage of history? Were they indeed Essenes? And if so, what exactly does that term mean?

The traditional images of the Essenes come down to us from Pliny, Philo and Josephus, who described them as a sect or sub-sect of 1st-century Judaism.[1] Pliny, as we have seen, depicted the Essenes as celibate hermits, residing, with 'only palm-trees for company', in an area that might be construed as Qumran.* Josephus, who is echoed by Philo, elaborates on this portrait. According to Josephus, the Essenes are celibate – although, he adds, almost as an afterthought, 'there is a second order of Essenes' who do marry.[2] The Essenes despise pleasure and wealth. They hold all possessions in common, and those who join their ranks must renounce private property. They elect their own leaders from amongst themselves. They are settled in every city of Palestine, as well as in isolated

---

*See p. 20.

communities, but, even in urban surroundings, keep themselves apart.

Josephus portrays the Essenes as something akin to a monastic order or an ancient mystery school. Postulants to their ranks are subjected to a three-year period of probation, the equivalent of a novitiate. Not until he has successfully undergone this apprenticeship is the candidate officially accepted. Full-fledged Essenes pray before dawn, then work for five hours, after which they don a clean loincloth and bathe – a ritual of purification performed daily. Thus purified, they assemble in a special 'common' room and partake of a simple communal meal. Contrary to later popular misconceptions, Josephus does not describe the Essenes as vegetarian. They are said to eat meat.

The Essenes, Josephus says, are well versed in the books of the Old Testament and the teachings of the prophets. They are themselves trained in the arts of divination, and can foretell the future by studying sacred texts in conjunction with certain rites of purification. In their doctrine, according to Josephus, the soul is immortal but trapped in the prison of the mortal and corruptible body. At death, the soul is set free and soars upwards, rejoicing. Josephus compares Essene teaching to that of 'the Greeks'. Elsewhere, he is more specific, likening it to the principles of the Pythagorean schools.[3]

Josephus mentions Essene adherence to the Law of Moses: 'What they reverence most after God is the Lawgiver, and blasphemy against him is a capital offence.'[4] On the whole, however, the Essenes are portrayed as pacifist, and on good terms with established authority. Indeed, they are said to enjoy the special favour of Herod, who 'continued to honour all the Essenes';[5] 'Herod had these Essenes in such honour and thought higher of them than their mortal nature required . . .'[6] But at one point, Josephus contradicts himself – or perhaps slips his guard. The Essenes, he says:

> despise danger and conquer pain by sheer will-power: death, if it comes with honour, they value more than life without end. Their spirit was tested to the utmost by the war with the Romans, who racked and twisted, burnt and broke them, subjecting them to

every torture yet invented in order to make them blaspheme the Lawgiver or eat some forbidden food.[7]

In this one reference, at variance with everything else Josephus says, his Essenes begin to sound suspiciously like the militant defenders of Masada, the Zealots or Sicarii.

With the exception of this one reference, Josephus' account was to shape popular images of the Essenes for most of the ensuing two thousand years. And when the *Aufklärung*, the so-called 'Enlightenment', began to encourage 'free-thinking' examination of Christian tradition, commentators began to make connections between that tradition and Josephus' Essenes. Thus, in 1770, no less a personage than Frederick the Great wrote definitively that 'Jesus was really an Essene; he was imbued with Essene ethics'.[8] Such apparently scandalous assertions proceeded to gain increasing currency during the latter half of the next century, and in 1863 Renan published his famous *Vie de Jésus*, in which he suggested that Christianity was 'an Essenism which has largely succeeded'.[9]

Towards the end of the 19th century, the revival of interest in esoteric thought consolidated the association of Christianity with the Essenes. Theosophy, through the teachings of H.P. Blavatsky, postulated Jesus as a magus or adept who embodied elements of both Essene and Gnostic tradition. One of Blavatsky's disciples, Anna Kingsford, developed a concept of 'esoteric Christianity'. This roped in alchemy as well and portrayed Jesus as a Gnostic thaumaturge who, prior to his public mission, had lived and studied with the Essenes. In 1889, such ideas were transplanted to the Continent through a book called *The Great Initiate*, by the French theosophist Edouard Schuré. The mystique surrounding the Essenes had by now begun to associate them with healing, to credit them with special medical training and to represent them as a Judaic equivalent of the Greek Therapeutae. Another influential work, *The Crucifixion by an Eye-Witness*, which appeared in German towards the end of the 19th century and in English around 1907, purported to be a genuine ancient text composed by an Essene scribe. Jesus was depicted as the son of Mary and an unnamed Essene teacher, whose fund of secret Essene medical knowledge enabled him not just to survive the Crucifixion, but also to appear to his disciples afterwards as if 'risen from the dead'. George Moore undoubtedly drew on this work when, in 1916, he published *The Brook Kerith* and scandalised Christian readers across the English-speaking world. Moore, too, portrayed Jesus as a protégé of Essene thought, who survives the Crucifixion and retires to an Essene community in the general vicinity of Qumran. Here, years later, he is visited by a fanatic named Paul, who, quite unknowingly, has come to promulgate a bizarre mythologised account of his career and, in the process, promote him to godhood.

The Essenes depicted in *The Brook Kerith* derive ultimately from the 'stereotyped' Essenes of Pliny, Josephus and Philo, imbued now with a mystical character which endeared them to esoteric-oriented writers of the late 19th and early 20th centuries. To the extent that educated readers knew anything of the Essenes at all, this was the prevailing image of them. And something of this image was retained even by more critical commentators, such as Robert Graves, who in other respects sought to demystify Christian origins.

When the Dead Sea Scrolls came to light, they seemed, on the surface at least, not to contain anything that conflicted with the prevailing image of the Essenes. It was only natural, therefore, that they should be associated with the established conceptions.

As early as 1947, when he first saw the Qumran texts, Professor Sukenik had suggested an Essene character for their authorship. Father de Vaux and his team also invoked the traditional image of the Essenes. As we have noted, de Vaux was quick to identify Qumran with the Essene settlement mentioned by Pliny. 'The community at Qumran', Professor Cross concurred, 'was an Essene settlement.'[10] It soon became regarded as an established and accepted *fact* that the Dead Sea Scrolls were essentially Essene in their authorship, and that the Essenes were of the familiar kind – pacifist, ascetic, celibate, divorced from public and particularly political issues.

The community at Qumran, the consensus view contends, built upon the much earlier remains of an abandoned Israelite fortress dating from the 6th century BC. The authors of the scrolls arrived at the site some time around 134 BC, and the major buildings were erected around 100 BC and thereafter – a chronology safely and uncontroversially pre-Christian. The community was said to have thrived until it was decimated by an earthquake, followed by a fire, in 31 BC. During the reign of Herod the Great (37–4 BC), Qumran was abandoned and deserted, and then, in the reign of Herod's successor, the ruins were reoccupied and rebuilding undertaken. According to the consensus, Qumran then flourished as a quietist, politically neutral and disengaged enclave until it was destroyed by the Romans in AD 68, during the war that also involved the sack of Jerusalem. After this the site was occupied by a Roman military garrison until the end of the 1st century. When Palestine rose in revolt again between AD 132 and 135, Qumran was inhabited by rebel 'squatters'.[11] It was a neat, conveniently formulated scenario which effectively defused the Dead Sea Scrolls of whatever explosive potential they might have. But the evidence seems to have been ignored when expediency and the stability of Christian theology so dictated.

There is a contradiction, quite apart from the geographical question, in de Vaux's assertion that the passage from Pliny, quoted here on page 20, refers to Qumran – a contradiction which pertains to the dating of the scrolls. Pliny is referring, in this passage, to the situation *after* the destruction of Jerusalem. The passage itself indicates that Engedi has likewise been destroyed – which it was. The Essene community, however, is described as still intact, and even taking in a 'throng of refugees'. Yet even de Vaux acknowledged that Qumran, like Jerusalem and Engedi, was destroyed during the revolt of AD 66–73. It would thus seem even more unlikely that Pliny's Essene community is in fact Qumran. What is more, Pliny's community, as he describes it, contains no women, yet there are women's graves among those at Qumran. It is still, of course, possible that the occupants of Qumran were Essenes, if not of Pliny's community, then of some other. If so, however, the Dead Sea Scrolls will themselves reveal how ill informed about the Essenes Pliny was.

The term 'Essene' is Greek. It occurs only in classical writers – Josephus, Philo and Pliny – and is written in Greek as 'Essenoi' or 'Essaioi'. Thus, if the inhabitants of Qumran were indeed Essenes, one would expect 'Essene' to be a Greek translation or transliteration of some original Hebrew or Aramaic word, by which the Qumran community referred to themselves.

Accounts of the Essenes by classical writers are not consistent with the life or thought of the community as revealed by either the external evidence of archaeology or the internal evidence of the texts themselves. Josephus, Philo and Pliny offer portraits of the Essenes which are often utterly irreconcilable with the testimony of Qumran's ruins and of the Dead Sea Scrolls. The evidence at Qumran, both internal and external, repeatedly contradicts their accounts. Some of these contradictions have been cited before, but it is worth reviewing the most important of them.

1. Josephus acknowledges that there is 'another order' of Essenes who do marry, but this, he indicates, is atypical.[12] In general, Josephus says, echoing Philo and Pliny, the Essenes are celibate. Yet the graves of women and children have been found among those excavated at Qumran. And the 'Community Rule' contains regulations governing marriage and the raising of children.

2. None of the classical writers ever mentions anything to suggest that the Essenes used a special form of calendar. The Qumran community, however, did – a unique, solar-based calendar, rather than the conventional Judaic calendar, which is lunar-based. If the Qumran community were indeed Essenes, surely so strikingly noticeable a characteristic would have been accorded some reference.

3. According to Philo, the Essenes differed from other forms of ancient Judaism in having no cult of animal sacrifices.[13] Yet the 'Temple Scroll' issues precise instructions for such sacrifices. And the ruins of Qumran revealed animal bones carefully placed in pots, or covered by pots, and buried in the ground under a thin covering of earth.[14] De Vaux speculated that these bones might be the remains of ritual meals. They might indeed. But they might equally be the remains of animal sacrifices, as stipulated by the 'Temple Scroll'.

4. The classical writers use the term 'Essene' to denote what they describe as a major sub-division of Judaism, along with

the Pharisees and Sadducees. Nowhere in the Dead Sea Scrolls, however, is the term 'Essene' found.

5. Josephus declares the Essenes to have been on congenial terms with Herod the Great, who, he says, 'had these Essenes in such honour and thought higher of them than their mortal nature required'.[15] Yet the Qumran literature indicates a militant hostility towards non-Judaic authorities in general, and towards Herod and his dynasty in particular. What is more, Qumran appears to have been abandoned and uninhabited for some years precisely because of persecution by Herod.

6. According to classical writers, the Essenes were pacifist. Philo specifically states that their numbers included no makers of weapons or armour.[16] Josephus emphatically distinguishes between the non-violent Essenes and the militantly messianic and nationalistic Zealots. Yet the ruins of Qumran include a defensive tower of a manifestly military nature, and what 'can only be described as a forge'.[17] As for the Qumran literature, it is often martial in the extreme, as exemplified by such texts as the 'War Scroll'. Indeed, the bellicose character of such texts would seem to have less in common with what Josephus says of the Essenes than with what he and others say of the so-called Zealots – which is precisely what Roth and Driver claimed the Qumran community to be, thereby incurring the fury of de Vaux and the international team.

The Qumran community wrote mostly not in Greek, but in Aramaic and Hebrew. So far as Aramaic and Hebrew are concerned, no accepted etymology for the origins of the term 'Essene' has hitherto been found. Even the classical writers were mystified by its derivation. Philo, for example, suggested that, in his opinion, the name stemmed from the Greek word for 'holy', '*oseeos*', and that the Essenes were therefore the '*Oseeotes*', or 'Holy Ones'.[18]

One theory has enjoyed a certain qualified currency among certain modern scholars, notably Geza Vermes of Oxford University. According to Vermes, the term 'Essene' derives from the Aramaic word '*assayya*', which means 'healers'.[19] This has fostered an image in some quarters of the Essenes as medical practitioners, a Judaic equivalent of the Alexandrian ascetics known as the 'Therapeutae'. But the word '*assayya*' does not occur anywhere in the corpus of Qumran literature; nor is there any reference to healing, to medical activities or to therapeutic work. To derive 'Essene' from '*assayya*', therefore, remains purely speculative; and there would be no reason to credit it at all unless there were no other options.

In fact, there *is* another option – not just a possibility, but a probability. If the Qumran community never refer to themselves as 'Essenes' or '*assayya*', they do employ a number of other Hebrew and Aramaic terms. From these terms, it is clear that the community did not have a single definitive name for themselves. They did, however, have a highly distinctive and unique concept of themselves, and this concept is reflected by a variety of appellations and designations.[20] The concept rests ultimately on the all-important 'Covenant', which entailed a formal oath of obedience, totally and eternally, to the Law of Moses. The authors of the Dead Sea Scrolls would thus refer to themselves as, for example, 'the Keepers of the Covenant'. As synonyms for 'Covenant' and 'Law', they would often use the same words that figure so prominently in Taoism – 'way', 'work' or 'works' ('*ma'asim*' in Hebrew). They would speak, for instance, of 'the Perfect of the Way', or 'the Way of Perfect Righteousness'[21] – 'way' meaning 'the work of the Law', or 'the way in which the Law functions', 'the way in which the Law works'. Variations of these themes run all through the Dead Sea Scrolls to denote the Qumran community and its members.

In the 'Habakkuk Commentary', Eisenman, continuing this line of thought, found one particularly important such variation – the '*Osei ha-Torah*', which translates as the 'Doers of the Law'.[22] This term would appear to be the source of the word 'Essene', for the collective form of '*Osei ha-Torah*' is '*Osim*', pronounced 'Oseem'. The Qumran community would thus have constituted, collectively, 'the *Osim*'. They seem, in fact, to have been known as such. An early Christian writer, Epiphanius, speaks of an allegedly 'heretical' Judaic sect which once occupied an area around the Dead Sea. This sect, he says, were called the 'Ossenes'.[23] It is fairly safe to conclude that the 'Essenes', the 'Ossenes' of Epiphanius and the '*Osim*' of the Qumran

28   Qumran, showing the marl terraces. The photograph was taken from
the ruins looking west towards the Judaean hills, with Cave 5 on the
extreme left and the two openings of Cave 4 just to the right. The original
entrance to Cave 4 can be seen above the right-hand opening.

29   The ruins of Qumran. Caves 4 and 5 can be seen at the end of the nearer eroded cliff-face.

30   The interior of Cave 4, Qumran, where the largest number of fragments were discovered in 1952. Fragments of up to 800 different scrolls were retrieved.

31   The Qumran ruins from the fortified tower. In the foreground are the remains of the circular weapons forge, to the left of which part of the water conduit has been exposed.

32   Remains of the main waterway
into the Qumran community.
The site had a complex water system
fed from seasonal water flowing in the
Wadi behind the ruins.

33   A cistern cut into the desert floor
on the rocky terraces near to the
Qumran ruins. Water control and
storage were vital to the survival of
such a community.

34   The water supply to Qumran depended upon this water tunnel carved through solid rock in the cliff-face. The water was dammed in the Wadi and directed through this tunnel.

35   The exit of the water tunnel. From here the water flowed down the waterway to the settlement itself.

36 Several of the 1,200 or so rock-covered graves slightly to the east of the ruins. Aligned north–south, contrary to normal Jewish practice, the graves appear to be unique to the Qumran-type of community. A small number of graves has been opened, and the remains of men, women and children found.

37　A dozen or so Qumran-type graves – aligned north–south – have been discovered some nine miles south of Qumran, at En el-Ghuweir. Clearly there was a settlement also on this site. The caves in the Wadi and cliffs behind may well have served as repositories for the same type of scrolls as were found near Qumran.

38　Ruins of a settlement at En el-Ghuweir near to the graves. The ruins have been dated to the Herodian period.

39   The pyramidal hill at Gamla in the Golan where the final citadel stood. Here, on 10 November 67 AD, 4,000 Zealots died fighting the Romans and another 5,000 killed themselves by jumping over the cliff. The Dead Sea Scrolls provide an insight into the rationale which lay behind these mass suicides.

40   The ruins of Masada where, on 15 April 75 AD, 960 Zealots – men, women and children – killed themselves rather than surrender to the Romans.

community were one and the same.

Thus the authors of the Dead Sea Scrolls may be thought of as 'Essenes', but not in the sense as defined and described by Josephus, Philo and Pliny. The accounts of the classical chroniclers prove to be altogether too circumscribed. They have also prevented many modern scholars from making the necessary connections – perhaps, in some cases, because it was not deemed desirable to do so. If the connections *are* made, a different and broader picture emerges – a picture in which such terms as 'Essene' and 'the Qumran community' will prove to be interchangeable with others. Eisenman effectively summarises the situation:

Unfortunately for the premises of modern scholarship, terms like: Ebionim, Nozrim, Hassidim, Zaddikim . . . turn out to be variations on the same theme. The inability to relate to changeable metaphor . . . has been a distinct failure in criticism.[24]

This, precisely, is what we are dealing with – changeable metaphors, a variety of different designations used to denote the same people or factions. Recognition of that point was urged as early as 1969 by an acknowledged expert in the field, Professor Matthew Black of St Andrews University, Scotland. The term 'Essene' was acceptable, Professor Black wrote:

provided we do not define Essenism too narrowly, for instance, by equating it exclusively with the Dead Sea group, but are prepared to understand the term as a general description of this widespread movement of anti-Jerusalem, anti-Pharisaic non-conformity of the period. It is from such an 'Essene-type' of Judaism that Christianity is descended.[25]

There is support for Professor Black's contention in the work of Epiphanius, the early Christian writer who spoke of the 'Ossenes'. Epiphanius states that the original 'Christians' in Judaea, generally called 'Nazoreans' (as in the Acts of the Apostles), were known as 'Jessaeans'. These 'Christians', or 'Jessaeans', would have conformed precisely to Professor Black's phraseology – a 'widespread movement of anti-Jerusalem, anti-Pharisaic non-conformity'. But there is an even more crucial connection.

Among the terms by which the Qumran community referred to themselves was 'Keepers of the Covenant', which appears in the original Hebrew as '*Nozrei ha-Brit*'. From this term derives the word '*Nozrim*', one of the earliest Hebrew designations for the sect subsequently known as 'Christians'.[26] The modern Arabic word for Christians, '*Nasrani*', derives from the same source. So, too, does the word 'Nazorean' or 'Nazarene', which, of course, was the name by which the 'early Christians' referred to themselves in both the Gospels and the Acts of the Apostles. Contrary to the assumptions of later tradition, it has nothing whatever to do with Jesus' alleged upbringing in Nazareth, which, the evidence (or lack of it) suggests, did not even exist at the time. Indeed, it seems to have been the very perplexity of early commentators encountering the unfamiliar term 'Nazorean' that led them to conclude Jesus' family came from Nazareth, which by then had appeared on the map.

To sum up, then, the 'Essenes' who figure in classical texts, the 'Ossenes' mentioned by Epiphanius, and the '*Osim*', the Qumran community, are one and the same. So, too, are the 'Jessaeans', as Epiphanius calls the 'early Christians'. So, too, are the '*Nozrei ha-Brit*', the '*Nozrim*', the '*Nasrani*' and the 'Nazoreans'. On the basis of this etymology, it becomes clear that we are indeed dealing with Professor Black's 'widespread movement', characterised, as Eisenman says, by shifting metaphor, a variety of slightly different designations used for the same people, shifting with time, translation and transliteration, just as 'Caesar' evolves into 'Kaiser' and 'Tsar'.

It would thus seem that the Qumran community was equivalent to the 'early Church' based in Jerusalem – the 'Nazoreans' who followed James, 'the Lord's brother'.[27] Indeed, the 'Habakkuk Commentary' states explicitly that Qumran's ruling body, the 'Council of the Community', was actually located at the time in Jerusalem.[28] And in Acts 9:2, the members of the 'early Church' are specifically referred to as 'followers of the Way' – a phrase identical with Qumran usage.

12
The Acts of the Apostles

Apart from the Gospels themselves, the most important book of the New Testament is the Acts of the Apostles. For the historian, in fact, Acts may be of even greater consequence. Like all historical documents issuing from a partisan source, it must, of course, be handled sceptically and with caution. One must also be cognisant of whom the text was written for, and whom it might have served, as well as what end. But it is Acts, much more than the Gospels, which has hitherto constituted the apparently definitive account of the first years of 'early Christianity'. Certainly Acts would appear to contain much basic information not readily to be found elsewhere. To that extent alone, it is a seminal text.

The Gospels, it is generally acknowledged, are unreliable as historical documents. Mark's, the first of them, was composed no earlier than the revolt of AD 66, and probably somewhat later. All four Gospels seek to evoke a period long predating their own composition – perhaps by as much as sixty or seventy years. They skim cursorily over the historical backdrop, focusing essentially on the heavily mythologised figure of Jesus and on his teachings. They are ultimately poetic and devotional texts, and do not even purport to be chronicles.

Acts is a work of a very different order. It cannot, of course, be taken as absolutely historical. It is, for one thing, heavily biased. Luke, the author of the text, was clearly drawing on a number of

175

different sources, editing and reworking material to suit his own purposes. There has been little attempt to unify either doctrinal statements or literary style. Even Church historians admit that the chronology is confused, the author having had no direct experience of many of the events he describes and being obliged to impose his own order upon them. Thus certain separate events are fused into a single occurrence, while single occurrences are made to appear to be separate events. Such problems are particularly acute in those portions of the text pertaining to events that predate the advent of Paul. Further, it would appear that Acts, like the Gospels, was compiled selectively, and was extensively tampered with by later editors.

Nevertheless, Acts, unlike the Gospels, aspires to be a form of chronicle over a continuous and extended period of time. Unlike the Gospels, it constitutes an attempt to preserve an historical record, and, at least in certain passages, to have been written by someone with a first-, or second-, hand experience of the events it describes. Although there is bias, the bias is a highly personal one; and this, to some extent, enables the modern commentator to read between the lines.

The narrative recounted in Acts begins shortly after the Crucifixion – generally dated at AD 30 but possibly as late as AD 36 – and ends somewhere between AD 64 and 67. Most scholars believe the narrative itself was composed, or transcribed, some time between AD 70 and 95. Roughly speaking, then, Acts is contemporary with some, if not all, of the Gospels. It may predate all four. It almost certainly predates the so-called Gospel of John, at least in the form that that text has come down to us.

The author of Acts is a well-educated Greek who identifies himself as Luke. Whether he is the same as 'Luke the beloved physician', mentioned as Paul's close friend in Colossians 4:14, cannot be definitively established, though most New Testament scholars are prepared to accept that he is. Modern scholars also concur that he would seem, quite clearly, to be identical with the author of Luke's Gospel. Indeed, Acts is sometimes regarded as the 'second half' of Luke's Gospel. Both are addressed to an unknown recipient named 'Theophilus'. Because both were written in Greek, many words and names have been translated into that language, and have probably, in a number of instances, altered in nuance, even in meaning, from their Hebrew or Aramaic originals. In any case, both Acts and Luke's Gospel were written specifically for a Greek audience – a very different audience from that addressed by the Qumran scrolls.

Although focusing primarily on Paul, who monopolises the latter part of its narrative, Acts also tells the story of Paul's relations with the community in Jerusalem composed of Jesus' immediate disciples under the leadership of James, 'the Lord's brother' – the enclave or faction who only later came to be called the first Christians and are now regarded as the early or original Church. In recounting Paul's association with this community, however, Acts offers only Paul's point of view. Acts is essentially a document of Pauline – or what is now deemed to be 'normative' – Christianity. Paul, in other words, is always the 'hero'; whoever opposes him, whether it be the authorities or even James, is automatically cast as villain.

Acts opens shortly after Jesus – referred to as 'the Nazorene' (in Greek '*Nazoraion*') – has disappeared from the scene. The narrative then proceeds to describe the organisation and development of the community or 'early Church' in Jerusalem and its increasing friction with the authorities. The community is vividly evoked in Acts 2:44–6: 'The faithful all lived together and owned everything in common; they sold their goods and possessions and shared out the proceeds among themselves according to what each one needed. They went as a body to the Temple every day but met in their houses for the breaking of bread . . .' (It is worth noting in passing this adherence to the Temple. Jesus and his immediate followers are usually portrayed as hostile to the Temple, where, according to the Gospels, Jesus upset the tables of the moneychangers and incurred the passionate displeasure of the priesthood.)

Acts 6:8 introduces the figure known as Stephen, the first official 'Christian martyr', who is arrested and sentenced to death by stoning. In his own defence, Stephen alludes to the murder of those who prophesied the advent of the 'Righteous One', or the 'Just One'. This terminology is specifically and uniquely Qumranic in character. The 'Righteous One' occurs repeatedly in the Dead Sea Scrolls as

177

'*Zaddik*'.[1] The 'Teacher of Righteousness' in the scrolls, '*Moreh ha-Zedek*', derives from the same root. And when the historian Josephus speaks of a teacher, apparently named 'Sadduc' or 'Zadok', as the leader of a messianic and anti-Roman Judaic following, this too would seem to be a faulty Greek rendering of the 'Righteous One'.[2] As portrayed in Acts, then, Stephen uses nomenclature unique and specifically characteristic of Qumran.

Nor is this the only Qumranic concern to figure in Stephen's speech. In his defence, he names his persecutors (Acts 7:53) – 'You who had the Law brought to you by angels are the very ones who have not kept it.' As Acts portrays it, Stephen is obviously intent on adherence to the Law. Again, there is a conflict here with orthodox and accepted traditions. According to later Christian tradition, it was the Jews of the time who made an austere and puritanical fetish of the Law. The 'early Christians' are depicted, at least from the standpoint of that stringency, as 'mavericks' or 'renegades', advocating a new freedom and flexibility, defying custom and convention. Yet it is Stephen, the first 'Christian martyr', who emerges as an advocate of the Law, while his persecutors are accused of dereliction.

It makes no sense for Stephen, a self-proclaimed adherent of the Law, to be murdered by fellow Jews extolling the same Law. But what if those fellow Jews were acting on behalf of a priesthood which had come to an accommodation with the Roman authorities – were, in effect, collaborators who, like many of the French under the German occupation, for example, simply wanted 'a quiet life' and feared an agitator or resistance fighter in their midst might lead to reprisals?[3] The 'early Church' of which Stephen is a member constantly stresses its own orthodoxy, its zealous adherence to the Law. Its persecutors are those who contrive to remain in good odour with Rome and, in so doing, lapse from the Law, or, in Qumran terms, transgress the Law, betray the Law.[4] In this context, Stephen's denunciation of them makes sense, as does their murder of him. And as we shall see, James – James 'the Just', the '*Zaddik*' or 'Righteous One', the 'brother of the Lord' who best exemplifies rigorous adherence to the Law – will subsequently, according to later tradition, suffer precisely the same fate as Stephen.

According to Acts, it is at the death of Stephen that Paul – then called Saul of Tarsus – makes his début. He is said to have stood watch over the discarded clothes of Stephen's murderers, though he may well have taken a more active role. In Acts 8:1, we are told that Saul 'entirely approved of the killing' of Stephen. And later, in Acts 9:21, Saul is accused of engineering precisely the kind of attack on the 'early Church' which culminated in Stephen's death. Certainly Saul, at this stage of his life, is fervent, even fanatic, in his enmity towards the 'early Church'. According to Acts 8:3, he 'worked for the total destruction of the Church: he went from house to house arresting both men and women and sending them to prison'. At the time, of course, he is acting as a minion of the pro-Roman priesthood.

Acts 9 tells us of Saul's conversion. Shortly after Stephen's death, he embarks for Damascus to ferret out members of the 'early Church' there. He is accompanied by his hit-squad and bears arrest warrants from his master, the high priest. As we have noted, this expedition is likely to have been not to Syria, but to the Damascus that figures in the 'Damascus Document'.[5]

En route to his destination, Saul undergoes some sort of traumatic experience, which commentators have interpreted as anything from sunstroke, to an epileptic seizure, to a mystical revelation (Acts 9:1–19; 22:6–16). A 'light from heaven' purportedly knocks him from his horse and 'a voice', issuing from no perceptible source, demands of him: 'Saul, Saul, why are you persecuting me?' Saul asks the voice to identify itself. 'I am Jesus, the Nazorene,' the voice replies, 'and you are persecuting me.' The voice further instructs him to proceed to Damascus, where he will learn what he must subsequently do. When this visitation passes and Saul regains a semblance of his former consciousness, he finds he has been stricken temporarily blind. In Damascus, his sight will be restored by a member of the 'early Church' and he will allow himself to be baptised.

A modern psychologist would find nothing particularly unusual in Saul's adventure. It may indeed have been produced by sunstroke or an epileptic seizure. It could equally well be ascribed to hallucination, hysterical or psychotic reaction or perhaps nothing more than the guilty conscience of a susceptible man with blood on his hands.

Saul, however, interprets it as a true manifestation of Jesus, whom he never knew personally; and from this his conversion ensues. He abandons his former name in favour of 'Paul'. And he will subsequently be as fervent in promulgating the teachings of the 'early Church' as he has hitherto been in extirpating them. He joins their community, becomes one of their apprentices or disciples. According to his letter to the Galatians (Gal. 1:17–18), he remains under their tutelage for three years, spending much of that time in Damascus. According to the Dead Sea Scrolls, the probation and training period for a newcomer to the Qumran community was also three years.[6]

After his three-year apprenticeship, Paul returns to Jerusalem to join the leaders of the 'community' there. Not surprisingly, most of them are suspicious of him, not being wholly convinced by his conversion. In Galatians 1:18–20, he speaks of seeing only James and Cephas. Everyone else, including the apostles, seems to have avoided him. He is obliged repeatedly to prove himself, and only then does he find some allies and begin to preach. Arguments ensue, however, and, according to Acts 9:29, certain members of the Jerusalem community threaten him. As a means of defusing a potentially ugly situation, his allies pack him off to Tarsus, the town (now in Turkey) where he was born. He is, in effect, being sent home, to spread the message there.

It is important to understand that this was tantamount to exile. The community in Jerusalem, like that in Qumran, was preoccupied almost entirely with events in Palestine. The wider world, such as Rome, was relevant only to the extent that it impinged or encroached on their more localised reality. To send Paul off to Tarsus, therefore, might be compared to a Provisional IRA godfather sending a new, ill-disciplined and overly energetic recruit to muster support among the 'Shining Path' guerrillas of Peru. If, by improbable fluke, he somehow elicits men, money, matériel or anything else of value, well and good. If he gets himself disembowelled instead, he will not be unduly missed, having been more nuisance than asset anyway.

Thus arises the first of Paul's three (according to Acts) sorties abroad. Among other places, it takes him to Antioch, and, as we learn from Acts 11:26, 'It was at Antioch that the disciples were first called "Christians".' Commentators date Paul's journey to Antioch at approximately AD 43. By that time, a community of the 'early Church' was already established there, which reported back to the sect's leadership in Jerusalem under James.

Some five or more years later, Paul is teaching in Antioch when a dispute arises over the content of his missionary work. As Acts 15 explains, certain representatives of the leadership in Jerusalem arrive in Antioch, perhaps, Eisenman suggests, with the specific purpose of checking on Paul's activities.[7] They stress the importance of strict adherence to the Law and accuse Paul of laxity. He and his companion, Barnabas, are summarily ordered back to Jerusalem for personal consultation with the leadership. From this point on, a schism will open and widen between Paul and James; and the author of Acts, so far as the dispute is concerned, becomes Paul's apologist.

In all the vicissitudes that follow, it must be emphasised that Paul is, in effect, the first 'Christian' heretic, and that his teachings – which become the foundation of later Christianity – are a flagrant deviation from the 'original' or 'pure' form extolled by the leadership. Whether James, 'the Lord's brother', was literally Jesus' blood kin or not (and everything suggests he was), it is clear that he knew Jesus, or the figure subsequently remembered as Jesus, personally. So did most of the other members of the community, or 'early Church', in Jerusalem – including, of course, Peter. When they spoke, they did so with first-hand authority. Paul had never had such personal acquaintance with the figure he'd begun to regard as his 'Saviour'. He had only his quasi-mystical experience in the desert and the sound of a disembodied voice. For him to arrogate authority to himself on this basis is, to say the least, presumptuous. It also leads him to distort Jesus' teachings beyond all recognition – to formulate, in fact, his own highly individual and idiosyncratic theology, and then to legitimise it by spuriously ascribing it to Jesus. For Jesus, adhering rigorously to Judaic Law, it would have been the most extreme blasphemy to advocate worship of any mortal figure, including himself. He makes this clear in the Gospels, urging his disciples, followers and listeners to acknowledge only God. In John 10:33–5, for example, Jesus is accused of the blasphemy of claiming

181

to be God. He replies, citing Psalm 82, 'Is it not written in your Law, I [meaning God in the psalm] said, you are Gods? So the Law uses the word gods of those to whom the word of God was addressed.'

Paul, in effect, shunts God aside and establishes, for the first time, worship of Jesus – Jesus as a kind of equivalent of Adonis, of Tammuz, of Attis, or of any one of the other dying and reviving gods who populated the Middle East at the time. In order to compete with these divine rivals, Jesus had to match them point for point, miracle for miracle. It is at this stage that many of the miraculous elements become associated with Jesus' biography, including, in all probability, his supposed birth of a virgin and his resurrection from the dead. They are essentially Pauline inventions, often wildly at odds with the 'pure' doctrine promulgated by James and the rest of the community in Jerusalem. It is hardly surprising, therefore, that James and his entourage should be disturbed by what Paul is doing.

Yet Paul knows full well what he is doing. He understands, with a surprisingly modern sophistication, the techniques of religious propaganda;[8] he understands what is necessary to turn a man into a god, and he goes about it more astutely than the Romans did with their emperors. As he himself pointedly acknowledges, he does not pretend to be purveying the historical Jesus, the individual whom James and Peter and Simeon knew personally. On the contrary, he acknowledges, in 2 Corinthians 11:3–4, that the community in Jerusalem are promulgating '*another Jesus*'. Their representatives, he says, call themselves 'servants of righteousness' – a characteristic Qumranic usage. They are now, to all intents and purposes, Paul's adversaries.

In accordance with instructions issued to him, Paul returns from Antioch to Jerusalem – around AD 48–9, it is generally believed – and meets with the community's leadership. Not surprisingly, another dispute ensues. If Acts is to be believed, James, for the sake of peace, agrees to compromise, thereby making it easier for 'pagans' to join the congregation. Somewhat improbably, he consents to relax certain aspects of the Law, while remaining adamant on others.

Paul pays lip service to the leadership. He still, at this point, needs their endorsement – not to legitimise his teachings, but to legitimise, and ensure the survival of, the communities he has founded abroad. He is already, however, bent on going his own way. He embarks on another mission of travel and preaching, punctuated (Acts 18:21) by another visit to Jerusalem. Most of his letters date from this period, between AD 50 and 58. It is clear from his letters that he has, by that time, become almost completely estranged from the leadership in Jerusalem and from their adherence to the Law.[9] In his missive to the Galatians (*c.* AD 57), he alludes scathingly to 'these people who are acknowledged leaders – not that their importance matters to me' (Gal. 2:6). His theological position has also deviated irreparably from those who adhere rigorously to the Law. In the same letter to the Galatians (2:16), he states that 'faith in Christ rather than fidelity to the Law is what justifies us, and . . . no one can be justified by keeping the Law'. Writing to the Philippians (3:9), he states: 'I am no longer trying for perfection by my own efforts, the perfection that comes from the Law . . .' These are the provocative and challenging statements of a self-proclaimed renegade. 'Christianity', as it will subsequently evolve from Paul, has by now severed virtually all connection with its roots, and can no longer be said to have anything to do with Jesus, only with Paul's image of Jesus.

By AD 58, Paul is again back in Jerusalem – despite pleas from his supporters who, obviously fearing trouble with the hierarchy, have begged him not to go. Again, he meets with James and the leadership of the Jerusalem community. Employing the now familiar Qumranic formulation, they express the worry they share with other 'zealots of the Law' – that Paul, in his preaching to Jews living abroad, is encouraging them to forsake the Law of Moses.[10] It is, of course, a justified accusation, as Paul has made clear in his letters. Acts does not record his response to it. The impression conveyed is that he lies, perjures himself and denies the charges against him. When asked to purify himself for seven days – thereby demonstrating the unjustness of the allegations and his continued adherence to the Law – he readily consents to do so.

A few days later, however, he again runs foul of those 'zealous for the Law', who are rather less temperate than James. On being seen at the Temple, he is attacked by a crowd of the pious. 'This', they claim in their anger, 'is the man who preaches to everyone everywhere . . . against the Law' (Acts 21:28ff.). A riot ensues, and Paul is dragged out of the Temple, his life in danger. In the nick of time, he is rescued by a Roman officer who, having been told of the disturbance, appears with an entourage of soldiers. Paul is arrested and put in chains – on the initial assumption, apparently, that he is a leader of the Sicarii, the Zealot terrorist cadre.

At this point, the narrative becomes increasingly confused, and one can only suspect that parts of it have been altered or expurgated. According to the existing text, Paul, before the Romans can trundle him off, protests that he is a Jew of Tarsus and asks permission to address the crowd who had just been trying to lynch him. Weirdly enough, the Romans allow him to do so. Paul then expatiates on his Pharisaic training under Gamaliel (a famous teacher of the time), on his initial hostility towards the 'early Church', on his role in the death of Stephen, on his subsequent conversion. All of this – or perhaps only a part of it, though one cannot be certain which part – provokes the crowd to new ire. 'Rid the earth of this man!' they cry. 'He is not fit to live!' (Acts 22:22)

Ignoring these appeals, the Romans carry Paul off to 'the fortress' – presumably the Antonia fortress, the Roman military and administrative headquarters. Here, they intend to interrogate him under torture. Interrogate him for what? To determine why he provokes such hostility, according to Acts. Yet Paul has already made his position clear in public – unless there are elements of his speech that, in a fashion not made clear by the text, the Romans deemed dangerous or subversive. In any case, torture, by Roman law, could not be exercised on any individual possessing full and official Roman citizenship – which Paul, having been born of a wealthy family in Tarsus, conveniently does. Invoking this immunity, he escapes torture, but remains incarcerated.

In the meantime, a group of angry Jews, forty or more in number, meet in secret. They vow not to eat or drink until they have brought about Paul's death. The sheer intensity and ferocity of this antipathy is worth noting. One does not expect such animosity – not to say such a preparedness for violence – from 'ordinary' Pharisees and Sadducees. Those who display it are obviously 'zealous for the Law'. But the only such passionate adherents of the Law in Palestine at the time were those whose sacred texts came subsequently to light at Qumran. Thus, for example, Eisenman calls attention to a pivotal passage in the 'Damascus Document' which declares of a man that 'if he transgresses after swearing to return to the Law of Moses with a whole heart and soul, then retribution shall be exacted from him'.[11]

How can the violent action contemplated against Paul be reconciled with the later popular image, put forward by the consensus, of placid, ascetic, quietist Essenes? The clandestine conclave, the fervent vow to eradicate Paul – these are more characteristic of the militant Zealots and their special assassination units, the dreaded Sicarii. Here again there is an insistent suggestion that the Zealots on the one hand, and the 'zealous for the Law' at Qumran on the other, were one and the same.

Whoever they are, the would-be assassins, according to Acts, are thwarted by the sudden and opportune appearance of Paul's hitherto unmentioned nephew, who somehow learns of their plot. This relative, of whom we know nothing more, informs both Paul *and* the Romans. That night, Paul is removed, for his own safety, from Jerusalem. He is removed with an escort of 470 troops – 200 infantry under the command of two centurions, 200 spearmen and 70 cavalry![12] He is taken to Caesarea, the Roman capital of Judaea, where he appears before the governor and Rome's puppet king, Agrippa. As a Roman citizen, however, Paul has a right to have his case heard in Rome, and he invokes this right. As a result, he is sent to Rome, ostensibly for trial. There is no indication of what he will be tried for.

After recounting his adventures on the journey – including a shipwreck – Acts ends. Or, rather, it breaks off, as if the author were interrupted in his work, or as if someone had removed the original ending and inserted a perfunctory finale instead. There are, of course, numerous later traditions – that Paul was imprisoned, that he obtained a personal audience with the emperor, that he was freed and went to Spain, that Nero ordered his execution, that he encountered Peter in Rome (or in prison in Rome), that he and Peter were executed together. But neither in Acts nor in any other reliable document is there a basis for any of these stories. Perhaps the original ending of Acts was indeed excised or altered. Perhaps Luke, the author, simply did not know 'what happened next' and, not being concerned with aesthetic symmetry, simply allowed himself to conclude lamely. Or perhaps, as Eisenman has suggested – and this possibility will be considered later – Luke did know, but deliberately cut short his narrative (or was cut short by later editors) in order to conceal his knowledge.

The last sections of Acts – from the riot inspired in the Temple on – are muddled, confused and riddled with unanswered questions. Elsewhere, however, Acts is ostensibly simple enough. On one level, there is the narrative of Paul's conversion and subsequent adventures. But behind this account looms a chronicle of increasing friction between two factions within the original community in Jerusalem, the 'early Church'. One of these factions consists of 'hardliners', who echo the teachings of Qumranic texts and insist on rigorous observance of the Law. The other, exemplified by Paul and his immediate supporters, want to relax the Law and, by making it easier for people to join the congregation, to increase the number of new recruits. The 'hardliners' are less concerned with numbers than with doctrinal purity, and seem to have only a cursory interest in events or developments outside Palestine; nor do they display any desire for an accommodation with Rome. Paul, on the other hand, is prepared to dispense with doctrinal purity. His primary objective is to disseminate his message as widely as possible and to assemble the largest possible body of adherents. In order to attain this objective, he goes out of his way to avoid antagonising the authorities and is perfectly willing to come to an accommodation with Rome, even to curry favour.

The 'early Church', then, as it appears in Acts, is rent by incipient schism, the instigator of which is Paul. Paul's chief adversary is the enigmatic figure of James, 'the Lord's brother'. It is clear that James is the acknowledged leader of the community in Jerusalem that becomes known to later tradition as the 'early Church'.[13] For the most part, James comes across as a 'hardliner', though he does – if Acts is to be believed – display a willingness to compromise on certain points. All the evidence suggests, however, that even this modest flexibility reflects some licence on the part of the author of Acts. James could not, obviously, have been excised from the narrative – his role, presumably, would have been too well-known. In consequence, he could only be played down somewhat, and portrayed as a conciliatory figure – a figure occupying a position somewhere between Paul and the extreme 'hardliners'.

In any case, the 'sub-text' of Acts reduces itself to a clash between two powerful personalities, James and Paul. Eisenman has demonstrated that James emerges as the custodian of the original body of teachings, the exponent of doctrinal purity and rigorous adherence to the Law. The last thing he would have had in mind was founding a 'new religion'. Paul is doing precisely that. Paul's Jesus is a full-fledged god, whose biography, miracle for miracle, comes to match those of the rival deities with whom he is competing for devotees – one sells gods, after all, on the same marketing principles that obtain for soap or pet food. By James's standards – indeed, by the standards of any devout Jew – this, of course, is blasphemy and apostasy. Given the passions roused by such issues, the rift between James and Paul would hardly have been confined, as Acts suggests it was, to the level of civilised debate. It would have generated the kind of murderous hostility that surfaces at the end of the narrative.

In the conflict between James and Paul, the emergence and evolution of what we call Christianity stood at a crossroads. Had the mainstream of its development conformed to James's teachings, there would have been no Christianity at all, only a particular species of Judaism which might or might not have emerged as dominant. As things transpired, however, the mainstream of the new movement gradually coalesced, during the next three centuries, around Paul and his teachings. Thus, to the undoubted posthumous horror of James and his associates, an entirely new religion was indeed born – a religion which came to have less and less to do with its supposed founder.

13
James 'The Righteous'

I f James played so important a role in the events of the time, why do we know so little about him? Why has he been relegated to the status of a shadowy figure in the background? Those questions can be answered simply enough. Eisenman stresses that James, whether he was literally Jesus' brother or not, had known Jesus personally in a way that Paul never did. In his teachings, he was certainly closer to 'the source' than Paul ever was. And his objectives and preoccupations were often at variance with Paul's – were sometimes, indeed, diametrically opposed. For Paul, then, James would have been a constant irritant. With the triumph of Pauline Christianity, therefore, James's significance, if it couldn't be obliterated completely, had, at the very least, to be diminished.

Unlike a number of personalities in the New Testament, James does seem to have been an historical personage, and, moreover, one who played a more prominent role in the affairs of his time than is generally recognised. There is, in fact, a reasonably copious body of literature pertaining to James, even though most of it lies outside the canonical compilation of the New Testament.

In the New Testament itself, James is mentioned in the Gospels as one of Jesus' brothers, though the context is generally vague or confusing and has obviously been tampered with. In Acts, as we have discussed, he assumes rather more prominence, though it is not until the second part of Acts that he emerges in any kind of perspective. Then, with Paul's letter to the Galatians, he is clearly identified as the leader of the 'early Church', who resides in Jerusalem and is attended by a council of elders.[1] Apart from those that impinge on Paul, however, one learns little of his activities, and even less about his personality and biography. Neither is the Letter of James in the New Testament of much value in this respect. The letter may indeed derive from a text by James, and Eisenman has drawn attention to its Qumranic style, language and imagery.[2] It contains (James 5:6) an accusation whose significance will become apparent shortly – an accusation to the effect that 'you murdered the righteous [or just] man'.[3] Again, however, no personal information is vouchsafed.

Such is James's role in scripture proper. But if one looks further afield, a portrait of James does begin to emerge. This is the research which Eisenman has been pursuing over the last few years. One source of information he has emphasised is an anonymous text of the 'early Church', the so-called 'Recognitions of Clement', which surfaced very early in the 3rd century. According to this document, James is preaching in the Temple when an unnamed 'enemy', accompanied by an entourage of followers, bursts in. The 'enemy' taunts James's listeners and drowns out his words with noise, then proceeds to inflame the crowd 'with revilings and abuse, and, like a madman, to excite everyone to murder, saying "What do ye? Why do ye hesitate? Oh, sluggish and inert, why do we not lay hands upon them, and pull all these fellows to pieces?" '[4] The 'enemy' does not confine himself to a verbal assault. Seizing a brand of wood, he begins to flail about with it at the assembled worshippers, and his entourage follow suit. A full-scale riot ensues:

> Much blood is shed; there is a confused flight, in the midst of which that enemy attacked James, and threw him headlong from the top of the steps; and supposing him to be dead, he cared not to inflict further violence upon him.[5]

James, however, is not dead. According to the 'Recognitions', his supporters carry him back to his house in Jerusalem. The next morning, before dawn, the injured man and his supporters flee the city, making their way to Jericho, where they remain for some time – presumably while James convalesces.[6]

For Eisenman, this attack on James is pivotal. He notes the

parallels between it and the attack on Stephen as recounted in Acts. He suggests that Stephen may be an invented figure, to disguise the fact that the attack – as Acts could not possibly have admitted – was really directed at James. And he points out that Jericho, where James flees for refuge, is only a few miles from Qumran. What is more, he argues, the flight to Jericho has a ring of historical truth to it. It is the kind of incidental detail that is unlikely to have been fabricated and interpolated, because it serves no particular purpose. As for the 'enemy', there would seem to be little doubt about his identity. The 'Recognitions of Clement' concludes:

> Then after three days one of the brethren came to us from Gamaliel . . . bringing us secret tidings that the enemy had received a commission from Caiaphas, the chief priest, that he should arrest all who believed in Jesus, and should go to Damascus with his letters . . .[7]

The surviving editions of Josephus' *Antiquities of the Jews* contain only one reference to James, which may or may not be later interpolation. The chronicle reports that the Sanhedrin, the religious high court, call before them James, 'the brother of Jesus who was called Christ'.[8] Accused (most improbably) of breaking the Law, James and certain of his companions are found guilty and accordingly stoned to death. Whether this account is accurate, doctored or wholly invented, the most important aspect of it is the date to which it refers. Josephus indicates that the events he has described occurred during an interval *between* Roman procurators in Judaea. The incumbent procurator had just died. His successor, Lucceius Albinus, was still *en route* to Palestine from Rome. During the interregnum, effective power in Jerusalem was wielded by the high priest, an unpopular man named Ananas. This allows the account of James's death to be dated at around AD 62 – only four years before the outbreak of the revolt in AD 66. Here, then, is at least some chronological evidence that James's death may have had something to do with the war that ravaged the Holy Land between AD 66 and 73. For further information, however, one must turn to later Church historians.

Perhaps the major source is Eusebius, 4th-century Bishop of

Caesarea (the Roman capital of Judaea) and author of one of the most important early Church histories. In accordance with the conventions of the time, Eusebius quotes at length from earlier writers, many of whose works have not survived. In speaking of James, he cites Clement, Bishop of Alexandria (*c.* AD 150–215). Clement refers to James, we are told, as 'the Righteous', or, as it is often translated, 'the Just' – '*Zaddik*' in Hebrew.[9] This, of course, is the by now familiar Qumranic usage, whence derives the 'Teacher of Righteousness', the leader of the Qumran community. According to Clement, Eusebius reports, James was thrown from a parapet of the Temple, then beaten to death with a club.[10]

Later in his chronicle, Eusebius quotes extensively from a 2nd-century Church historian, Hegesippus. All of Hegesippus' works were reputedly extant as late as the 16th or 17th century. Everything has since disappeared, though copies may well exist in the Vatican, as well as in the library of one or another monastery – in Spain, for example.[11] At present, however, almost everything we have by Hegesippus is contained in the excerpts from his work cited by Eusebius.

Quoting Hegesippus, Eusebius states that James 'the Righteous' 'was holy from his birth':

> he drank no wine . . . ate no animal food; no razor came near his head; he did not smear himself with oil, and took no baths. He alone was permitted to enter the Holy Place [the Holy of Holies in the Temple], for his garments were not of wool but of linen [i.e. priestly robes]. He used to enter the Sanctuary alone, and was often found on his knees beseeching forgiveness for the people, so that his knees grew hard like a camel's . . . Because of his unsurpassable righteousness, he was called the Righteous and . . . 'Bulwark of the people' . . .[12]

At this point, it is worth interrupting the text to note certain intriguing details. James is said to wear linen, or priestly robes. This was the prerogative of those who served in the Temple and belonged to one of the priestly families, traditionally the Sadducean 'aristocracy' who, during the 1st century, came to an accommodation with Rome and the Herodian dynasty of Roman puppets. Again, Eisenman points

191

out, Epiphanius, another Church historian, speaks of James wearing
the mitre of the high priest.[13] Then, too, only the high priest was
allowed to enter the Holy of Holies, the inner sanctum and most
sacred spot in the Temple. What, then, can James be doing there –
and without eliciting any explanation or expression of surprise from
Church historians, who seem to find nothing untoward or irregular
in his activities? Did he, perhaps, by virtue of his birth, have some
legitimate right to wear priestly apparel and enter the Holy of
Holies? Or might he have been acting, as Eisenman suggests, in the
capacity of a kind of 'opposition high priest' – a rebel who, defying
the established priesthood's accommodation with Rome, had taken
upon himself the role they had betrayed?[14] Certainly the established
priesthood had no affection for James. According to Hegesippus,
the 'Scribes and Pharisees' decide to do away with him, so that the
people 'will be frightened and not believe him'. They proclaim that
'even the Righteous one has gone astray',[15] and invoke a quote from
the Old Testament – in this case from the prophet Isaiah (Isa. 3:10)
– to justify their actions. They note that Isaiah had prophesied the
death of the 'Righteous One'. In murdering James, therefore, they
will simply be bringing Isaiah's prophecy to fulfilment. But also,
in using this quote from Isaiah, they are following a technique
employed in both the Dead Sea Scrolls and the New Testament.
Eisenman points out that, just as this quote is used in order to
describe the death of James, so the Qumran community employs
similar 'Righteousness' passages from the New Testament in order
to describe the death of the 'Teacher of Righteousness'.[16] Eusebius
goes on to describe the death of James in the following manner:

> So they went up and threw down the Righteous one. They said
> to each other 'let us stone James the Righteous', and began to stone
> him, as in spite of his fall he was still alive . . . While they pelted
> him with stones . . . [a member of a particular priestly family]
> called out: 'Stop! What are you doing . . .' Then one of them, a
> fuller, took the club which he used to beat clothes, and brought it
> down on the head of the Righteous one. Such was his martyrdom
> . . . Immediately after this Vespasian began to besiege them.[17]

Vespasian, who became emperor in AD 69, commanded the

Roman army that invaded Judaea to put down the revolt of AD 66. Here again, then, is a chronological connection between James's death and the revolt. But Eusebius goes further. The connection for him is more than just chronological. The entire 'siege of Jerusalem', he says, meaning presumably the whole of the revolt in Judaea, was a direct consequence of James's death – 'for no other reason than the wicked crime of which he had been the victim'.[18]

To support this startling contention, Eusebius invokes Josephus. The passage of Josephus he quotes, although no longer to be found in any extant version of Josephus, was unquestionably what Josephus wrote, because Origen, one of the earliest and most prolific of the Church Fathers, quotes precisely the same passage. Referring to the revolt of AD 66 and the Roman invasion that followed, Josephus states that 'these things happened to the Jews in requital for James the Righteous, who was a brother of Jesus known as Christ, for though he was the most righteous of men, the Jews put him to death'.[19]

From these fragments pertaining to James, a scenario begins to take form. James, the acknowledged leader of the 'early Church' in Jerusalem, represents a faction of Jews who, like the Qumran community, are 'zealous for the Law'. This faction is understandably hostile towards the Sadducee priesthood and the high priest Ananas (appointed by Herod[20]), who have betrayed their nation and their religion by concluding an accord with the Roman administration and its Herodian puppet-kings. So intense is this hostility that James arrogates to himself the priestly functions which Ananas has compromised.[21] Ananas' supporters respond by contriving James's death. Almost immediately thereafter, the whole of Judaea rises in revolt, and Ananas is himself one of the first casualties, assassinated as a pro-Roman collaborator. As the rebellion gains momentum, Rome is forced to react, and does so by dispatching an expeditionary force under Vespasian. The result is the war which witnesses the sack of Jerusalem and the destruction of the Temple in AD 68, and which does not end until the fall of Masada in AD 73.

The only uncertain element in this scenario is the nature and magnitude of the part played by James's death. Did it merely coincide chronologically? Or was it, as Josephus and Eusebius assert, the primary causal factor? The truth, almost certainly, lies somewhere in between: the revolt stemmed from enough contributing factors for the historian not to have had to fall back on James's death as a sole explanation. On the other hand, the evidence unquestionably indicates that James's death was not just a marginal incident. It would seem to have had at least something to do with the course of public events.

In any case James, as a result of Eisenman's analysis, indubitably emerges as a more important personage in 1st-century history than Christian tradition has hitherto acknowledged. And the 'early Church' emerges in a very different light. It is no longer a congregation of devotees eschewing politics and public affairs, pursuing a course of personal salvation and aspiring to no kingdom other than that of heaven. On the contrary, it becomes one of the manifestations of Judaic nationalism at the time – a body of militant individuals intent on upholding the Law, deposing the corrupt Sadducee priesthood of the Temple, toppling the dynasty of illegitimate puppet-kings and driving the occupying Romans from the Holy Land. In all these respects, it conforms to conventional images of the Zealots.

But what has all this to do with Qumran and the Dead Sea Scrolls?

From the Acts of the Apostles, from Josephus and from early Christian historians, there emerges a coherent, if still incomplete, portrait of James, 'the Lord's brother'. He appears as an exemplar of 'righteousness' – so much so that 'the Just', or 'the Righteous', is appended as a sobriquet to his name. He is the acknowledged leader of a 'sectarian' religious community whose members are 'zealous for the Law'. He must contend with two quite separate and distinct adversaries. One of these is Paul, an outsider who, having first persecuted the community, then converts and is admitted into it, only to turn renegade, prevaricate and quarrel with his superiors, hijack the image of Jesus and begin preaching his own doctrine – a doctrine which draws on that of the community, but distorts it. James's second adversary is from outside the community – the high priest Ananas, head of the Sadducee priesthood. Ananas is a notoriously corrupt and widely hated man. He has also betrayed both the God and the people of Israel by collaborating with the Roman administration and their Herodian puppet-kings. James publicly challenges Ananas and eventually meets his death at the hands of Ananas' minions; but Ananas will shortly be assassinated in turn. All of this takes place against a backdrop of increasing social and political unrest and the impending invasion of a foreign army.

With this scenario in mind, Eisenman turned to the Dead Sea Scrolls, and particularly the 'Habakkuk Commentary'. When the fragmentary details of the Qumran texts had been assembled into a coherent sequence, what emerged was something extraordinarily similar to the chronicle of Acts, Josephus and early Christian historians. The scrolls told their own story, at the centre of which was a single protagonist, the 'Teacher of Righteousness' – an exemplar of the same virtues associated with James. Like James, the 'Teacher' was the acknowledged leader of a 'sectarian' religious community whose members were 'zealous for the Law'. And like James, the 'Teacher' had to contend with two quite separate and distinct adversaries.

One of these was dubbed the 'Liar', an outsider who was admitted to the community, then turned renegade, quarrelled with the 'Teacher' and hijacked part of the community's doctrine and membership. According to the 'Habakkuk Commentary', the 'Liar' 'did not listen to the word received by the Teacher of Righteousness from the mouth of God'.[22] Instead, he appealed to 'the unfaithful of the New Covenant in that they have not believed in the Covenant of God and have profaned His holy name'.[23] The text states explicitly that 'the Liar . . . flouted the Law in the midst of their whole congregation'.[24] He 'led many astray' and raised 'a congregation on deceit'.[25] He himself is said to be 'pregnant with [works] of deceit'.[26] These, of course, are precisely the transgressions of which Paul is accused in Acts – transgressions which lead, at the end of Acts, to the attempt on his life. And Eisenman stresses Paul's striking hypersensitivity to charges of prevarication and perjury.[27] In 1 Timothy 2:7, for example, he asserts indignantly, as if defending himself, that 'I am telling the truth and no lie'. In II Corinthians 11:31, he swears that: 'The God and Father of the Lord Jesus . . . knows that I am not lying.' These are but two instances; Paul's letters reveal an almost obsessive desire to exculpate himself from implied accusations of falsity.

According to the Dead Sea Scrolls, the 'Liar' was the adversary of the 'Teacher of Righteousness' from within the community. The 'Teacher's' second adversary was from outside. This was the 'Wicked Priest', a corrupt representative of the establishment who had betrayed his function and his faith.[28] He conspired to exterminate the 'Poor' – those 'zealous for the Law' – said to be scattered about Jerusalem and other places. He harried the 'Teacher of Righteousness' wherever the 'Teacher' sought refuge. At the hands of the 'Wicked Priest's' minions, the 'Teacher' suffered some serious injury and possibly – the text is vague on the matter – death. Subsequently, the 'Wicked Priest' was himself assassinated by followers of the 'Teacher', who, after killing him, 'took vengeance upon his body of flesh' – that is, defiled his corpse.[29] The parallels between the 'Wicked Priest' of the scrolls and the historical figure of the high priest Ananas are unmistakable.

In his book on James, Eisenman explores these parallels – James, Paul and Ananas on the one hand, the 'Teacher of Righteousness', the 'Liar' and the 'Wicked Priest' on the other – in exhaustive detail. He goes through the 'Habakkuk Commentary' and other texts line by line, comparing them with information vouchsafed by Acts, by Josephus and by early Christian historians. In our own pages, it would be impossible to do adequate justice to the weight of evidence he amasses. But the conclusions of this evidence are inescapable. The 'Habakkuk Commentary' and certain other of the Dead Sea Scrolls are referring to the same events as those recounted in Acts, in Josephus and in the works of early Christian historians.

This conclusion is reinforced by the striking and pervasive recurrence of Qumranic philosophy and imagery in Acts, in the Letter of James and in Paul's copious epistles. It is also reinforced by the revelation that the place for which Paul embarks and in which he spends three years as a postulant is in fact Qumran, not the city in Syria. Even the one fragment that would not, at first, appear to fit – the fact that the persecution and death of James occurs quite specifically in Jerusalem, while the Dead Sea Scrolls have been assumed to chronicle events in Qumran – is explained within the texts themselves. The 'Habakkuk Commentary' states explicitly that the leadership of the community were in Jerusalem at the relevant time.[30]

There is another point which Eisenman stresses as being particularly important. In the Letter to the Romans (1:17), Paul states that 'this is what reveals the justice of God to us: it shows how faith leads to faith, or as scripture says: the upright man finds life through faith'. The same theme appears in the Letter to the Galatians (3:11): 'the Law will not justify anyone in the sight of God, because we are told: the righteous man finds life through faith'.

These two statements constitute, in effect, 'the starting-point of the theological concept of faith'. They are ultimately, as Eisenman says, 'the foundation piece of Pauline theology'.[31] They provide the basis on which Paul is able to make his stand against James – is able to extol the supremacy of faith, while James extols the supremacy of the Law.

From where does Paul derive this principle of the supremacy of faith? It was certainly not an accepted part of Judaic teaching at the time. In fact, it derives from the original Book of Habakkuk, a text of Old Testament apocrypha believed to date from the mid-7th century BC. According to Chapter 2, Verse 4 of the Book of Habakkuk, 'the upright man will live by his faithfulness'. Paul's words in his letters are clearly an echo of this statement; and the Book of Habakkuk is clearly the 'scripture' to which Paul refers.

More important still, however, is the 'Habakkuk Commentary' – the gloss and exegesis on part of the Book of Habakkuk found among the Dead Sea Scrolls. The 'Habakkuk Commentary' cites the same statement and then proceeds to elaborate upon it:

> *But the righteous shall live by his faith.* Interpreted, this concerns all those who observe the Law in the House of Judah, whom God will deliver from the House of Judgment because of their suffering and because of their faith in the Teacher of Righteousness.[32]

This extraordinary passage is tantamount, in effect, to a formulation of early 'Christian' doctrine. It states explicitly that suffering, and faith in the 'Teacher of Righteousness', constitute the path to deliverance and salvation. From this passage in the Dead Sea Scrolls, Paul must have derived the foundation for the whole of his own

197

theology. But the passage in question declares unequivocally that suffering and faith in the 'Teacher of Righteousness' will lead to deliverance only among 'those who observe the Law in the House of Judah'.[33] It is just such emphasis on adherence to the Law that Paul contrives to ignore, thereby precipitating his doctrinal dispute with James and the other members of the 'early Church'.

14
Zeal for the Law

According to Robert Eisenman, the Qumran community emerges from the Dead Sea Scrolls as a movement of a very different nature to that of the Essenes of popular tradition. This movement has centres not just in Qumran, but in a number of other places as well, including Jerusalem. It can exercise considerable influence, can wield considerable power, can command considerable support. It can dispatch Paul, as well as many others, on embassies of recruitment and fund-raising abroad. It can organise riots and public disturbances. It can plot assassinations (such as that attempted on Paul at the end of Acts and, subsequently, that of Ananas). It can put forward its own legitimate alternative candidate for the position of the Temple's high priest. It can capture and hold strategically important fortresses such as Masada. Most significantly of all, it can galvanise the entire population of Judaea around it and instigate a full-fledged revolt against Rome – a revolt which leads to a major conflict of seven years' duration and necessitates the intervention not of a few detachments, but of an entire Roman army. Given the range and magnitude of these activities, it is clear that traditional images of the Essenes and of the 'early Church' are woefully inadequate. It is equally clear that the movement which manifested itself through the Qumran community and the 'early Church' also manifested itself through other groups generally deemed to be separate – the 'Zadokites', for example, the Zealots and the Sicarii.

Eisenman's research has revealed the underlying simplicity of what had previously seemed a dauntingly complicated situation.

As he says, 'terms like: *Ebionim, Nozrim, Hassidim, Zaddikim* (i.e., Ebionites, Palestinian Christians, Essenes, and Zadokites), turn out to be variations on the same theme'[1], while 'the various phraseologies the community at Qumran used to refer to itself, e.g. 'sons of light' . . . do not all designate different groups, but function as interchangeable metaphors'.[2]

The militant Zealots and Sicarii will prove similarly to be variations on the same theme, manifestations of the same movement. This movement is militant, nationalistic, revolutionary, xenophobic and messianic in character. Although rooted in Old Testament times, it coalesces during the Maccabean period of the 2nd century BC; but the events of the 1st century of the Christian era will imbue it with a new and particularly ferocious momentum. At the core of the movement lies the question of dynastic legitimacy – legitimacy not just of the ruling house, but of the priesthood. In the beginning, indeed, priestly legitimacy is the more important.

The legitimacy of the priesthood had become crucial in Old Testament times. It was supposed to descend lineally from Aaron through the Tribe of Levi. Thus, throughout the Old Testament, the priesthood is the unique preserve of the Levites. The Levite high priests who attend David and Solomon are referred to as 'Zadok' – though it is not clear whether this is a personal name or an hereditary title.[3] Solomon is anointed by Zadok, thereby becoming 'the Anointed One', the 'Messiah' – '*ha-mashi'ah*' in Hebrew. But the high priests were themselves *also* anointed and were also, in consequence, 'Messiahs'. In Old Testament times, then, the people of Israel are, in effect, governed by two parallel lines of 'Messiahs', or 'Anointed Ones'. One of these lines presides over spiritual affairs and descends from the Tribe of Levi through Aaron. The other, in the form of the kingship, presides over secular affairs and traces itself, through David, to the Tribe of Judah. This, of course, explains the references in the Dead Sea Scrolls to 'the Messiah(s) of Aaron and of Israel', or 'of Aaron and of David'. The principle is essentially similar to that whereby, during the Middle Ages in Europe, Pope and Emperor were supposed to preside jointly over the Holy Roman Empire.

The priestly line invoking a lineage from Aaron maintained their status until the Babylonian invasion of 587 BC. In 538 BC, when the 'Babylonian Captivity' ended, the priesthood quickly re-established itself, again claiming a descent (metaphorical, if not literal) from Aaron. In 333 BC, however, Alexander the Great overran the Holy Land. For the next 160-odd years, Palestine was to be ruled by a succession of Hellenistic, or Greek-oriented, dynasties. The priesthood, during this period, spawned a bewildering multitude of claimants, many of whom adapted, partially or completely, to Hellenistic ways, Hellenistic life-styles, Hellenistic values and attitudes. As is often the case in such circumstances, the general liberalising tendency engendered a 'hard-line' conservative reaction. There arose a movement which deplored the relaxed, heterodox and 'permissive' atmosphere, the indifference to old traditions, the defilement and pollution of the ancient 'purity', the defiance of the sacred Law. This movement undertook to rid Palestine of Hellenised collaborators and libertines, who had, it was felt, by their very presence, desecrated the Temple.

According to the first book of Maccabees, the movement first asserted itself – probably around 167 BC – when Mattathias Maccabaeus, a country priest, was ordered by a Greek officer to sacrifice on a pagan altar, in defiance of Judaic law. Enraged by this blasphemous sight, Mattathias, who 'burned with zeal for the Law' (1 Macc. 2:26), summarily killed a fellow Jew who complied, along with the Greek officer. In effect, as Eisenman has said, Mattathias thus became the first 'Zealot'.[4] Immediately after his action in the Temple, he raised the cry of revolt: 'Let everyone who is zealous for the Law and supports the Covenant come out with me' (1 Macc. 2:27). Thereupon, he took to the countryside with his sons, Judas, Simon, Jonathan and two others, as well as with an entourage called the 'Hasidaeans' – 'mighty warriors of Israel, every one who offered himself willingly for the Law' (1 Macc. 2:42). And when Mattathias, a year or so later, lay on his deathbed, he exhorted his sons and followers to 'show zeal for the Law and give your lives for the Covenant of our fathers' (1 Macc. 2:50).

On Mattathias's death, control of the movement passed to his son, Judas, who 'withdrew into the wilderness, and lived like wild animals in the hills with his companions, eating nothing but wild plants to avoid contracting defilement' (2 Macc. 5:27). This attests to what will eventually become an important principle and ritual – that of purifying oneself by withdrawing into the wilderness and, as a species of initiation, living for a time in seclusion. Here, Eisenman suggests, is the origin of remote communities such as Qumran, the first foundation of which dates from Maccabean times.[5] It is, in effect, the equivalent of the modern 'retreat'. In the New Testament, of course, the supreme exemplar of self-purification in remote solitude is John the Baptist, who 'preached in the wilderness' and ate 'locusts and honey'. But it must be remembered that Jesus, too, undergoes a probationary initiatory experience in the desert.

From the fastnesses to which they had withdrawn, Judas Maccabaeus, his brothers and his companions embarked on a prolonged campaign of guerrilla operations which escalated into a full-scale revolt and mobilised the people as a whole. By 152 BC, the Maccabeans had wrested control of the Holy Land, pacified the country and installed themselves in power. Their first act, on capturing the Temple, was to 'purify' it by removing all pagan trappings. It is significant that though the Maccabeans were simultaneously *de facto* kings and priests, the latter office was more important to them. They hastened to regularise their status in the priesthood, as custodians of the Law. They did not bother to call themselves kings until the fourth generation of their dynasty, between 103 and 76 BC.

From the bastion of the priesthood, the Maccabeans promulgated the Law with fundamentalist ferocity. They were fond of invoking the Old Testament legend of the 'Covenant of Phineas', which appears in the Book of Numbers.[6] Phineas was said to be a priest and a grandson of Aaron, active after the Hebrews had fled Egypt under Moses and established themselves in Palestine. Shortly thereafter, their numbers are devastated by plague. Phineas turns on one man in particular, who has taken a pagan foreigner to wife; seizing a spear, he promptly dispatches the married couple. God, at that point, declares that Phineas is the only man to 'have the same zeal as I have'. And He makes a covenant with Phineas. Henceforth, in reward for his zeal for his God (1 Macc.

2:54), Phineas and his descendants will hold the priesthood for all time.

Such was the figure to whom the Maccabean priesthood looked as a 'role model'. Like Phineas, they condemned all relations, of any kind, with pagans and foreigners. Like Phineas, they insisted on, and sought to embody, 'zeal for the Law'. This 'xenophobic antagonism' to foreign ways, foreign wives etc. was to be passed on as a legacy, and 'would seem to have been characteristic of the whole Zealot/Zadokite orientation'.[7]

Whether the Maccabeans could claim a literal pedigree from Aaron and from David is not certain. Probably they couldn't. But their 'zeal for the Law' served to legitimise them. During their dynasty, therefore, Israel could claim both a priesthood and a monarchy that conformed more or less to the stringent criteria of Old Testament authority.

All of this ended, of course, with the accession of Herod in 37 BC, installed as a puppet by the Romans who had overrun Palestine a quarter of a century before. At first, before he had consolidated his position, Herod was also preoccupied by questions of legitimacy. Thus, for example, he contrived to legitimise himself by marrying a Maccabean princess. No sooner was his position secure, however, than he proceeded to murder his wife and her brother, rendering the Maccabean line effectively extinct. He also removed or destroyed the upper echelons of the priesthood, which he filled with his own favourites and minions. These are the 'Sadducees' known to history through biblical sources and through Josephus. Eisenman suggests that the term 'Sadducee' was originally a variant, or perhaps a corruption, of 'Zadok' or '*Zaddikim*' – the 'Righteous Ones' in Hebrew, which the priesthood of the Maccabeans unquestionably were.[8] The 'Sadducees' installed by Herod were, however, very different. They were firmly aligned with the usurping monarch. They enjoyed an easy and comfortable life of prestige and privilege. They exercised a lucrative monopoly over the Temple and everything associated with the Temple. And they had no concept whatever of 'zeal for the Law'. Israel thus found itself under the yoke of a corrupt illegitimate monarchy and a corrupt illegitimate priesthood, both of which were ultimately instruments of pagan Rome.

As in the days of Mattathias Maccabaeus, this situation inevitably provoked a reaction. If Herod's puppet priests became the 'Sadducees' of popular tradition, their adversaries – the 'purists' who remained 'zealous for the Law' – became known to history under a variety of different names.[9] In certain contexts – the Qumran literature, for example – these adversaries were called 'Zadokites' or 'Sons of Zadok'. In the New Testament, they were called 'Nazorenes' – and, subsequently, 'early Christians'. In Josephus, they were called 'Zealots' and 'Sicarii'. The Romans, of course, regarded them as 'terrorists', 'outlaws' and 'brigands'. In modern terminology, they might be called 'messianic revolutionary fundamentalists'.[10]

Whatever the terminology one uses, the religious and political situation in Judaea had, by the beginning of the 1st century AD, provoked widespread opposition to the Herodian régime, the pro-Herodian priesthood and the machinery of the Roman Empire, which sustained and loomed behind both. By the 1st century AD, there were thus two rival and antagonistic factions of 'Sadducees'. On the one hand, there were the Sadducees of the New Testament and Josephus, the 'Herodian Sadducees'; on the other hand, there was a 'true' or 'purist' Sadducee movement, which repudiated all such collaboration and remained fervently loyal to three traditional governing principles – a priesthood or priestly 'Messiah' claiming descent from Aaron, a royal 'Messiah' claiming descent from David and, above all, 'zeal for the Law'.[11]

It will by this time have become clear to the reader that 'zeal for the Law' is not a casually used phrase. On the contrary, it is used very precisely in the way that such phrases as 'brethren of the craft' might be used in Freemasonry; and whenever the phrase, or some variant of it, occurs, it offers a vital clue to the researcher, indicating to him a certain group of people or movement. Given this fact, it becomes strained and disingenuous to argue – as adherents of the consensus do – that there must be some distinction between the Qumran community, who extol 'zeal for the Law', and the Zealots of popular tradition.

The Zealots of popular tradition are generally acknowledged to have been founded at the dawn of the Christian era by a figure known as Judas of Galilee, or, more accurately perhaps, Judas of Gamala. Judas launched his revolt immediately after the death of Herod the Great in 4 BC. One particularly revealing aspect of this revolt is cited by Josephus. At once, 'as soon as mourning for Herod was over', public demand was whipped up for the incumbent Herodian high priest to be deposed and another, 'of greater piety and purity', to be installed in his place.[12] Accompanied by a priest known as 'Sadduc' – apparently a Greek transliteration of 'Zadok', or, as suggested by Eisenman, *Zaddik*, the Hebrew for 'Righteous One' – Judas and his followers promptly raided the royal armoury in the Galilean city of Sepphoris, plundering weapons and equipment for themselves. Around the same time – either just before or just after – Herod's palace at Jericho, near Qumran, was attacked by arsonists and burned down.[13] These events were to be followed by some seventy-five years of incessant guerrilla warfare and terrorist activity, culminating in the full-scale military operations of AD 66–73.

In *The Jewish Wars*, written in the volatile aftermath of the revolt, Josephus states that Judas of Galilee had founded 'a peculiar sect of his own'.[14] Josephus' second major work, however, *Antiquities of the Jews*, was composed a quarter of a century or so later, when the general atmosphere was rather less fraught. In this work, therefore, Josephus could afford to be more explicit.[15] He states that Judas and Sadduc 'became zealous', implying something tantamount to a conversion – a conversion to some recognised attitude or state of mind. Their movement, he says, constituted 'the fourth sect of Jewish philosophy', and the youth of Israel 'were zealous for it'.[16] From the very beginning, the movement was characterised by Messianic aspirations. Sadduc embodied the figure of the priestly Messiah descended from Aaron. And Judas, according to Josephus, had an 'ambitious desire of the royal dignity' – the status of the royal Messiah descended from David.[17]

Judas himself appears to have been killed fairly early in the fighting. His mantle of leadership passed to his sons, of whom there were three. Two of them, Jacob and Simon, were well-known 'Zealot' leaders, captured and crucified by the Romans some time between AD 46 and 48. The third son (or perhaps grandson), Menahem, was one of the chief instigators of the revolt of AD 66. In its early days, when the revolt still promised to be successful, Menahem is described as making a triumphal entry into Jerusalem, 'in the state of a king' – another manifestation of messianic dynastic ambitions.[18] In AD 66, Menahem also captured the fortress of Masada. The bastion's last commander, known to history as Eleazar, was another descendant of Judas of Galilee, though the precise nature of the relationship has never been established.

The mass suicide of 'Zealot' defenders at Masada has become a familiar historical event, the focus of at least two novels, a cinema film and a television mini-series. It has already been referred to in this book, and there will be occasion to look at it more closely shortly. Masada, however, was not the only instance of such mass suicide. In AD 67, responding to the rebellion sweeping the Holy Land, a Roman army advanced on Gamala in Galilee, the original home of Judas and his sons. Four thousand Jews died trying to defend the town. When their efforts proved futile, another five thousand committed suicide. This reflects something more than mere political opposition. It attests to a dimension of religious fanaticism. Such a dimension is expressed by Josephus, who, speaking of the 'Zealots', says: 'They . . . do not value dying any kinds of death, nor indeed do they heed the deaths of their relations and friends, nor can any such fear make them call any man Lord . . .'[19] To acknowledge a Roman emperor as a god, which Rome demanded, would have been, for the 'Zealots', the most outrageous blasphemy.[20] To such a transgression of the Law, death would indeed have been preferable.

'Zeal for the Law' effectively brings the 'Zealots' – usually envisaged as more or less secular 'freedom fighters' – into alignment with the fervently religious members of the Qumran community; and, as we have already noted, Qumranic texts were found in the ruins of Masada. 'Zeal for the Law' also brings the 'Zealots' into alignment with the so-called 'early Church', to whose adherents the same 'zeal' is repeatedly ascribed. The figure cited in the Gospels as 'Simon Zelotes', or 'Simon the Zealot', attests to at least one 'Zealot' in Jesus' immediate entourage; and Judas Iscariot, whose name may well derive from the Sicarii, might be another. Most revealing of all, however, is Eisenman's discovery – the original Greek term used to denote members of the 'early Church'. They are called, quite explicitly, '*zelotai* of the Law' – that is, 'Zealots'.[21]

There thus emerges, in 1st-century Palestine, a kind of fundamentalist dynastic priesthood claiming either genealogical or symbolic descent from Aaron and associated with the expected imminent advent of a Davidic or royal Messiah.[22] This priesthood maintains itself in a state of perpetual self-declared war with the Herodian dynasty, the puppet priests of that dynasty and the occupying Romans. Depending on their activities at a given moment, and the perspective from which they are viewed, the priesthood and its supporters are variously called 'Zealots', 'Essenes', 'Zadokites', 'Nazoreans' and a number of other things – including, by their enemies, 'brigands' and 'outlaws'. They are certainly not passive recluses and mystics. On the contrary, their vision, as Eisenman says, is 'violently apocalyptic', and provides a theological corollary to the violent action with which the 'Zealots' are usually associated.[23] This violence, both political and theological, can be discerned in the career of John the Baptist – executed, according to the Gospels of Matthew and Mark, for condemning the marriage of Herod Antipas to his niece because it 'is against the Law for you to have her'. And, indeed, Eisenman has even suggested that John the Baptist may have been the mysterious 'Sadduc' who accompanied Judas of Galilee, leader of the 'Zealots' at the time of Jesus' birth.[24]

To recapitulate, then, there emerge, from the confusing welter of sobriquets and nomenclature, the configurations of a broad movement in which 'Essenes', 'Zadokites', 'Nazoreans', 'Zealots' and other such supposed factions effectively fuse. The names prove to be merely different designations – or, at most, different manifestations – of the same religious and political impetus, diffused throughout the Holy Land and beyond, from the 2nd century BC on. The ostensibly separate factions would have been, at most, like the variety of individuals, groups and interests which coalesced to form the single movement known as the 'French Resistance' during the Second World War. At most. For Robert Eisenman personally, any distinction between them is but a matter of degree; they are all variations on the same theme. But even if some subtle gradations between them did exist, they would still have been unified by their joint involvement in a single ambitious enterprise – the ridding of their land of Roman occupation, and the reinstatement of the old legitimate Judaic monarchy, together with its rightful priesthood.

That enterprise, of course, did not end with the destruction of Jerusalem and Qumran between AD 68 and 70, nor with the fall of Masada in AD 73. In the immediate aftermath of the débâcle, large numbers of 'Zealots' and Sicarii fled abroad, to places where there were sizeable Judaic populations – to Persia, for example, and to Egypt, especially Alexandria. In Alexandria, they attempted to mobilise the local Jewish population for yet another uprising against Rome. They met with little success, some six hundred of them being rounded up and handed over to the authorities. Men, women and children were tortured in an attempt to make them acknowledge the emperor as a god. According to Josephus, 'not a man gave in or came near to saying it'. And he adds:

> But nothing amazed the spectators as much as the behaviour of young children; for not one of them could be constrained to call Caesar Lord. So far did the strength of a brave spirit prevail over the weakness of their little bodies. [25]

Here again is that strain of fanatical dedication – a dedication that cannot be political in nature, that can only be religious.

More than sixty years after the war that left Jerusalem and the Temple in ruins, the Holy Land erupted again in a new revolt, led by the charismatic Messianic figure known as Simeon bar Kochba, the 'Son of the Star'. According to Eisenman, the terminology suggests that Simeon was in reality descended by blood from the 'Zealot' leaders of the previous century. [26] In any case, the image of the 'Star' had certainly figured prominently among them during the period culminating with the first revolt. [27] And, as we have noted, the same image figures repeatedly in the Dead Sea Scrolls. It derives ultimately from a prophecy in the Book of Numbers (24:17): 'a star from Jacob takes the leadership, a sceptre arises from Israel'. The 'War Rule' invokes this prophecy, and declares that the 'Star', or the 'Messiah', will, together with the 'Poor' or the 'Righteous', repel invading armies. Eisenman has found this 'Star' prophecy in two other crucial places in the Qumran literature.[28] One, the 'Damascus Document', is particularly graphic: 'The star is the Interpreter of the Law who shall come to Damascus; as it is written . . . the sceptre is the Prince . . .'[29]

Josephus, as well as Roman historians such as Suetonius and Tacitus, reports how a prophecy was current in the Holy Land during the early 1st century AD, to the effect that 'from Judaea would go forth men destined to rule the world'.[30] According to Josephus, the promulgation of this prophecy was a major factor in the revolt of AD 66. And, needless to say, the 'Star' prophecy finds its way into Christian tradition as the 'Star of Bethlehem', which heralds Jesus' birth.[31] As 'Son of the Star', then, Simeon bar Kochba enjoyed an illustrious symbolic pedigree.

Unlike the revolt of AD 66, Simeon's insurrection, commencing in AD 132, was no ill-organised conflagration resulting, so to speak, from spontaneous combustion. On the contrary, much prolonged and careful planning went into the enterprise. Jewish smiths and craftsmen pressed into Roman service would, for example, deliberately forge slightly sub-standard weapons. When these were rejected by the Romans, they would be collected and stored for use by the rebels. From the war of the previous century, Simeon had also learned that there was no point in capturing and holding fortresses such as Masada. To defeat the Romans, a campaign based on mobility, on hit-and-run tactics, would be necessary. This led to the construction of vast underground networks of rooms, corridors and tunnels. In the period prior to the revolt, Simeon used these networks for training. Subsequently, once hostilities had begun, they served as bases and staging areas, enabling the rebels to launch a sudden lightning assault, then disappear – the kind of ambush with which American soldiers, to their cost, became familiar during the war in Vietnam.[32] But Simeon did not confine himself solely to guerrilla operations. His army included many volunteers from abroad, many mercenaries and professional soldiers with considerable military experience. Indeed, surviving records discovered by archaeologists have revealed that a number of Simeon's officers and staff spoke only Greek.[33] With such well-trained forces at his disposal, he could, on occasion, meet the Romans in pitched battle.

Within the first year of the revolt, Simeon had destroyed at least one complete Roman legion, and probably a second.[34] Palestine had been effectively cleared of Roman troops. Jerusalem had been recaptured and a Judaic administration installed there. The campaign came within a hair's-breadth of total success. It failed primarily because Simeon was let down by his expected allies. According to his overall grand design, his troops were to be supported by forces from Persia, where a great many Jews still resided and enjoyed the sympathetic favour of the reigning dynasty. Just when Simeon most needed these reinforcements, however, Persia itself was invaded from the north by marauding hill tribes, who effectively pinned down Persian resources, leaving Simeon bereft of his promised support.[35]

In Syria, safely outside Palestine, the Romans regrouped under the personal leadership of the Emperor Hadrian, with Julius Severus, formerly governor of Britain, as his second-in-command. Another full-scale invasion ensued, involving as many as twelve legions, some eighty thousand troops. In a two-pronged advance, they fought their way from post to post down the entire length of the Holy Land. Eventually Simeon was cornered, making his last stand at Battir, his headquarters, a few miles west of Jerusalem, in AD 135.

During the entire course of the revolt, Simeon's troops were in constant occupation of Qumran. Coins found in the ruins attest to their presence in what would, after all, have been a site of considerable strategic importance. It is thus possible, despite the claims of Father de Vaux, that some, at least, of the Dead Sea Scrolls were deposited in Qumran as late as Simeon's time.

15
Zealot Suicide

Once the broad messianic movement of 1st-century Palestine is seen in perspective, and once the apparently diverse sects are seen as integral parts of it, a number of hitherto inexplicable elements and anomalies slip into place. Thus, for example, the apocalyptic and eschatological ferocity of John the Baptist begins to make sense, as does his role in the events recounted by the Gospels. Thus, too, can one account for a number of theologically awkward passages and incidents pertaining to Jesus' own career. There is, as we have noted, at least one 'Zealot' in his following, and possibly more. There is the violence of his action in overturning the tables of the money-changers at the Temple. There is his execution not by Judaic but by Roman authorities, in a fashion specifically reserved for political offenders. There are numerous other instances, which the authors of this book have examined at length elsewhere. Finally, there are Jesus' own words:

> Do not suppose that I have come to bring peace to the earth; it is not peace I have come to bring, but a sword. For I have come to set a man against his father, a daughter against her mother . . . (Matt. 10:34–5)

And, more tellingly still, in unmistakably Qumranic phraseology:

> Do not imagine that I have come to abolish the Law or the Prophets. I have come not to abolish but to complete [or ful-fil] them . . . not one dot, not one little stroke shall disappear

211

from the Law until its purpose is achieved. Therefore the man who infringes even one of the least of these commandments and teaches others to do the same will be considered the least in the Kingdom of Heaven. (Matt. 5:17–19)[1]

In this passage, it is almost as if Jesus had anticipated Paul's advent. Certainly he could not have warned against it any more specifically. By the standards he lays down, Paul's status in the Kingdom of Heaven cannot be much higher than that of official pariah-in-residence.

Another anomaly that emerges in a fresh light is the fortress of Masada, and the character and mentality of its tenacious defenders. When the Holy Land rose in revolt in AD 66, Masada was one of the first strongholds to be seized – by Menahem, the son or grandson of Judas of Galilee, founder of the 'Zealots'. Perched high on a sheer-sided mountain overlooking the south-western shore of the Dead Sea, some thirty-three miles below Qumran, the place became the rebels' most important bastion, the supreme symbol and embodiment of resistance. Long after that resistance had collapsed elsewhere, Masada continued to hold out. Jerusalem, for example, was occupied and razed within two years of the insurrection's outbreak – in AD 68. Masada remained impregnable, however, until AD 74. From within its walls, some 960 defenders withstood repeated assaults and a full-scale siege by a Roman army estimated to have numbered fifteen thousand.

Despite the tenacity of this resistance, Masada's position, by the middle of April AD 74, had become hopeless. Cut off from reinforcement, entirely encircled by Roman troops, the garrison no longer had any prospect of withstanding a general assault. The besieging Romans, after bombarding the fortress with heavy siege machinery, had constructed an immense ramp running up the mountainside and, on the night of 15 April, prepared for their final onslaught. The garrison, under the command of Eleazar ben Jair, came to their own decision. The men killed their wives and children. Ten men were then chosen to kill their comrades. Having done so, they proceeded to draw lots, choosing one to dispatch the remaining nine. After he had performed this task, he set fire to what remained of the buildings in the fortress and killed himself. Altogether, 960 men, women and children perished. When the Romans burst through the gate the following morning, they found only corpses amid the ruins.

Two women and five children escaped the carnage, supposedly having hidden in the water conduits under the fortress while the rest of the garrison killed themselves. Josephus recounts the testimony of one of the women – drawing, he says, on her interrogation by Roman officers.[2] According to Josephus, she furnished a detailed account of what transpired on the last night of the siege. If this account is to be believed (and there is no reason why it shouldn't), Eleazar, the commander of the fortress, exhorted his followers to their mass suicide by his charismatic and persuasive eloquence:

> Ever since primitive man began to think, the words of our ancestors and of the gods, supported by the actions and spirits of our forefathers, have constantly impressed on us that life is the calamity for man, not death. Death gives freedom to our souls and lets them depart to their own pure home where they will know nothing of any calamity; but while they are confined within a mortal body and share its miseries, in strict truth they are dead.
>
> For association of the divine with the mortal is most improper. Certainly the soul can do a great deal when imprisoned in the body; it makes the body its own organ of sense, moving it invisibly and impelling it in its actions further than mortal nature can reach. But when, freed from the weight that drags it down to earth and is hung about it, the soul returns to its own place, then in truth it partakes of a blessed power and an utterly unfettered strength, remaining as invisible to human eyes as God Himself. Not even while it is in the body can it be viewed; it enters undetected and departs unseen, having itself one imperishable nature, but causing a change in the body; for whatever the soul touches lives and blossoms, whatever it deserts withers and dies: such is the superabundance it has of immortality.[3]

According to Josephus, Eleazar concludes: 'Let us die unenslaved by our enemies, and leave this world as free men in company with our wives and children. That is what the Law ordains.'[4]

On occasion, Josephus is unreliable. When he is so, however, it shows. In this instance, there is certainly no reason to doubt his word; and the excavations of Masada conducted in the 1960s tend to support his version of events. It is, of course, probable that he embellished Eleazar's speeches somewhat, making them perhaps more eloquent (and long-winded) than they might actually have been, availing himself of some poetic licence. But the general tenor of the narrative rings true, and has always been accepted by historians. What is more, Josephus had a unique and first-hand understanding of the mentality that dictated the mass suicide at Masada. At the beginning of the revolt, he himself had been a rebel commander in Galilee. In AD 67, his forces were besieged by the Romans under Vespasian at Jotapata – now Yodefat, near Sepphoris. When the town fell, many of its defenders committed suicide rather than submit to capture. Many others, including Josephus himself, fled and hid in caves. According to his own account, he found himself in one cave with forty other fugitives. Here, as at Masada, lots were drawn as to who would kill his comrades. Whether 'by chance', as Josephus suggests, or by 'the providence of God', or perhaps by a fiddle which aided and abetted one or the other, he and another man ended up as the sole survivors. Persuading his companion to surrender, he then himself defected to the victorious Romans.[5] He does not emerge from the adventure in any very creditable light, of course. But even if he himself could not live up to them, he was no stranger to 'Zealot' attitudes, including their preparedness for self-immolation in the name of the Law.

In reality, there was a fairly sophisticated logic governing such self-immolation, which would not have been readily apparent to Josephus' readers, either at the time or subsequently. The mass suicides at Masada, at Gamala and at other sites are explained by Eisenman as resting ultimately on the uniquely 'Zealot' concept of resurrection. This concept derived primarily from two Old Testament prophets, Daniel and Ezekiel, both of whose texts were found among the Dead Sea Scrolls at Qumran. Daniel (Daniel 12:2) was the first to give expression to the concept in any developed form: 'Of those who lie sleeping in the dust of the earth many will awake, some to everlasting life, some to shame and everlasting disgrace.' He speaks, too, of an imminent 'Kingdom of Heaven', and of 'End

Times', of the 'coming of an anointed Prince', of a 'Son of Man' on whom 'was conferred sovereignty' (Daniel 7:13–14).

In Ezekiel, the relevant passage is the famous vision of a valley filled with dry bones, all of which, God announces, will live again:

> I mean to raise you from your graves . . . and lead you back to the soil of Israel. And you will know that I am Yahweh, when I open your graves and raise you from your graves . . . And I shall put my spirit in you, and you will live . . .' (Ezekiel 37:12–14)

So important was this passage deemed to be that a copy of it was found buried under the floor of the synagogue at Masada.[6]

The concept of resurrection derived from Daniel and Ezekiel was picked up and adopted by the original 'zealots for the Law', the Maccabees. Thus, in the second book of Maccabees, it is used to encourage martyrdom for the sake of the Law. In 2 Maccabees 14:42, an Elder of Jerusalem kills himself rather than be captured and suffer outrages. In 2 Maccabees 6:18ff., a priest and teacher of the Law kills himself as an 'example of how to make a good death . . . for the venerable and holy laws'. This incident, according to Eisenman, is the prototype for the establishment of later Zealot mentality. The principle finds its fullest expression in 2 Maccabees 7, where seven brothers submit to death by torture rather than transgress the Law:

> Said one brother, '. . . you may discharge us from this present life, but the king of the world will raise us up, since it is for his laws that we die, to live again for ever.'
>
> Another said, 'It was heaven that gave me these limbs; for the sake of his laws I disdain them; from him I hope to receive them again.'
>
> The next said to his tormentors, 'Ours is the better choice, to meet death at men's hands, yet relying on God's promise that we shall be raised up by him; whereas for you . . . there can be no resurrection, no new life.'

Here then, in the pre-Christian book of Maccabees, is the principle of bodily resurrection that will figure so prominently in later Christian theology. It is available, however, as the third of the above speeches makes clear, only to the righteous, to those 'zealous for the Law'.

215

But there is another point of relevance in the passage devoted to the death of the seven brothers. Just before the last of them is to be executed, his mother is brought in to see him. She has been urged to plead with him to submit and thereby save himself. Instead, she says to him that 'in the day of mercy I may receive you back in your brothers' company' (2 Macc. 7:29). At the end of time, those who die together will be resurrected together. Thus Eleazar, in his exhortation to the garrison of Masada, urges them to die 'in company with our wives and children. That is what the Law ordains.' Not the Law of the 'Sadducee' establishment or of later Judaism – only the Law of the so-called 'Zealots'. Had the women and children in the fortress been left alive, they would not have been exterminated by the victorious Romans. But they would have been separated from their menfolk and from each other. And many of them would have been enslaved, raped, consigned to Roman army brothels and thereby defiled, bereft of their ritual purity according to the Law. At Masada, separation and defilement were feared more than death, since death, for the 'Righteous', would have been only temporary. Here then, among the ferocious defenders of Masada, is a principle of bodily resurrection virtually identical to that of later Christianity.

The garrison who defended Masada can hardly be reconciled with traditional images of placid, peace-loving Essenes – who, according to adherents of the consensus, made up the community at Qumran. And indeed, as we have noted, adherents of the consensus continue to insist that no connection can possibly have existed between the Qumran community and the garrison at Masada, despite the discovery at Masada of texts identical to some of those found at Qumran – found at Qumran and, in at least two instances, found nowhere else – and despite the use by the defenders of Masada of precisely the same calendar as that used by the Qumran material: a unique solar calendar, in contrast to the lunar calendar of the official 'Sadducee' establishment and of later rabbinical Judaism.

Once again, there can be discerned the configuration of what Eisenman has described: a broad messianic nationalistic movement in which a number of supposed factions, if there was ever any distinction between them, effectively merged. Eisenman's explanation accommodates and accounts for what has previously seemed a welter of contradictions and anomalies. It makes sense, too, of the mission on which Paul is dispatched by James and the hierarchy of the so-called 'early Church' – the 'Nazorean' enclave – in Jerusalem. In biblical times, it must be remembered, 'Israel' was not just a territory, not just a particular tract of land. Even more important, 'Israel' denoted a people, a tribe, a 'host'. When Paul and other 'evangelists' are sent forth by the hierarchy in Jerusalem, their purpose is to make converts to the Law – that is, to 'Israel'. What would this have meant in practical terms, if not the recruitment of an army? Since Old Testament times, and especially since the 'Babylonian Captivity', the 'tribe of Israel' had been scattered across the Mediterranean world and beyond, on into Persia – where, at the time of Simeon bar Kochba's rising in AD 132, there was still enough sympathy to elicit at least a promise of support. Were not the emissaries of the Jerusalem hierarchy sent to tap this potentially immense source of manpower – to 'call to the colours' the dispersed people of 'Israel' to drive the Roman invaders from their native soil and liberate their homeland? And Paul, in preaching a wholly new religion rather than mustering recruits, was, in effect, depoliticising, demilitarising and emasculating the movement.[7] This would, of course, have been a far more serious matter than merely lapsing from dogma or certain ritual observances. It would have been, in fact, a form of treason. For the Law, as it figures in the Dead Sea Scrolls, is not wholly confined to dogma and ritual observances. Running throughout the Qumran texts, as a sacred duty, there is clearly a thrust to build a legitimate messianic persona, whether royal, or priestly, or both. By implication, this would involve the re-establishment of the ancient monarchy and priesthood, to drive out the invader, to reclaim and purify the Holy Land for the people chosen by God to inhabit it. In the words of the 'War Scroll': 'The dominion of the [invaders] shall come to an end . . . the sons of righteousness shall shine over all the ends of the earth.'[8]

16

Paul – Roman Agent or Informer?

With this grand design in mind, it is worth looking again at the confused and sketchy description of the events that occur towards the end of the Acts of the Apostles. Paul, it will be remembered, after a prolonged evangelistic mission abroad, has again been summoned to Jerusalem by James and the irate hierarchy. Sensing trouble, his immediate supporters exhort him repeatedly, at each stage of his itinerary, not to go; but Paul, never a man to shrink from a confrontation, remains deaf to their appeals. Meeting with James and other members of the community's leadership, he is again castigated for laxity in his observation of the Law. Acts does not record Paul's response to these charges, but it would appear, from what follows, that he perjures himself, denying the accusations against him, which his own letters reveal to have been justified.[1] In other words, he recognises the magnitude of his offence; and however fierce his integrity, however fanatic his loyalty to 'his' version of Jesus, he acknowledges that some sort of compromise is, this time, necessary. Thus, when asked to purify himself for seven days and thereby demonstrate the unjustness of the allegations against him, he readily consents to do so. Eisenman suggests that James may have been aware of the true situation and that Paul may well have been 'set up'. Had he refused the ritual of purification, he would have declared himself openly in defiance of the Law. By acceding to the ritual, he became, even more than before,

218

the 'Liar' of the 'Habakkuk Commentary'. Whatever the course of action he chose, he would have damned himself – which may have been precisely what James intended.[2]

In any case, and despite his exculpatory self-purification, Paul continues to inspire enmity in those 'zealous for the Law' – who, a few days later, attack him in the Temple. 'This', they proclaim, 'is the man who preaches to everyone everywhere . . . against the Law' (Acts 21:28). The ensuing riot is no minor disturbance:

> This roused the whole city: people came running from all sides; they seized Paul and dragged him out of the Temple, and the gates were closed behind them. They would have killed him if a report had not reached the tribune of the cohort that there was rioting all over Jerusalem. (Acts 21:30–31)

The cohort is called out – no fewer than six hundred men – and Paul, in the nick of time, is rescued, presumably to prevent civil upheaval on an even greater scale. Why else would the cohort bother to save the life of one heterodox Jew who'd incurred the wrath of his fellows? The sheer scale of the tumult attests to the kind of currency, influence and power the so-called 'early Church' must have exercised in Jerusalem at the time – *among Jews!* Clearly, we are dealing with a movement within Judaism itself, which commands loyalty from much of the city's populace.

Having rescued him from the incensed mob, the Romans arrest Paul – who, before he is marched off to prison, asks permission to make a self-exonerating speech. Inexplicably, the Romans acquiesce to his request, even though the speech serves only to further inflame the mob. Paul is then carried off for torture and interrogation. As was asked previously, interrogation about what? Why torture and interrogate a man who has offended his co-religionists on fine points of orthodoxy and ritual observance? There is only one explanation for the Romans taking such an interest – that Paul is suspected of being privy to information of a political and/or military nature.

The only serious political and/or military adversaries confronting the Romans were the adherents of the nationalistic movement – the 'Zealots' of popular tradition. And Paul, the evangelist of the 'early Church', was under threat from those 'zealous for the Law' – forty

219

The Dead Sea Scrolls Deception

or more of them in number – who were plotting to kill him, vowing not to eat or drink until they had done so. Saved from this fate by his hitherto unmentioned nephew, he is bundled, under escort, out of Jerusalem to Caesarea, where he invokes his right as a Roman citizen to make a personal appeal to the emperor. While in Caesarea, he hobnobs in congenial and intimate fashion with the Roman procurator, Antonius Felix. Eisenman has emphasised that he is also intimate with the procurator's brother-in-law, Herod Agrippa II, and with the king's sister – later the mistress of Titus, the Roman commander who will destroy Jerusalem and eventually become emperor.[3]

These are not the only suspicious elements looming in the background of Paul's biography. From the very beginning, his apparent wealth, his Roman citizenship and his easy familiarity with the presiding establishment have differentiated him from his fellows and from other members of the 'early Church'. Obviously, he has influential connections with the ruling élite. How else could so young a man have become the high priest's hatchet man? In his letter to the Romans (16:11), moreover, he speaks of a companion strikingly named 'Herodion' – a name obviously associated with the reigning dynasty, and most unlikely for a fellow evangelist. And Acts 13:1 refers to one of Paul's companions in Antioch as 'Manaen, who had been brought up with Herod the Tetrarch'. Here, again, there is evidence of high-level aristocratic affiliation.[4]

Startling though the suggestion may be, it does seem at least possible that Paul was some species of Roman 'agent'. Eisenman was led to this conclusion by the scrolls themselves, then found the references in the New Testament to support it. And indeed, if one combines and superimposes the materials found at Qumran with those in Acts, together with obscure references in Paul's letters, such a conclusion becomes a distinct possibility. But there is another possibility as well, possibly no less startling. Those last muddled and enigmatic events in Jerusalem, the nick-of-time intervention of the Romans, Paul's heavily escorted departure from the city, his sojourn in luxury at Caesarea, his mysterious and utter disappearance from the stage of history – these things find a curious echo in our own era. One is reminded of beneficiaries of the 'Witness Protection

Program' in the States. One is also reminded of the so-called 'supergrass phenomenon' in Northern Ireland. In both cases, a member of an illicit organisation – dedicated to organised crime or to paramilitary terrorism – is 'turned' by the authorities. He consents to give evidence and testify, in exchange for immunity, protection, relocation and money. Like Paul, he would incur the vengeful wrath of his colleagues. Like Paul, he would be placed under seemingly disproportionate military and/or police protection. Like Paul, he would be smuggled out under escort. Having co-operated with the authorities, he would then be given a 'new identity' and, together with his family, resettled somewhere theoretically out of reach of his vindictive comrades. So far as the world at large was concerned, he would, like Paul, disappear.

Does Paul, then, belong in the company of history's 'secret agents'? Of history's informers and 'supergrasses'? These are some of the questions generated by Robert Eisenman's research. But in any case, Paul's arrival on the scene set a train of events in motion that was to prove irreversible. What began as a localised movement within the framework of existing Judaism, its influence extending no further than the Holy Land, was transformed into something of a scale and magnitude that no one at the time can have foreseen. The movement entrusted to the 'early Church' and the Qumran community was effectively hijacked and converted into something that could no longer accommodate its progenitors. There emerged a skein of thought which, heretical at its inception, was to evolve in the course of the next two centuries into an entirely new religion. What had been heresy within the framework of Judaism was now to become the orthodoxy of Christianity. Few accidents of history can have had more far-reaching consequences.

Postscript

The story of the scrolls is, needless to say, unfinished. The plot continues to unfold, to take new twists and turns. Even as this book is being prepared for publication, other books and articles are appearing in print, conferences are being convened, media coverage is intensifying, various protagonists are making new statements; and developments will be accelerated by the departure of John Strugnell and the appointment of a new editor-in-chief. We have attempted to chronicle events as late as the winter of 1990–91, but events will continue to evolve beyond then, and will, in so doing, inevitably leave aspects of our account behind.

In the meantime, the struggle to effect the release of unpublished Qumran material, still kept sequestered by the international team and the Ecole Biblique, continues. Thus, for example, Oxford University Press now has a complete set of photographs of the scrolls, but access to them is still restricted. Thus, the newly created Israeli 'Oversight Committee' is going about its work, though with how much efficacy remains to be seen. Certain texts scheduled for recent publication have so far failed to meet their deadlines, and whether this will prove true for others as well also remains to be seen. Publication of yet other material has been promised, but is likely to be presented in accordance with the consensus view and to conform to the established orthodoxy of interpretation. There remains, too, the plan by Professors Eisenman and Davies to pursue action through the Israeli High Court. Although premature disclosure of this plan

225

by *Biblical Archaeology Review*[1] effectively put the international team on their guard and prompted them to plug as many legal loopholes as possible, it also had the effect of goading the 'Oversight Committee' to more active efforts. It is therefore possible that the mere prospect of legal action may have accomplished as much as such action itself would have done.

At the same time, an ever-increasing phalanx of supporters is gathering around Robert Eisenman, and his cause is being espoused by more and more scholars of influence and prominence. It continues to be widely publicised by the media. To the extent that the public has an opinion on the matter at all, that opinion is beginning to tilt markedly in Eisenman's favour.

As for Eisenman himself, he is pursuing his campaign on new fronts. In 1988, he had pointed out that the excavations at Qumran were far from complete, far from exhaustive. The surrounding terrain is, in fact, ideal for the preservation of manuscripts, and virtually all experts in the field agree that there are more discoveries to be made. It is not just possible, but probable, that additional scroll material still exists, buried under landslides and rock-falls. Many caves have yet to be excavated properly – that is, through the rubble of fallen roofs and down to bed-rock. Other caves, previously explored only by the Bedouin, have to be explored anew, since the Bedouin tended to overlook some concealed documents and to leave behind many fragments; and, in any case, officially sanctioned Bedouin excavations effectively ceased with the 1967 war. There are other sites in the general vicinity of Qumran that have yet to be thoroughly explored. Nine miles to the south, for example, on the shores of the Dead Sea, at a place called En el-Ghuweir, an Israeli archaeologist found Qumran-style graves and the ruins of a Qumran-style (albeit smaller) residence.[2] It is certainly reasonable to suppose that the caves in the nearby wadis, hitherto unexcavated, may also be repositories for scrolls.

With these facts in mind, Eisenman determined to embark on his own archaeological explorations. His primary objective was, of course, to look for additional scroll material. Such material might – as proved to be the case with the 'Temple Scroll' – be entirely new. But even if it duplicated material already in the hands of the international team, it would render pointless any continued suppression. Quite apart from the prospect of additional scroll material, however, Eisenman wanted to build up as complete a picture as possible of the population in the entire region, from Qumran on south towards Masada. There might have been, he concluded, other Qumran-style communities. In consequence, he undertook to look for evidence of any other kind – evidence of water control, for example, such as terraces, aqueducts and cisterns, which might have been constructed to sustain livestock and support agriculture.

To date, Michael Baigent has accompanied Robert Eisenman and his team of archaeologists and volunteers on two exploratory expeditions, in January 1989 and in January 1990. In the first of them, they concentrated on the excavation of a cave roughly a mile south of Qumran, some 500 feet up the cliff. The cave opened into a series of chambers extending at least eighty feet back into the rock. Part of the interior had a smooth floor made of palm fronds and packed mud. No scrolls came to light, but a number of Iron Age remains were found – a juglet, an oil lamp, and, uniquely, an arrow shaft and arrowhead in perfect preservation after 3,000 years. The expedition proved, for the first time, that some at least of the caves around Qumran had been inhabited – not just used as temporary refuges during brief periods of danger, but occupied on a more permanent basis.

The second expedition endeavoured to explore as much as possible of the Dead Sea coast south of Qumran and the adjacent cliff-face. The purpose of this undertaking was to compile an inventory of all hitherto unexplored caves that might warrant subsequent exhaustive excavation. Dividing itself into small teams, the expedition searched some thirteen miles of cliff, rising precipitously as high as 1,200 feet. Apart from caves, there were found the remains of artificial terraces and walls, of constructions for water control and irrigation – all attesting to human inhabitation and cultivation. Altogether, 137 habitable caves were located and subjected to preliminary examination without excavation. Of these, 83 were deemed worthy of systematic excavation: they will become the focus of future archaeological activity.

Of particular and revolutionary importance to any such activity will be a new system of 'high-tech' ground radar known as 'Subsurface Interface Radar' (SIR). We had been discussing with Eisenman the likelihood of there being other caves in the vicinity of Qumran and along the shore of the Dead Sea, as well as of caves, rooms, cellars, passages and/or other subterranean structures under the ruins of Qumran itself. De Vaux, the only person to attempt any excavation of the actual site, never looked for anything of the sort, never really probed beneath the surface. Yet it is virtually unknown for a construction of the kind attested to by the Qumran ruins *not* to have underground chambers, passages, dungeons or escape tunnels. It is generally acknowledged that something of the sort must indeed exist. But some fairly major excavations would be necessary, involving much trial and error and probably damage to the site.

The prospect, therefore, of finding anything under Qumran seemed, *a priori*, doomed in advance by the magnitude of what would have been entailed. But in the autumn of 1988 we chanced on a newspaper article about a 'secret burial vault' of possible relevance to Shakespearean scholars, found under a church near Stratford-on-Avon. What interested us about this article was the fact that the vault had apparently been located by a species of underground radar scanning system, operated by a firm based in the south of England.

The possibilities offered by SIR proved exciting indeed. It was a terrestrial equivalent of a ship-based sonar recording system. The apparatus was portable. When moved at a constant speed over the ground, it produced a computer-generated image of subterranean features. The image in turn was produced through the building up of a profile of 'interfaces' – that is, points at which earth or rock or any other substance of density and solidity gave way to air. The entire system was thus ideal for locating underground caves and cavities. At the very least, it would register interfaces 30 feet below the surface. Under good conditions, it could penetrate as deep as 120 feet.

The manager of the company that operated the radar proved keen to help. He had, it transpired, read and enjoyed the books we had previously published. The prospect of his equipment being employed at Qumran intrigued him. He even offered to come along on an expedition and operate the apparatus himself. As a result of this offer, Eisenman's 1990 expedition made a special point of noting sites warranting investigation by radar. We are now waiting for permission from the Israeli government to bring the equipment into the country and employ it at Qumran.

The Dead Sea Scrolls found in 1947 were not the first such ancient texts to come to light in the Judaean desert. Indeed, there are reports of such texts being found as early as the 3rd century AD. The theologian Origen, one of the early Church Fathers, is alleged to have made one such discovery. According to the Church historian Eusebius, Origen found several different versions of Old Testament texts, some of which had been lost for many years. He is said to have 'hunted them out of their hiding places and brought them to light'.[3] One version of the psalms, we are told, 'was found at Jericho in a jar during the reign of Antoninus, Son of Severus'.[4] This reference allows us to date the discovery to somewhere between AD 211 and 217.

More intriguing still is a letter dating from some time shortly before AD 805, written by Timotheus, Patriarch of Seleucia, to another ecclesiastic:

> We learned from trustworthy Jews who were being instructed . . . in the Christian faith that ten years ago, near Jericho, some books were found in a cave . . . the dog of an Arab hunter followed an animal into a cave and didn't return. The Arab went in after it and found a small cave in which there were many books. The Arab went to Jerusalem and told the Jews there who then came out in large numbers and found books of the Old Testament and other books in Hebrew characters. As the person who told this story to me was a learned man . . . I asked him about the many references in the New Testament which are referred to as originating in the Old Testament but which cannot be found there . . . He said: they exist and can be found in the books from the cave . . .[5]

Similar discoveries have continued to occur through the centuries, up until modern times. One of the most famous is that of Moses

William Shapira, an antique dealer with a shop in Jerusalem in the late 19th century.[6] In 1878, Shapira was told of some Arabs who, on the run from the authorities, had sought refuge in what is now Jordanian territory, on the eastern shore of the Dead Sea. Here, in a cave at Wadi Mujib, directly across the Dead Sea from En Gedi, they were reported to have found a number of old bundles of rags which they tore open, hoping to find valuables of some kind. They found only a number of dark leather scrolls. One of the Arabs took these away with him and later claimed that possession of them had brought him luck. This was said to be his reason for not wanting to sell them – or for raising the price.

Shapira, who sold antiquities to European collectors and museums, was intrigued. Through a sheik with whom he was friendly, he managed to purchase what purported to be the entire corpus of material. This comprised fifteen strips of parchment, each about three-and-a-half by seven inches in size. After studying his acquisition for some weeks, Shapira realised that what he had was an ancient version of the Book of Deuteronomy, one which differed markedly from the established biblical text.

In 1883, after a number of vicissitudes and consultations with experts, Shapira brought his scroll fragments to London. He was preceded by great excitement and extensive coverage in the press. British experts pronounced the fragments genuine, and translations of them were published in *The Times*. The Prime Minister, William Gladstone, came to see them and discussed their possible purchase with Shapira. A sum of £1 million was apparently mentioned – a staggering figure for the time.

The French government sent a prominent scholar, one of Shapira's old enemies, across the Channel to examine the fragments and compile a report. Shapira refused to let the Frenchman inspect the fragments closely or to handle them. The Frenchman was allowed only a cursory look at two or three fragments. He was then reduced, by Shapira's intransigence, to spending two days looking at two additional fragments on display in a glass case, jostled by other visitors to the museum. Out of spite, and a probably justified exasperation, the Frenchman at last pronounced the fragments to be forgeries. Other scholars, without even bothering to look at the fragments, echoed this conclusion, and the affair quickly degenerated into farce. Shapira had effectively ruined himself. Repudiated and discredited, he shot himself in a Rotterdam hotel room on 9 March 1884. His scroll fragments were purchased by a London antiquarian book-dealer for £10 5s.

Since then, they have disappeared – though they might conceivably still turn up in someone's attic or among the belongings of some private collector. According to the last attempt to trace them, they may have been taken to Australia with the effects of a dealer in antiquities.

A number of modern authorities – including Allegro, who made a special study of Shapira – have become convinced that Shapira's fragments were probably genuine. Had they been discovered this century rather than last, Allegro maintained, they would in all likelihood have proved to be as valid as the material found at Qumran.[7] But in the late 19th century, egos, scholarly reputations and vested interests were as much 'on the line' as they are today. As a result, something of potentially priceless value has, almost certainly, been irretrievably lost.

At the same time, discoveries such as Shapira's continue to be made. Thus, for example, in the late 1970s, when we ourselves had little more than a cursory knowledge of the Dead Sea Scrolls and other such documents, we were telephoned by a friend from Paris, a collector of antiques. He asked if, on virtually no notice, we could meet him at a restaurant in London, not far from Charing Cross. Michael Baigent, who'd done much professional photography, was particularly requested. He was asked to bring a camera along – and keep it hidden.

Baigent found our associate in the company of three other men – an American collector, a Palestinian dealer and a Jordanian engineer. He accompanied them to a nearby bank, where they were ushered into a small private room and two wooden chests were produced, each locked with three padlocks. 'We don't know what's in these chests,' one of the bank's officials said pointedly. 'We don't *want* to know what's in them.' The officials then left, locking Baigent and his four companions in the room.

A telephone call was made to Jerusalem and some sort of permission was obtained. The Jordanian engineer then produced a bunch of keys and proceeded to open the two chests. Inside, there were literally hundreds of thin cardboard sheets, each holding (attached by adhesive tape!) a dozen or so fragments of ancient parchment and/or papyrus. The fragments obviously spanned a considerable period of time, derived from a number of diverse sources and had been inscribed in several different languages – Aramaic, for example, Hebrew, Greek and Arabic. As might be expected of so eclectic and haphazard an assemblage, not everything was of value. Many of the fragments proved subsequently to be worthless – receipts and documents pertaining to ancient commercial transactions that might have been ferreted out of some archaic rubbish tip. But there were others as well.

The collection had come to London through the clandestine scroll market active in Jerusalem and Bethlehem during the 1950s and 1960s, and had been brought out of Israel during, or shortly after, the 1967 war. It was now supposedly being offered for sale to a certain unnamed European government, for an alleged price of £3 million. Baigent was asked to make a selection of photographs, to be displayed as samples of what was available. He took approximately a hundred photographs. But there were hundreds of sheets and, altogether, upwards of two thousand fragments, most of them relatively large.

In the dozen or so years since this incident, we have heard nothing further about the collection. If a sale was indeed negotiated, it was done so quietly, with no public announcement of any kind. Alternatively, the entire collection may still be sequestered in its London bank, or in some other similar depository elsewhere, or amongst the treasures of some private dealer.

Transactions such as the one to which we'd been peripherally privy were not, we subsequently learned, at all uncommon. During the course of the next decade, our research was to bring us into contact with an intricate network of antique dealers and collectors engaged in subterranean scroll traffic. This network is international and deals on a scale comparable to that of networks trafficking in

paintings or gems. Hundreds of thousands of pounds can be produced on virtually immediate notice and be transferred on the basis
of a handshake.

Two factors have conduced to the dissemination of the underground scroll market. One was the action of Yadin and the Israeli
military in the immediate aftermath of the 1967 war, when the dealer
known as Kando was held for interrogation and forced to divulge the
existence of the 'Temple Scroll'. Not surprisingly, this action upset
the existing 'truce' and fostered a profound mistrust between Israeli
and Arab dealers. As a result, much material found by the Bedouin,
which would ordinarily have passed into Israeli hands, now finds its
way illegally to Amman or Damascus or even further afield. From
there, it passes to the West via such routes as Turkey or the Lebanon.

A second spur to the subterranean scroll market was a law
instituted under the auspices of UNESCO, according to which any
antiquities smuggled out of a country must be returned to their point
of origin. This law was made retroactive. In consequence, individuals
who had invested large sums in scroll material, or hoped to obtain
large sums for scroll material, could not afford to make their holdings
public. In effect, the law drove the clandestine traffic in scrolls even
further underground – and, of course, caused a dramatic increase in
prices.

How does the underground scroll trade operate? Much of it
is controlled by certain families well known in the antique trade,
who supply many of the legal antiquities on sale in Israel and
abroad. During the course of the last half-century, these families
have established their own intelligence networks, which maintain
close contacts with the Bedouin and keep abreast of all rumours,
whispers, legends and reported discoveries of antiquarian interest.
When a potentially fruitful site is located, the land will be rented
for a year and a large black Bedouin tent – ostensibly a domicile
– will be erected. At night, excavations will be conducted under
the tent. When all antiquities of value have been removed, the tent
will be dismantled and its occupants will move on. A similar process
occurs in towns, and particularly in Jerusalem, which has proved
especially fertile territory. Sites will be rented for short periods
or, if necessary, purchased. If a house does not already exist, one

will be constructed. The occupants will then excavate downwards from the cellar to bedrock.

Through such procedures as these, much scroll material has found its way into the hands of private collectors and investors. This material entirely circumvents the world of 'official' archaeology and biblical scholarship. Indeed, the world of 'official' archaeology and biblical scholarship often does not even realise it exists. Unknown to the academics, there is at present a substantial quantity of Qumran and related material in the hands of collectors or for sale. We ourselves know of numerous fragments. We know of a well-preserved copy of one Qumran text, called the 'Book of Jubilees'. We know of a handful of letters by Simeon bar Kochba. And there are substantial grounds for believing that other documents – documents of a much more explosive nature, utterly unique and undreamed of by the world of scholarship – also exist.

In the course of the next ten to twenty-five years, major developments can be expected from any or all of three distinct quarters. One of these comprises the territory explored at length in the preceding pages. The campaign continues to prise from the hands of the international team the Qumran material in their possession. As we have seen, this campaign is steadily gaining ground. As public opinion mobilises itself – as the Israeli authorities become more attentive to the matter, as the Israeli *public* becomes outraged by the situation, and as more and more scholars rally to Robert Eisenman's cause – the prospect of *all* the texts now held by the international team being released becomes more imminent. Indeed, there are reasons to suppose that a complete facsimile edition, including photographs of all hitherto unpublished texts, may not be so very long in coming.

At the same time, there is also the possibility, enhanced by each new archaeological expedition Eisenman and his colleagues undertake to Qumran and the shores of the Dead Sea, that wholly new material may come to light. This possibility will be further enhanced – now that the Israeli government has granted permission for its use – by deployment of the 'Subsurface Interface Radar' system.

Finally, there is the clandestine scroll market, which may at any moment cough up something of unprecedented consequence –

234

something hitherto kept secret, at last released into public domain. As we have said, such material exists. The question is simply if and when those who hold it decide it can be divulged.

Whatever the quarter or quarters from which new material might issue, fresh and, in some cases, very major revelations are bound to be forthcoming. As this occurs, we can expect ever more light to be shed on biblical history, on the character of ancient Judaism, on the origins of both Christianity and Islam. One should not, of course, expect a disclosure of such magnitude as to 'topple the Church', or anything as apocalyptic as that. The Church today, after all, is less a religious than a social, cultural, political and economic institution. Its stability and security rest on factors quite remote from the creed, the doctrine and the dogma it promulgates. But some people, at any rate, may be prompted to wonder whether the Church – an institution so demonstrably lax, biased and unreliable in its own scholarship, its own version of its history and origins – should necessarily be deemed reliable and authoritative in its approach to such urgent contemporary matters as overpopulation, birth control, the status of women and the celibacy of the clergy.

Ultimately, however, the import of the Qumran texts resides in something more than their potential to embarrass the Church. The real import of the Qumran texts resides in what they have to reveal of the Holy Land, that soil which, for so many centuries, has voraciously soaked up so much human blood – blood shed in the name of conflicting gods or, to be more accurate, not very dissimilar versions of the same God. Perhaps the documents yet to be divulged may confront us a little more inescapably with the scale and pointlessness of our own madness – and shame us, thereby, at least by a degree or so, in the general direction of sanity. The Dead Sea Scrolls offer a new perspective on the three great religions born in the Middle East. The more one examines those religions, the more one will discern not how much they differ, but how much they overlap and have in common – how much they derive from essentially the same source – and the extent to which most of the quarrels between them, when not precipitated by simple misunderstanding, have stemmed less from spiritual values than from politics, from greed, from selfishness and the presumptuous arrogance of

235

interpretation. Judaism, Christianity and Islam are all, at present, beset by a resurgent fundamentalism. One would like to believe – though this may be too much to hope for – that greater understanding of their common roots might help curb the prejudice, the bigotry, the intolerance and fanaticism to which fundamentalism is chronically prone.

17 January 1991

Notes and References

Note

The full bibliographical details, when not cited here, are to be found in the Bibliography.

Preface

1 Eisenman, *Maccabees, Zadokites, Christians and Qumran*, p.xvi.

1   The Discovery of the Scrolls

1 The true story of the discovery will probably never be known. All the various accounts differ in certain details. Arguments over the correct sequence of events continued into the 1960s. For the different accounts, see: Allegro, *The Dead Sea Scrolls*, pp.17ff.; Brownlee, 'Muhammad Ed-Deeb's own Story of his Scroll Discovery', pp. 236ff.; 'Edh-Dheeb's Story of his Scroll Discovery', pp.483ff.; 'Some New Facts Concerning the Discovery of the Scrolls of 1Q', pp.417ff.; Harding, *The Times*, 9 August 1949, p.5; Samuel, 'The Purchase of the Jerusalem Scrolls', pp.26ff.; *Treasure of Qumran*, pp.142ff.; Trever, 'When was Qumran Cave 1 Discovered?', pp.135ff.; *The Untold Story of Qumran*, pp.25ff.; Wilson, *The Dead Sea Scrolls 1947–1969*, pp.3ff.
2 See, for example, Brownlee, op. cit., p.486, and n.6; Allegro, op. cit., p.20.
3 Wilson, op. cit., p.4.
4 Van der Ploeg, *The Excavations at Qumran*, pp.9–13.
5 Interviews, Miles Copeland, 10 April and 1 May 1990. A search of CIA archives requested under the provisions of the Freedom of Information Act has failed to locate the photographs.

6 Interview, 21 May 1990.
7 Yadin, *The Message of the Scrolls*, pp.15–24, quoting Sukenik's private journal.
8 Ibid., p.14.
9 Trever, *The Untold Story of Qumran*, p.85.
10 *Time Magazine*, 15 April 1957, p.39.
11 Allegro, op. cit., pp.38–9.
12 Ibid., p.41.
13 Pliny, *Natural History*, V, xv.
14 De Vaux, *Archaeology and the Dead Sea Scrolls*, pp.134–5.
15 Reports of this survey can be found in the following: de Vaux, 'Exploration de la région de Qumran', pp.540ff.; Reed, 'The Qumran Caves Expedition of March 1952', pp.8ff.
16 Ibid.
17 Allegro, *The Treasure of the Copper Scroll*, p.35.
18 *Time Magazine*, op. cit., p.38.
19 Yadin, op. cit., p.40.
20 Ibid., pp.41–52.
21 Sharon to Eisenman, 16 January 1990.

2 The International Team

1 Pryce-Jones, 'A New Chapter in the History of Christ?', p.12ff.
2 Ibid., p.14.
3 Ibid.
4 Pryce-Jones to authors, 11 January 1990.
5 Interview, Magen Broshi, 12 November 1989.
6 Interview, Frank Cross, 18 May 1990.
7 Private communication.
8 Interview, Abraham Biran, 4 December 1989.
9 Interview, James Robinson, 3 November 1989.
10 North, 'Qumran and its Archaeology', p.429.
11 Interview, Norman Golb, 1 November 1989.
12 Interview, Shemaryahu Talmon, 8 November 1989.
13 *Time Magazine*, 14 August 1989, p.44.
14 *BAR*, May/June 1989, p.57; September/October 1989, p.20.
15 Interview, James Robinson, 3 November 1989.
16 See Robinson, 'The Jung Codex: the Rise and Fall of a Monopoly'; see also Robinson, 'Getting the Nag Hammadi Library into English'.
17 A total of three volumes of *Discoveries in the Judaean Desert* dealing

with the Cave 4 fragments have been published to date. There remain, so far as the projected publication schedule is concerned, fifteen further volumes dealing with Cave 4 texts and one more of Cave 11.

18 *New York Times*, 26 June 1989, p.B4.
19 *BAR*, September/October 1985, p.6.
20 Ibid., p.66. The magazine adds: 'Obviously, the existence of this factor is controversial and disputed.'
21 Ibid., p.66.
22 *New York Times*, op. cit., pp.B1, B4.
23 *The Chronicle of Higher Education*, 5 July 1989, p.A7.
24 Cross, *The Ancient Library of Qumran*, p.30.
25 Allegro, *The Dead Sea Scrolls*, p.50.
26 This letter and many following are to be found in the private correspondence file of John Allegro's papers.

3 The Scandal of the Scrolls

1 Wilson, *The Dead Sea Scrolls 1947–1969*, p.77.
2 Ibid., pp.97–8.
3 Ibid., p.97.
4 Interview, Philip Davies, 10 October 1989.
5 There was, however, one 'rash' statement made by Wilson which, for the record, should be dismissed. De Vaux told Wilson a story of events during the Six Day War, when, according to Wilson's report, the Israeli troops, upon entering the grounds of the Ecole Biblique on 6 June 1967, sat priests, two at a time, as hostages in the open courtyard. The threat was that they should be shot if any sniper fire should come from the buildings of the Ecole or the associated Monastery of St Stephen. See Wilson, op. cit., p.259. Interviews in Israel have indicated that this event did not take place but was a tale foisted upon Wilson by de Vaux. Wilson did not apparently check this statement with any Israeli sources.
6 Interview, Shemaryahu Talmon, 8 November 1989.
7 Given to the Académie des Inscriptions et Belles-Lettres on 26 May 1950. Reported in *Le Monde*, 28–9 May 1950, p.4.
8 Brownlee, 'The Servant of the Lord in the Qumran Scrolls I', p.9.
9 Allegro to Strugnell, in a letter undated but written between 14 and 31 December 1955.
10 Ibid.
11 Ibid.

12 *New York Times*, 5 February 1956, p.2.
13 Ibid.
14 *The Times*, 8 February 1956, p.8.
15 Allegro to de Vaux, 9 February 1956.
16 Allegro to de Vaux, 20 February 1956.
17 Ibid.
18 Allegro to de Vaux, 7 March 1956.
19 Ibid.
20 Allegro to Cross, 6 March 1956.
21 *The Times*, 16 March 1956, p.11.
22 *The Times*, 20 March 1956, p.13.
23 Ibid.
24 Allegro to Strugnell, 8 March 1957.
25 Smyth, 'The Truth about the Dead Sea Scrolls', p.33.
26 Ibid., p.34.
27 Allegro to Claus-Hunno Hunzinger, 23 April 1956.
28 Harding to Allegro, 28 May 1956.
29 *The Times*, 1 June 1956, p.12.
30 Allegro to Harding, 5 June 1956.
31 Ibid.
32 Ibid.
33 Allegro to Cross, 5 August 1956.
34 Allegro to de Vaux, 16 September 1956.
35 Allegro to team member (name withheld), 14 September 1959.
36 Team member (name withheld) to Allegro, 21 October 1959.
37 Allegro to de Vaux, 16 September 1956.
38 Ibid.
39 *BAR*, March/April 1990, p.24. This text is catalogued as 4Q246 and forms part of Milik's collection.
40 Allegro to Cross, 31 October 1957.
41 Ibid.
42 Allegro to James Muilenburg, 31 October 1957.
43 Allegro to Muilenburg, 24 December 1957.
44 Ibid.
45 Allegro to Dajani, 10 January 1959.
46 Ibid.
47 *The Times*, 23 May 1970, p.22.
48 *The Times*, 19 May 1970, p.2.
49 *The Times*, 26 May 1970, p.9.
50 *The Daily Telegraph*, 18 May 1987, p.11.

51   *The Times*, 5 October 1970, p.4.
52   Wilson, op. cit., p.125.
53   Vermes, *The Dead Sea Scrolls: Qumran in Perspective*, pp.23–4.
54   *Times Literary Supplement*, 3 May 1985, p.502.
55   Ibid.
56   Eisenman has pointed to mention of 'the Poor' in the *War Scroll*; see
      Eisenman, op. cit., p.43, n.23; p.62, n.105. This text states that the
      Messiah will lead 'the Poor' to victory against the armies of Belial
      (*The War Scroll*, XI,14 (Vermes, p.116 – Vermes for his own reasons
      translates 'Belial' as 'Satan')). For a more detailed discussion, see
      Eisenman, 'Eschatological "Rain" Imagery in the War Scroll from
      Qumran and in the Letter of James', p.182.
57   Interview, Emile Puech, 7 November 1989.
58   This fragment is coded 4Q246. See *BAR*, March/April 1990, p.24.
      It is to this document that Allegro was alluding in his letter of 16
      September 1956 (see above p.56).
59   Ibid.

4   *Opposing the Consensus*

1   *The Times*, 23 August 1949, p.5.
2   Ibid.
3   Jean Carmignac, review of Roth, *The Historical Background of the
     Dead Sea Scrolls*. See *Revue de Qumran*, no.3, 1959 (vol.i, 1958–9),
     p.447.
4   De Vaux made this assertion in 'Fouilles au Khirbet Qumran',
     Revue biblique, vol.lxi (1954), p.233. He repeated it in his 'Fouilles
     de Khirbet Qumran', *Revue biblique*, vol.lxiii (1956), p.567, and in
     'Les manuscrits de Qumran et l'archéologie', *Revue biblique*, vol.lxvi
     (1959), p.100.
5   Roth, 'Did Vespasian Capture Qumran?', *Palestine Exploration
     Quarterly*, July–December 1959, pp.122ff.
6   Driver, *The Judaean Scrolls*, p.3.
7   De Vaux, review of Driver, *The Judaean Scrolls*. See *New Testament
     Studies*, vol.xiii (1966–7), p.97.
8   Ibid., p.104.
9   Albright, in M. Black, ed. *The Scrolls and Christianity*, p.15.
10   Eisenman to authors, 13 June 1990.
11   Eisenman to authors, 27 September 1989.
12   *BAR*, September/October 1985, p.66.

13 Ibid., p.6.
14 Ibid., p.66.
15 Ibid., p.70. *BAR* first called for the publication of the unpublished scrolls in May 1985.
16 Ibid.
17 Benoit to Cross, Milik, Starcky and Puech, Strugnell, E. Ulrich, Avi (sic) Eitan, 15 September 1985.
18 Eitan to Benoit, 26 December 1985.
19 Interview, Yuval Ne'eman, 16 January 1990.
20 Ibid.
21 Eisenman, *Maccabees, Zadokites, Christians and Qumran*, p.xvi.
22 Eisenman to authors, 5 July 1990.
23 It is called '*MMT*' from the first letters of three Hebrew words occurring in the opening line: *Miqsat Ma'aseh ha-Torah*, 'Some rulings upon the Law'. The text essentially gives the position of the Qumran community on a selection of rules from the Torah.
24 *Catalogue of the Dead Sea Scrolls*, 07/04/81.
25 Eisenman to authors, 15 September 1990.
26 A copy of this timetable was published in *BAR*, July/August 1989, p.20. Mrs Ayala Sussman of the Israeli Department of Antiquities confirmed for us that this was the timetable. Interview with Ayala Sussman, 7 November 1989.
27 Letter, Eisenman and Davies to Strugnell, 16 March 1989.
28 Letter, Eisenman and Davies to Drori, 2 May 1989.
29 Ibid.
30 Ibid.
31 Letter, Strugnell to Eisenman, 15 May 1989.
32 *BAR*, September/October 1989, p.20.
33 Letter, Strugnell to Eisenman, 15 May 1989.
34 Davies, 'How not to do Archaeology: The Story of Qumran', pp.203–4.

5 Academic Politics and Bureaucratic Inertia

1 Florentino Garcia-Martinez to Eisenman, 4 October 1989.
2 *New York Times*, 9 July 1989, p.E26.
3 *BAR*, May/June 1990, p.67.
4 *BAR*, July/August 1990, p.44.
5 *BAR*, July/August 1989, p.18.
6 *BAR*, November/December 1989, p.74.

7   *BAR*, July/August 1989, p.18.
8   Ibid., p.19.
9   *Los Angeles Times*, 1 July 1989, Part II, pp.20–21.
10 *International Herald Tribune*, 16 November 1989, p.2.
11 *BAR*, July/August 1990, p.47.
12 *Time Magazine*, 14 August 1989, p.44.
13 *BAR*, March/April 1990, cover.
14 *BAR*, July/August 1990, p.6.
15 Interview, Ayala Sussman, 7 November 1989.
16 Ibid.
17 Ibid.
18 Interview, Shemaryahu Talmon, 8 November 1989.
19 Ibid.
20 Ibid.
21 Interview, Shemaryahu Talmon, 9 November 1989.
22 Interview, Jonas Greenfield, 9 November 1989.
23 Conversation with Ayala Sussman, 10 November 1989.
24 Ibid.
25 Ibid.
26 Interview, Hilary Feldman, 4 December 1989.
27 Ibid.

6   The Onslaught of Science

1   Letter, Allegro to Muilenburg, 24 December 1957.
2   Letter, Strugnell to Allegro, 3 January 1956.
3   Wilson, *The Dead Sea Scrolls 1947–1969*, p.138.
4   Allegro's suspicions about the international team were raised during
    his summer at the 'Scrollery' in 1957. They crystallised during the
    débâcle of his television programme, the filming of which took
    place in Jerusalem, Qumran and Amman in October 1957. He
    planned to try to break up the international team and open the
    scrolls to all qualified scholars. Then, in a letter to Awni Dajani
    (curator of the Palestine Archaeological Museum) dated 10 January
    1959, Allegro wrote: 'I think it would be a ripe opportunity to take
    over the whole Museum, scrolls and all . . .' Allegro returned to this
    theme in September 1966. On 13 September of that year he wrote to
    Awni Dajani saying that he was very concerned about the situation
    and that the Jordanian government should act. It is clear, though,
    from a letter of 16 September 1966 (to Joseph Saad), that Allegro had

been told that the Jordanian government was planning to nationalise the museum at the end of the year. Allegro then began a series of letters regarding the preservation of the scrolls and ideas for raising funds for research and publication. Then, as adviser on the scrolls to the Jordanian government, he produced a report on the present state and the future of scroll research which he sent to King Hussein on 21 September 1966. The same day he also sent a copy of the report to the Jordanian Prime Minister. The Jordanian government nationalised the museum in November 1966.

5   *BAR*, July/August 1990, p.6.
6   Interview, Philip Davies, 10 October 1989.
7   Interview, Norman Golb, 1 November 1989.
8   *Palestine Exploration Fund Quarterly Statement*, 1887, p.16.
9   De Rosa, *Vicars of Christ*, p.179.
10 For a detailed account of the personal and political machinations which lay behind the promulgation of this dogma, see Hasler, *How the Pope became Infallible*.
11 Ibid., p.246.
12 Fogazzaro, *The Saint*, p.242.
13 Schroeder, *Père Lagrange and Biblical Inspiration*, p.13, n.7.
14 Ibid., p.15.
15 Letter, Allegro to Cross, 5 August 1956.
16 Murphy, *Lagrange and Biblical Renewal*, p.60.
17 Ibid.
18 Ibid., p.62.
19 Ibid., p.64.
20 Ibid.
21 Ibid., 61–2.
22 De Vaux to Golb, 26 March 1970.
23 Interview, Norman Golb, 1 November 1989.
24 *BAR*, July/August 1990, p.45.
25 *BAR*, January/February 1990, p.10.
26 *Jerusalem Post Magazine*, 29 September 1989, p.11.

7   The Inquisition Today

1   *New Catholic Encyclopaedia*, vol.xi, p.551.
2   Ibid.
3   *Annuario pontificio*, 1989, p.1187.
4   *Annuario pontificio*, 1956, p.978.

5   *Annuario pontificio*, 1973, p.1036.

6   *Annuario pontificio*, 1988, p.1139.

7   *New Catholic Encyclopaedia*, vol.xi, p.551.

8   Benjamin Wambacq, 'The Historical Truth of the Gospels', *The Tablet*, 30 May 1964, p.619.

9   Ibid.

10 Hebblethwaite, *Synod Extraordinary*, p.54. According to Pope John Paul II, 'the Congregation for the Doctrine of the Faith has no other purpose than to preserve from all danger . . . the authenticity and integrity of . . . faith'; see Hebblethwaite, *In the Vatican*, p.90.

11 *Annuario pontificio*, 1969, pp.967, 1080.

12 Schillebeeckx argues that the 'apostolic right' – the rights of the local leaders of Church communities – 'has priority over the Church order which has in fact grown up'. See *Ministry: A Case for Change*, p.37.

13 Küng, *Infallible? An Enquiry*, p.196.

14 Ibid., p.102.

15 Ibid., p.18.

16 Küng, 'The Fallibility of Pope John Paul II', *Observer*, 23 December 1979, p.11.

17 Ibid.

18 *Sunday Times*, 2 December 1984, p.13.

19 Ibid.

20 *Observer*, 27 May 1990, p.1.

21 *Independent*, 27 June 1990, p.10.

22 *The Times*, 27 June 1990, p.9.

8   The Dilemma for Christian Orthodoxy

1   *The Community Rule*, III, 7ff. (Vermes, p.64). (As Vermes's translations of the Dead Sea Scroll texts are the easiest to obtain for the English speaking reader, page references to his work will be added.)

2   Acts, 2:44–6.

3   *The Community Rule*, I, 11ff. (Vermes, p.62).

4   Ibid., VI, 2–3 (Vermes, p.69).

5   Ibid., VI, 22–3 (Vermes, p.70).

6   Eisenman, in *James the Just in the Habakkuk Pesher*, p.32, n.16, draws important parallels between the ruling council of Qumran and that of the 'early Church' in Jerusalem, under James.

7   *The Commentary on Psalm 37*, III, 11 (Vermes, p.291). See also

Eisenman, *Maccabees, Zadokites, Christians and Qumran*, p.108 (*Ebion/ Ebionim*), and pp.xiv, xvi, and 62–3.

8 *The War Scroll*, XIV, 7 (Vermes, p.120).

9 *The Community Rule*, VIII, 21 (Vermes, p.73). See also Eisenman, *Maccabees, Zadokites, Christians and Qumran*, p.42, n.21; pp. 89–90; p.109 for *Tamimei-Derech*.

10 *The Community Rule*, X, 21–2 (Vermes, p.77).

11 *The Community Rule*, VIII, 7 (Vermes, p.72). See also Eisenman, *Maccabees, Zadokites, Christians and Qumran*, p.80.

12 *The Community Rule*, I, 1 (Vermes, p.61–2).

13 *The Habakkuk Commentary*, VIII, 2–3 (Vermes, p.287). See also Eisenman, *James the Just in the Habakkuk Pesher*, pp.37–40.

14 *The Community Rule*, I, 2–3 (Vermes, pp.61–2).

15 *The Community Rule*, VIII, 22ff. (Vermes, p.73). See also Eisenman, *Maccabees, Zadokites, Christians and Qumran*, p.xii.

16 *The Community Rule*, II, 19 (Vermes, p.63).

17 Driver, *The Judaean Scrolls*, pp.316–30; Talmon, *The World of Qumran from Within*, pp.147–85.

18 *The Community Rule*, VI, 4–6 (Vermes, p.69).

19 *The Messianic Rule*, II, 20–21 (Vermes, p.102).

20 Danielou, *The Dead Sea Scrolls and Primitive Christianity*, p.27.

9 The Scrolls

1 *Newsweek*, 27 February 1989, p.55.

2 *The Community Rule*, VII, 3 (Vermes, p.71; Vermes gives the words: 'whoever has deliberately lied'; these words do not exist in the Hebrew original, which reads 'if he has spoken unwittingly').

3 Ibid, I, 16ff. (Vermes, p.62).

4 Ibid., III, 6ff. (Vermes, pp.64).

5 Ibid., V, 9 (Vermes, p.67).

6 Ibid., IX, 23 (Vermes, p.75; translated by Vermes as 'zealous for the Precept', which tends to obscure this important phrase).

7 Ibid, VI, 16ff. (Vermes, p.71).

8 Ibid., VIII, 3ff. (Vermes, p.72). See also Eisenman, *Maccabees, Zadokites, Christians and Qumran*, p.42, n.21; for a detailed discussion, see *James the Just in the Habakkuk Pesher*, p.8.

9 *The Community Rule*, IX, 11 (Vermes, p.74).

10 *The War Scroll*, VI, 7 (Vermes, p.111; Vermes calls this document 'The War Rule').

11   Ibid., XI, 7 (Vermes, p.116; Vermes translates 'Messiah' as 'Thine anointed' which obscures the import of this passage). See also Eisenman, 'Eschatological "Rain" Imagery in the War Scroll from Qumran and in the Letter of James', pp.180–82.

12   *The Temple Scroll*, LXVI, 10ff. (Vermes, p.158). See also Eisenman's appendix to *James the Just in the Habakkuk Pesher*, entitled 'The "Three Nets of Belial" in the Zadokite Document and "balla/BELA" in the Temple Scroll', pp.87–94.

13   Eisenman, ibid., p.89.

14   Ibid., demonstrating the niece-marriage connection to Herodians.

15   Parts of eight copies of the 'Damascus Document' were found in Cave 4, parts of another in Cave 5 and one more in Cave 6.

16   Eisenman, appendix to *James the Just in the Habakkuk Pesher*, 'The "Three Nets of Belial" in the Zadokite Document and "balla/bela" in the Temple Scroll', pp.87–94.

17   *The Damascus Document*, VIII, 21–21b (Vermes, p.90). (All line numbers for this document are from the edition of C. Rabin.)

18   Ibid., XX, 15 (Vermes, p.90).

19   Ibid., MS 'A', VII, 18–20 (Vermes, p.89).

20   Ibid., VII, 21a (Vermes, p.88); XX, 1 (Vermes, p.90); XII, 23 (Vermes, p.97); XIII, 20 (Vermes, p.98); XIV, 19 (Vermes, p.99).

21   See Eisenman, *Maccabees, Zadokites, Christians and Qumran*, p.68, n.120; p.69, n.122.

22   Ibid., p.42, n.19. In addition to the documents we have mentioned, reference to the 'Liar' or to those who reject the Law can be found in the Psalm 37 Commentary and other Qumran texts.

23   Ibid., p.xv.

24   Josephus, *The Jewish Wars*, VI, vi. See aso Driver, *The Judaean Scrolls*, pp.211–14; Eisenman, *James the Just in the Habakkuk Pesher*, p.27.

10   *Science in the Service of Faith*

1   See, for example, Vermes, *The Dead Sea Scrolls in English*, pp.29, 31; de Vaux, *Archaeology and the Dead Sea Scrolls*, pp.116–17.

2   Driver, *The Judaean Scrolls*, p.211.

3   De Vaux, in *New Testament Studies*, vol.xiii (1966–7), p.91.

4   Ibid., p.93.

5   Ibid.

6   Eisenman, in *Maccabees, Zadokites, Christians and Qumran*, exposes de Vaux's treatment of Driver; see p.47, n.47; p.56, n.92; p.57, n.93; p.72, n.129; p.83 (n.155).

7   North, 'Qumran and its Archaeology', p.434.

8   A British architect with previous experience of repairing earthquake-damaged buildings was in charge of the reconstruction of the Qumran ruins for the Jordanian government prior to the war of 1967. He stated that there was no evidence that the Qumran buildings were damaged by earthquake and gave, as his opinion, that the crack in the cistern was caused by the weight of water coupled with faulty construction or repair. See Steckoll, 'Marginal Notes on the Qumran Excavations', p.34.

9   Callaway, *The History of the Qumran Community*, p.45.

10 Milik, *Ten Years of Discovery in the Wilderness of Judaea*, p.52.

11 De Vaux, 'Fouilles au Khirbet Qumran', p.233. This article appeared in 1954.

12 De Vaux, in *New Testament Studies*, vol.xiii (1966–7), p.104.

13 De Vaux, 'Les Manuscrits de Qumran et l'archéologie', p.100.

14 Cross, *The Ancient Library of Qumran*, p.47.

15 Roth, 'Did Vespasian capture Qumran?', p.124.

16 De Vaux, *L'archéologie et les manuscrits de la mer morte*, p.32, n.1; *Archaeology and the Dead Sea Scrolls*, p.40, n.1. In addition, it is worth noting that in the absence of any complete publication of de Vaux's excavation results certain doubts linger about all his coin discoveries. The Israeli coin expert Ya'acov Meshorer told Eisenman that neither he nor anyone else he knew had ever seen de Vaux's coins. Eisenman, *Maccabees, Zadokites, Christians and Qumran*, p.93, n.173. See also p.94, n.175 for the so-called '10th Legion' coin.

17 De Vaux, *Archaeology and the Dead Sea Scrolls*, p.67.

18 Ibid., pp.19, 22, 34, 37, 44–5. It is difficult to be precise about the exact numbers of coins found and their identification until the long-delayed publication of de Vaux's final report on the excavation. The archaeological reports published in *Revue biblique* have, by de Vaux's own admission, been incorrect with regard to the coin identification. See ibid, p.19, n.3.

19 Ibid., p.109.

20 Eisenman, op. cit., p.34.

21 Ibid., p.92 (n.168).

22 De Vaux, op. cit., p.43.

23 Driver, op. cit., p.396.

24 Ibid., p.394.

25 De Vaux, in *New Testament Studies*, vol.xiii (1966–7), p.99, n.1.

26 Danielou, *The Dead Sea Scrolls and Primitive Christianity*, pp.121–2.

27 De Vaux, *Archaeology and the Dead Sea Scrolls*, p.28. See also Eisenman, op. cit., p.94, n.174.

28 Cross, op. cit., p.51.

29 Driver, op. cit., p.397.

30 Golb, 'The Dead Sea Scrolls', p.182. In *Science Times*, 21 November 1989, p.C8, Golb said of Qumran, 'There's nothing to show it was anything but a fortress.'

31 Golb, 'The Problem of Origin and Identification of the Dead Sea Scrolls', p.5.

32 Cross, op. cit., pp.86–7.

33 Cross, 'The Development of the Jewish Scripts', in Wright, *The Bible and the Ancient Near East*, p. 135. See also Eisenman, op. cit., pp.28–31; p.82, n.155; p.84, n.156 and n.157; p.86, n.158 and n.159; p.87, n.161; p.88, n.163.

34 Cross, ibid., p.191, n.20.

35 Birnbaum, *The Hebrew Scripts*, p.130. This was first pointed out by Eisenman, op. cit., p.85 (n.157).

36 Eisenman, op. cit., p.85 (n.157).

37 Davies, 'How Not to do Archaeology: the Story of Qumran', p.206.

38 Eisenman, op. cit., p.29.

39 Ibid., p.30.

40 Eisenman to authors, 7 July 1990.

41 Roth, 'The Zealots and Qumran: The Basic Issue', p.84.

11   The Essenes

1 The main classical references to the Essenes are found in:
Josephus, *Life*; *The Jewish Wars*, II, viii; *Antiquities of the Jews*, XVIII, i
Philo Judaeus, *Every Good Man is Free*, XII–XIII; *Hypothetica*, 11
Pliny, *Natural History*, V, xv.

2 Josephus, *The Jewish Wars*, II, viii.

3 Josephus, *Antiquities of the Jews*, XV, x.

4 Josephus, *The Jewish Wars*, II, viii.

5 Josephus, *Antiquities of the Jews*, XV, x.

6 Ibid. This close relationship between the Essenes of Josephus' description and King Herod the Great was explored in detail in Eisenman, 'Confusions of Pharisees and Essenes in Josephus',

a paper delivered to the Society of Biblical Literature Conference in New York, 1981.

7 Josephus, *The Jewish Wars*, II, viii.
8 Quoted by Dupont-Sommer, *The Essene Writings from Qumran*, p.13.
9 Ibid.
10 Cross, *The Ancient Library of Qumran*, pp.37–8.
11 The standard elaboration of the consensus hypothesis is in de Vaux, *Archaeology and the Dead Sea Scrolls*, pp.3–45.
12 Josephus, *The Jewish Wars*, II, viii.
13 Philo Judaeus, *Every Good Man is Free*, XII.
14 De Vaux, *Archaeology and the Dead Sea Scrolls*, pp.12–14.
15 Josephus, *Antiquities of the Jews*, XV, x. See also on this, Eisenman, *James the Just in the Habakkuk Pesher*, p.79.
16 Philo Judaeus, *Every Good Man is Free*, XII.
17 Cross, *The Ancient Library of Qumran*, p.51.
18 Philo Judaeus, *Every Good Man is Free*, XII.
19 Vermes, 'The Etymology of "Essenes" ', p.439. See also Vermes, *The Dead Sea Scrolls: Qumran in Perspective*, p.126.
20 Eisenman, *Maccabees, Zadokites, Christians and Qumran*, p.6.
21 Ibid., p.108 (*Derech*, 'the Way'; *ma'aseh*, 'works'/'acts'); p.109 (*Tamimei-Derech*, 'the Perfect of the Way'; *Tom-Derech*, 'Perfection of the Way'). See also the discussion on p.41, n.17.
22 Ibid., p.109.
23 Epiphanius of Constantia, *Adversus octoginta haereses*, I, i, Haeres xx (Migne, 41, col.273).
24 Eisenman, op. cit., p.44, n.30.
25 Black, 'The Dead Sea Scrolls and Christian Origins', in Black, *The Scrolls and Christianity*, p.99.
26 Eisenman, *James the Just in the Habakkuk Pesher*, p.99 (*Nozrei ha-Brit*).
27 Ibid., pp.vii–x.
28 *The Habakkuk Commentary*, XII, 7ff. (Vermes, p.289).

12 The Acts of the Apostles

1 Eisenman, *Maccabees, Zadokites, Christians and Qumran*, pp. xiii, 4–6.
2 Josephus, *Antiquities of the Jews*, XVIII, i. See also ibid., p.59, n.99.
3 Eisenman, op. cit., pp.10–11, 22–3. For arguments regarding the 'Stephen' episode being a reworking of an attack upon James as recorded in the *Recognitions of Clement* (I, 70), see p.76, n.144, and also *James the Just in the Habakkuk Pesher*, p.4, n.11; p.39.

4   Eisenman, *Maccabees, Zadotites, Christians and Qumran*, p.41, n.17.

5   Ibid., p.68, n.120; p.69, n.122. Eisenman sees both 'Damascus' references as generically parallel.

6   *The Community Rule*, VI, 14–23 (Vermes, p.70). The sense is not entirely clear: this novitiate period was at least two years with the third year being the first of full membership; or, the novitiate itself took three years with the fourth year being the first of full membership. See Vermes, *The Dead Sea Scrolls in English*, p.7.

7   Eisenman, *James the Just in the Habakkuk Pesher*, pp.30–32.

8   Eisenman points to the psychological attitude demonstrated in Paul's first letter to the Corinthians where he, among other precepts, explains the necessity of 'winning':

> So though I am not a slave of any man I have made myself the slave of everyone so as to win as many as I could. I made myself a Jew to the Jews, to win the Jews . . . To those who have no Law, I was free of the Law myself . . . to win those who have no Law . . . All the runners at the stadium are trying to win, but only one of them gets the prize. You must run in the same way, meaning to win. (1 Corinthians 9:19–27).

9   Eisenman, *James the Just in the Habakkuk Pesher*, pp.30–32.

10   Ibid.; see also p.57, n.39 (where Eisenman reviews Paul's 'defamation of the Jerusalem leadership' in his letters).

11   *The Damascus Document*, XV, 12–14 (Vermes, p.92).

12   Acts 23:23 states unequivocally that there were 200 soldiers, 200 auxiliaries and 70 cavalry as the escort.

13   Eisenman, *James the Just in the Habakkuk Pesher*, p.3.

13   James 'The Righteous'

1   While Acts never explicitly states that James is the 'leader' of the Jerusalem community, in Acts 15:13–21 and 21:18 he has a prominent role. The latter tellingly states that 'Paul went . . . to visit James, and all the elders were present'. This puts the elders in a subordinate position to James. Paul, in his letter to the Galatians (2:9), states: 'James, Cephas and John, these leaders, these pillars'. Later, this same letter (2:11–12) clearly shows that Cephas is subordinate to James (Cephas = Peter). John is barely mentioned in Acts after the introduction of Paul.

Later Church writers specifically call James the leader of the early 'Christians'.

2   For example, James 2:10: 'if a man keeps the whole of the Law, except for one small point at which he fails, he is still guilty of breaking it all'. See Eisenman, *James the Just in the Habakkuk Pesher*, p.2, n.6; p.21, n.1; p.25; p.58 (n.39).

3   In the Greek text it reads as here. Curiously, *The Jerusalem Bible* translated primarily by de Vaux and the members of the Ecole Biblique obscures the sense with the reading: 'It was you who condemned the innocent and killed them . . .'

4   *Recognitions of Clement*, I, 70.

5   Ibid.

6   Eisenman, when discussing this incident, notes that six weeks later, when in Caesarea, Peter mentions that James was still limping as a result of his injury. As Eisenman says, 'Details of this kind are startling in their intimacy and one should hesitate before simply dismissing them as artistic invention.' See Eisenman, op. cit, p.4, n.11.

7   *Recognitions of Clement*, I, 71.

8   Josephus, *Antiquities of the Jews*, XX, ix.

9   Eusebius, *The History of the Church*, 2, 1; 2, 23.

10   Ibid., 2, 1.

11   A number of the older monasteries in Spain have, since their foundation, systematically collected all available texts both orthodox and heretical. As these monasteries have never been plundered, their holdings remain intact. Unfortunately, access to their libraries is severely restricted.

12   Eusebius, op. cit., 2, 23.

13   Eisenman, op. cit., p.3.

14   Ibid.

15   Eusebius, op. cit., 2, 23.

16   Eisenman, op. cit., p.10.

17   Eusebius, op. cit., 2, 23.

18   Ibid.

19   Ibid. See also Eisenman, op. cit., p.28, n.12; p.60, n.40 (referring to Origen, *Contra celsum*, 1.47; 2.13).

20   Herod Agrippa II.

21   Eisenman, op. cit., pp.63–5.

22   *The Habakkuk Commentary*, II, 2 (Vermes, p.284).

23   Ibid., II, 3–4 (Vermes, p.284).

24   Ibid., V, 11–12 (Vermes, p.285).
25   Ibid., X, 9–10 (Vermes, p.288).
26   Ibid., X, 11–12 (Vermes, p.288).
27   For a comprehensive review of Paul's sensitivity to the charge of lying, see Eisenman, op. cit., p.39, n.24.
28   Eisenman, op. cit., p.viii, points out the important difference between the 'Liar' and the 'Wicked Priest'. This distinction must be made before any historical sense can be made of the texts. The consensus position is that the 'Liar' and the 'Wicked Priest' are the same person. See Vermes, *The Dead Sea Scrolls in English*, p.30.
29   *The Habakkuk Commentary*, IX, 2 (Vermes, p.287). See Eisenman, op. cit., pp.50–51, where he explains that the passage would read more accurately as: 'they took vengeance upon the flesh of his corpse'. This relates the passage very closely to the known facts of Ananas' death. See also Eisenman, 'Interpreting "*Arbeit Galuto*" in the Habakkuk *Pesher*', which connects this phrase to the Sanhedrin trial of James.
30   *The Habakkuk Commentary*, XII, 7ff. (Vermes, p.289).
31   Eisenman to authors, 22 August 1990.
32   *The Habakkuk Commentary*, VIII, 1ff. (Vermes, p.287). See also Eisenman, op. cit., pp.37–9, for a discussion of this reference to 'faith'.
33   Eisenman, ibid.

14   Zeal for the Law

1   Eisenman, *Maccabees, Zadokites, Christians and Qumran*, p.44, n.30.
2   Ibid., p.6.
3   Ibid., p.8; p.45, n.36 (quoting Wernberg-Møller).
4   Ibid., p.12; p.49, n.58; see also p.26.
5   Ibid., p.12.
6   Ibid., p.13; p.49, n.58. See Numbers 25:7ff. Mattathias invokes this covenant in his dying speech (1 Macc. 2:54): 'Phinehas our father, because he was deeply zealous, received the covenant of everlasting priesthood.' (Revised Standard Version)
7   Eisenman to authors, 29 August 1990.
8   Ibid., pp.13–16; p.45, n.36.
9   Ibid., p.44, n.30.
10   Ibid., p.10.
11   Ibid., p.90, n.164. This terminology of 'purist' and 'Herodian'

Sadducees derives from Eisenman. The 'purist' Sadducees, or the 'Zealots', were, after 4 BC, 'Messianic' in their ideology. Hence Eisenman refines his terminology on occasion to speak of the post-4 BC groups rather as 'Messianic Sadducees' and 'Boethusian Sadducees' – the latter after Simon ben Boethus, whom Herod established as high priest. In our text, we have retained the simpler division into 'purist' and 'Herodian' groups. This approach provides the key to understanding the *'MMT'* document.

12 Josephus, *The Jewish Wars*, II, i. See Eisenman, op. cit., pp.25–6.
13 Josephus, op. cit., II, iv.
14 Ibid., II, viii.
15 Eisenman, op. cit., p.53, n.79; p.75, n.140.
16 Josephus, *Antiquities of the Jews*, XVIII, i.
17 Ibid., XVII, x.
18 Josephus, *The Jewish Wars*, II, xvii.
19 Josephus, *Antiquities of the Jews*, XVIII, i.
20 This material received an early public airing in a paper given by Eisenman to the Society of Biblical Literature at its meeting in New York in 1981, 'Confusions of Pharisees and Essenes in Josephus'.
21 *The Interlinear Greek–English New Testament*, Acts 21:20.
22 Eisenman, op. cit., pp.5–9.
23 Ibid., p.58, n.95.
24 Ibid., pp.36–7; p.90, n.164; p.96 (n.179).
25 Josephus, *The Jewish Wars*, VII, x; the translation of G.A. Williamson is used here (*The Jewish War*, pp.392–3).
26 Eisenman, op. cit., p.96, n.180.
27 Ibid., pp.25–6.
28 Ibid., p.73, n.132; listing *The Damascus Document*, VII, 18–21; *The War Scroll*, XI, 5ff.; *A Messianic Testimonia* (4QTest), 9–13.
29 *The Damascus Document*, VII, 18–21.
30 Tacitus, *The Histories*, V, xiii; the translation of K. Wellesley is used here (p.279). See also Suetonius, *The Twelve Caesars*, Vespasian, 4; translation by R. Graves (p.281).
31 Eisenman, op. cit., p.25.
32 Gichon, 'The Bar Kochba War', p.88.
33 Ibid., p.92.
34 Ibid., pp.89–90.
35 Gichon to authors, 12 January 1990.

15 Zealot Suicide

1 The last sentence of this quote from Matthew is a pure Qumran-style statement opposing the methods of 'the Liar'.
2 Josephus, *The Jewish Wars*, VII, ix.
3 Ibid., VII, viii; the translation used is that of G.A. Williamson, *The Jewish War*, p.387.
4 Ibid. (Williamson, p.390).
5 Ibid., III, viii.
6 Yadin, *Masada*, pp.187–8. Yadin makes nothing of this fact. See Eisenman, *Maccabees, Zadokites, Christians and Qumran*, p.22; p.67 n.117.
7 Ibid., p.62 n.105.
8 *The War Scroll*, I, 6–8 (Vermes, p.105).

16 Paul – Roman Agent or Informer?

1 Especially 1 Corinthians 9:19–27. See above, Chapter 11, n.8.
2 Eisenman to authors, 24 August 1990.
3 Eisenman, *James the Just in the Habakkuk Pesher*, p.16, n.39; p.59, n.39.
4 Eisenman, *Maccabees, Zadokites, Christians and Qumran*, p.62, n.105, makes the point that 'Paul's "Gentile mission", overriding the demands of the Law and addressed equally "to Jews and Gentiles alike" . . . is perfectly in line with the exigencies of Herodian family policy.' Eisenman has made a detailed examination of all the evidence surrounding Paul's links with the ruling families in a paper 'Paul as Herodian' delivered to the Society of Biblical Literature, 1983.

Postscript

1 *BAR*, July 1989, p.21.
2 Bar-Adon, 'Another Settlement of the Judean Desert Sect'.
3 Eusebius, *The History of the Church*, VI, 16 (p.256).
4 Ibid.
5 Braun, 'Ein Brief des Katholikos Timotheos I', p.305.
6 The full story of Shapira is told in Allegro, *The Shapira Affair*.
7 Ibid., pp.114–19.

Bibliography

Albright, W.F. *The Archaeology of Palestine*, rev. edn (Harmondsworth, 1963)

Allegro, J.M. *The Treasure of the Copper Scroll* (London, 1960)
 The Sacred Mushroom and the Cross (London, 1970)
 The Dead Sea Scrolls: A Reappraisal, 2nd edn (Harmondsworth, 1975)
 The Dead Sea Scrolls and the Christian Myth (Newton Abbot, 1979)

Annuario pontificio (Vatican City; published annually)

Avigad, N. and Yadin, Y. *A Genesis Apocryphon* (Jerusalem, 1956)

Baillet, M. 'Fragments du document de Damas, Qumran, grotte 6', *Revue biblique*, vol. lxiii (1956), pp.513ff.

Bar-Adon, P. 'Another Settlement of the Judean Desert Sect at En el-Ghuweir on the Shores of the Dead Sea', *Bulletin of the American Schools of Oriental Research*, no.227 (Oct. 1977), pp.1ff.

Birnbaum, S.A. *The Hebrew Scripts* (Leiden, 1971)

Black, M. *The Scrolls and Christian Origins* (London, 1961)

Black, M., ed. *The Scrolls and Christianity* (London, 1969)

Bonsirven, J. 'Révolution dans l'histoire des origines chrétiennes?', *Etudes*, vol.cclxviii (Jan.–Mar. 1951)

Braun, O. 'Ein Brief des katholikos Timotheos I über biblische Studien des 9. Jahrhunderts', *Oriens Christianus*, vol.1 (1901), pp.299ff.

Brownlee, W.H. 'A Comparison of the Covenanters of the Dead Sea Scrolls with pre-Christian Jewish Sects', *The Biblical Archaeologist*, vol. xiii, no.3 (Sept. 1950), pp.50ff.
 'The Servant of the Lord in the Qumran Scrolls I', *Bulletin of the American Schools of Oriental Research*, no.132 (Dec. 1953), pp.8ff.
 'Muhammad ed-Deeb's own Story of his Scroll Discovery', *Journal of Near Eastern Studies*, vol.xv (Jan.–Oct. 1956), pp. 236ff.

256

'Edh-Dheeb's Story of his Scroll Discovery', *Revue de Qumran*, no.12, vol.iii (1962), pp.483ff.

'Some new facts concerning the discovery of the Scrolls of 1Q', *Revue de Qumran*, no.15, vol.iv (1963), pp.417ff.

The Meaning of the Qumran Scrolls for the Bible (Oxford, 1964)

Bruce, F.F. *Second Thoughts on the Dead Sea Scrolls* (London, 1956)

Burrows, M. *The Dead Sea Scrolls of St. Marks Monastery*, 2 vols (New Haven, 1950–51)

The Dead Sea Scrolls (London, 1956)

Callaway, P.R. *The History of the Qumran Community* (Sheffield, 1988)

Charles, R.H. *The Apocrypha and Pseudepigrapha of the Old Testament*, 2 vols (Oxford, 1913)

Cross, F.M. *The Ancient Library of Qumran* (London, 1958)

Cullmann, O. 'The Significance of the Qumran Texts for Research into the Beginnings of Christianity', *Journal of Biblical Literature*, vol.lxxiv, part IV (Dec. 1955), pp.213ff.

Cupitt, D. *The Sea of Faith: Christianity in Change* (London, 1984)

Danielou, J. *The Dead Sea Scrolls and Primitive Christianity*, trans. S. Attanasio (Westport, 1979)

Davies, A.P. *The Meaning of the Dead Sea Scrolls* (New York, 1956)

Davies, P.R. *The Damascus Covenant* (Sheffield, 1983)

Behind the Essenes (Atlanta, 1987)

'How Not to do Archaeology: The Story of Qumran', *Biblical Archaeologist* (Dec. 1988), pp.203ff.

Discoveries in the Judaean Desert, series:

vol.i, Milik, J.T. and Barthelemy, D (1955)

vol.ii, Benoit, P., Milik, J.T. and de Vaux, R. (1961)

vol.iii, Baillet, M., Milik, J.T. and de Vaux, R. (1962)

vol.iv, Sanders, J.A. (1965)

vol.v, Allegro, J.M. (1968)

vol.vi, Milik, J.T. (1977)

vol.vii, Baillet, M. (1982)

vol.viii, Tov, E. (1990)

Driver, G.R. *The Hebrew Scrolls* (Oxford, 1951)

The Judaean Scrolls (Oxford, 1965)

Dunn, J.D.G. *Jesus, Paul and the Law* (London, 1990)

Dupont-Sommer, A. *The Dead Sea Scrolls: A Preliminary Survey*, trans. E.M. Rowley (Oxford, 1952)

The Jewish Sect of Qumran and the Essenes, trans. R.D. Barnett (London, 1954)

Bibliography

Les écrits ésséniens découverts près de la Mer Morte (Paris, 1959)

The Essene Writings from Qumran, trans. G. Vermes (Oxford, 1961)

Eisenman, R.H. *Maccabees, Zadokites, Christians and Qumran* (Leiden, 1983)

James the Just in the Habakkuk Pesher (Leiden, 1986)

'The Historical Provenance of the "Three Nets of Belial" Allusion in the Zadokite Document and *Balla/Bela* in the Temple Scroll', *Folia orientalia*, vol.xxv (1988), pp.51ff.

'Eschatological "Rain" Imagery in the War Scroll from Qumran and in the Letter of James', *Journal of Near Eastern Studies*, vol.xlix, no.2 (April 1990)

'Interpreting *"Abeit-Galuto"* in the Habakkuk *Pesher*', *Folia orientalia*, vol.xxvii (1990)

Epiphanius of Constantia. *Adversus octoginta haereses*, I, i, Haeres xx, in J.-P. Migne, *Patrologiae cursus completus, series graeca*, vol.41 (Paris, 1858)

Epistle of Barnabas, in *The Ante-Nicene Fathers*, vol.i, ed. A.C. Coxe (Grand Rapids, 1985), pp.137ff.

Eusebius of Caesarea *The History of the Church from Christ to Constantine*, trans. G.A. Williamson (Harmondsworth, 1981)

Feldman, L.H. and Hata, G. *Josephus, Judaism and Christianity* (Detroit, 1987)

Josephus, the Bible and History (Detroit, 1989)

Fisk, R. *Pity the Nation* (London, 1990)

Fitzmyer, J.A. 'The Qumran Scrolls, the Ebionites and their Literature', *The Scrolls and the New Testament*, ed. K. Stendahl (London, 1958), pp.208ff.

The Dead Sea Scrolls: Major Publications and Tools for Study, 2nd edn (Missoula, 1977)

Fogazzaro, A. *The Saint*, trans. M. Prichard-Agnetti (London, 1906)

Fritsch, C.T. 'Herod the Great and the Qumran Community', *Journal of Biblical Literature*, vol.lxxiv, part III (Sept. 1955), pp.173ff.

Gallarati-Scotti, T. *The Life of Antonio Fogazzaro*, trans. M. Prichard-Agnetti (London, 1922)

Gaster, T.H. *The Dead Sea Scriptures* (New York, 1956)

Gichon, M. 'The Bar Kochba War – A Colonial Uprising against Imperial Rome (131/2–135 CE)', *Revue internationale d'histoire militaire*, no.42 (1979), pp.82ff.

'Who Were the Enemies of Rome on the Limes Palaestinae', *Studien zu den Militärgrenzen Roms*, iii (Stuttgart, 1986)

Gilkes, A.N. *The Impact of the Dead Sea Scrolls* (London, 1962)

Bibliography

Golb, N. 'The Problem of Origin and Identification of the Dead Sea Scrolls', *Proceedings of the American Philosophical Society*, vol.cxxiv, no.1 (1980), pp.1ff.

    'The Dead Sea Scrolls', *The American Scholar* (spring, 1989), pp. 177ff.

Graves, R. *King Jesus*, 4th edn (London, 1960)

    The White Goddess (London, 1977)

Hasler, A.B. *How the Pope became Infallible*, trans. P. Heinegg (New York, 1981)

Hebblethwaite, P. *Synod Extraordinary* (London, 1986)

    In the Vatican (Oxford, 1988)

The Interlinear Greek–English New Testament, trans. A. Marshall (London, 1967)

The Jerusalem Bible, ed. A. Jones (after R. de Vaux) (London, 1966)

Josephus, F. *Antiquities of the Jews: A History of the Jewish Wars and Life of Flavius Josephus, Written by Himself*, trans. W. Whiston (London, n.d.)

    The Jewish War, trans. G.A. Williamson (Harmondsworth, 1978)

Kahle, P.E. *The Cairo Geniza* (London, 1947)

Kenyon, K. *Digging up Jericho* (London, 1957)

Knibb, M.A. *The Qumran Community* (Cambridge, 1987)

Kuhn, K.G. 'Les rouleaux de cuivre de Qumran', *Revue biblique*, vol.lxi (1954), pp.193ff.

Küng, H. *Infallible?*, trans. E. Mosbacher (London, 1971)

Ladouceur, D.J. 'Josephus and Masada', *Josephus, Judaism and Christianity*, ed. L.H. Feldman and G. Hata (Detroit, 1987), pp.95ff.

Leon-Dufour, X. *The Gospels and the Jesus of History*, trans. J. McHugh (London, 1968)

Lloyd, S. *Foundations in the Dust*, rev. edn (London, 1980)

Maier, J. *The Temple Scroll* (Sheffield, 1985)

Metzger, B.M., ed. *The Apocrypha of the Old Testament* (New York, 1965)

Milik, J.T. *Ten Years of Discovery in the Wilderness of Judaea*, trans. J. Strugnell (London, 1959)

Murphy, R. *Lagrange and Biblical Research* (Chicago, 1966)

Negoitsa, A. 'Did the Essenes Survive the 66–71 War?', *Revue de Qumran*, no.24, vol.vi (1959), pp.517ff.

Nemoy, L. 'Al-Qirqisani's Account of the Jewish Sects and Christianity', *Hebrew Union College Annual*, vol.vii (1930), pp.317ff.

Neusner, J. *Judaism in the Beginning of Christianity* (London, 1984)

New Catholic Encyclopaedia, 14 vols (New York, 1967)

North, R. 'Qumran and its Archaeology', *The Catholic Biblical Quarterly*, vol.xvi, no.4 (Oct. 1954), pp.426ff.

The Oxford Dictionary of the Christian Church, ed. F.L. Cross and E.A. Livingstone, 2nd edn (Oxford, 1983)

Pearlman, M. *The Dead Sea Scrolls in the Shrine of the Book* (Jerusalem, 1988)

Philo Judaeus *On the Contemplative Life*, trans. F.H. Colson (Cambridge, Mass., and London, 1967)

    Every Good Man is Free, trans. F.H. Colson (Cambridge, Mass., and London, 1967)

Pliny *Natural History*, trans. H. Rackham and W.H.S. Jones, 10 vols (London, 1938–42)

Ploeg, J. van der *The Excavations at Qumran*, trans. K. Smyth (London, 1958)

Pryce-Jones, D. 'A New Chapter in the Story of Christ', *Daily Telegraph Magazine*, 19 July 1968, pp.12ff.

Pritz, R.A. *Nazarene Jewish Christianity* (Jerusalem and Leiden, 1988)

Rabin, C. *Qumran Studies* (Oxford, 1957)

Rabin, C., ed. *The Zadokite Documents*, 2nd rev. edn (Oxford, 1958)

Recognitions of Clement, trans. Thomas Smith, in the *Ante-Nicene Library*, 25 vols, vol.iii (Edinburgh, 1867)

Reed, W.L. 'The Qumran Caves Expedition of March 1952', *Bulletin of the American Schools of Oriental Research*, no.135 (October, 1954), pp.8ff.

Robinson, J.M. 'The Jung Codex: The Rise and Fall of a Monopoly', *Religious Studies Review*, no.3 (Jan. 1977), pp.17ff.

    'Getting the Nag Hammadi Library into English', *Biblical Archaeologist*, vol.xlii (Fall 1979), p.239

Rosa, P. de *Vicars of Christ* (London, 1989)

Roth, C. *The Historical Background of the Dead Sea Scrolls* (Oxford, 1958)

    'The Zealots and Qumran: The Basic Issue', *Revue de Qumran*, vol.ii, no.5 (1959), pp.81ff.

    'Did Vespasian Capture Qumran?', *Palestine Exploration Quarterly* (July–Dec. 1959), pp.122ff.

    'Qumran and Masadah: A Final Clarification Regarding the Dead Sea Sect', *Revue de Qumran*, no.17, vol.v (1964), pp.81ff.

Rowley, H.H. 'The Qumran Sect and Christian Origins', *Bulletin of the John Rylands Library*, vol.xliv, no.1 (Sept. 1961), pp.119ff.

Samuel, A.Y. 'The Purchase of the Jerusalem Scrolls', *The Biblical Archaeologist*, vol.xii, no.2 (May, 1949), pp.26ff.

    Treasure of Qumran (London, 1968)

La Sainte Bible, traduite . . . sous la direction de L'Ecole Biblique de

Jérusalem (Paris, 1956)

Schillebeeckx, E. *Ministry: A Case for Change*, trans. J. Bowden (London, 1981)

Schroeder, F.J. *Père Lagrange and Biblical Inspiration* (Washington, 1954)

Silberman, N.A. *Digging for God and Country* (New York, 1982)

Smith, M. 'The Dead Sea Sect in Relation to Ancient Judaism', *New Testament Studies*, vol.vii (1960–61), pp.347ff.

Smyth, K. 'The Truth about the Dead Sea Scrolls', *The Irish Digest* (June 1956), pp.31ff.

Steckoll, S.H. 'Preliminary Excavation Report in the Qumran Cemetery', *Revue de Qumran*, no.23, vol.vi (1968), pp.323ff.

'Marginal Notes on the Qumran Excavations', *Revue de Qumran*, no.25, vol.vii (1969), pp.33ff.

Stendahl, K., ed. *The Scrolls and the New Testament* (London, 1958)

Stutchbury, H.E. and Nicholl, G.R. 'Khirbet Mazin', *Annual of the Department of Antiquities of Jordan*, vols.vi–vii (1962), pp.96ff.

Suetonius *The Twelve Caesars*, trans. R. Graves (Harmondsworth, 1979)

Sukenik, E.L. *The Dead Sea Scrolls of the Hebrew University* (Jerusalem, 1955)

Tacitus *The Histories*, trans. K. Wellesley, rev. edn (Harmondsworth, 1988)

Talmon, S. *The World of Qumran from Within* (Jerusalem, 1989)

Trever, J. 'When was Qumran Cave 1 Discovered?', *Revue de Qumran*, no.9, vol.iii (1961), pp.135ff.

The Untold Story of Qumran (London, 1966)

Vaux, R. de 'A Propos des manuscrits de la mer morte', *Revue biblique*, vol.lvii (1950), pp.417ff.

'Exploration de la région de Qumran', *Revue biblique*, vol. lx (1953), pp.540ff.

'Fouille au Khirbet Qumran', *Revue biblique*, vol.lx (1953), pp.83ff.

'Fouilles au Khirbet Qumran', *Revue biblique*, vol.lxi (1954), pp.206ff.

'Fouilles de Khirbet Qumran', *Revue biblique*, vol.lxiii (1956), pp. 533ff.

'Les manuscrits de Qumran et l'archéologie', *Revue biblique*, vol.lxvi (1959), pp.87ff.

Archaeology and the Dead Sea Scrolls, rev. edn (Oxford, 1977)

Vermes, G. 'The Etymology of "Essenes" ', *Revue de Qumran*, no.7, vol.ii (1960), pp.427ff.

The Dead Sea Scrolls: Qumran in Perspective (London, 1977)

Jesus the Jew (London, 1977)

'The Essenes and History', *Journal of Jewish Studies*, vol.xxxii, no.1 (1981), pp.18ff.

Jesus and the World of Judaism (London, 1983)

The Dead Sea Scrolls in English, 3rd edn (Sheffield, 1987)

Webb, J. *The Flight from Reason* (London, 1971)

The Harmonious Circle (London, 1980)

Wilson, E. *The Scrolls from the Dead Sea* (London, 1955)

The Dead Sea Scrolls 1947–1969, rev. edn (Glasgow, 1977)

Wright, G.E., ed. *The Bible and the Ancient Near East* (London, 1961)

Yadin, Y. *The Message of the Scrolls* (London, 1957)

'What the Temple Scroll Reveals', *Daily Telegraph Magazine*, 19 July 1968, pp.15ff.

Masada (London, 1975)

Bar-Kokhba (London, 1978)

The Temple Scroll (London, 1985)

Index

'Keepers of the Covenant', 172, 173-4
Kesey, Ken, 62
Khirbet Qumran, *see* Qumran
King, Philip, 89
Kingsford, Anna, 167
Koenen, Ludwig, 86
Koldeway, Robert, 107
Küng, Hans, 122-4

Lagrange, Father Albert, 111-13, 118
Last Supper, timing of, 135-6
Leary, Timothy, 62
Leo XIII, Pope, 110, 111, 112, 118
'Liar, the', 149, 146-7, 195-6, 219
Life of Jesus, The (Renan), 107-8, 167
Lippens, Captain Philippe, 16
Loisy, Alfred, 109-10, 112
Loza, José, 119
Lucceius Albinus, 190
Luke's Gospel, 66, 176-7

Maccabeans, 201-3
Maccabees, Zadokites, Christians and Qumran (Eisenman), xvii, 75
Mark's Gospel, 175
Martyr, Justin, 65-6
Masada, fortress of, xvi, 69, 132, 193, 199, 208; mass suicide at, 206, 212-14, 216
Mattathias Maccabaeus, 201, 204
Mayhew, Christopher, 62
Menahem, 205-6, 212
Messiah figure, 133, 141-2, 147; of Aaron and of David, 200, 204, 205
Metternich, Prince, 109
Milik, Father Josef, 29, 32, 34, 35, 38, 48, 49, 58, 85, 88, 91; and the 'Copper Scroll', 53, 54, 55-6; on the archaeological evidence at Qumran, 154-5; controls and withholds Qumran material, 66, 86-7, 99-100, 116, 117
Ministry: A Case for Change (Schillebeeckx), 122
MMT document, 77, 78, 91

Mogilany Resolution, 85-6, 90
Moore, George, 168
Moses, 120, 145
Muhammad adh-Dhib (Muhammad the Wolf), 6
Murphy-O'Connor, Jerome, 100

Nabokov, Vladimir, xvii, 41
Nag Hammadi Scrolls, 32, 35-6, 37, 86, 129-30
Name of the Rose, The (Eco), xviii, 32
Nazoreans (Nazarenes), 174, 217
Ne'eman, Yuval, 73, 74-5, 76
Neusner, Jacob, 89
New Testament, 43; on James, 188-9
New York Times: 'The Vanity of Scholars', 85
Nietzsche, F., 108
North, Robert, 32, 153
'Notes in the Margin' (Sturgill), 51

Old Testament, 112, 113-14
Origen, 193, 229
Origin of Species, The (Darwin), 108
Orlinsky, Harry, 24
Oversight Committee, 89-90, 91, 92, 93-4, 95, 225, 226

palaeography, dating by, 160-4
Palestine Archaeological Museum, *see* Rockefeller Museum
Palestine Exploration Fund, 106
Paul, Saint, xiii-xiv, xviii, 134-5, 176, 177, 178-87, 199, 218-21; as 'the Liar', 195; conversion of, 147-8, 179-80; and James, 182, 183, 188, 189, 194, 197-8, 217, 218-19; and Jesus, 212
Paul VI, Pope, 121
Peter, Saint, 133, 181, 182, 185
Philo Judaeus: on the Essenes, 165, 168, 169, 170, 171, 173
Phineas, Covenant of, 202-3
Pius IX, Pope, 109
Pius X, Pope, 110, 120
Pius XII, Pope, 114

Index